In Celebration of Golf

By the same author

Great Opens: Historic British and American Championships 1913–1975
Golf to Remember (with Peter Alliss)
Golf for the Connoisseur

IN CELEBRATION OF
GOLF

Edited by
Michael Hobbs

Foreword by Henry Cotton

CHARLES SCRIBNER'S SONS
New York

Library of Congress Catalog Card Number 82-60402
ISBN 0-684-17800-1

Contents

PART II MISCELLANY

Illustrations

Acknowledgements

Grateful acknowledgement is made to the following for permission to use copyright material owned by them. If any holders of rights have been inadvertently overlooked the publisher offers apologies and promise of correction in later editions.

Cassell Ltd for *Grand Slam Golf* by Gary Player

Cassell Ltd and Random House, Inc for *The World of Golf* by Charles Price

David & Charles for *Great Opens* by Michael Hobbs

The Estate of the late Bernard Darwin for *Out of the Rough* by Bernard Darwin

Vivienne, Lady Glenavy for *How to Become a Scratch Golfer* by Patrick Campbell

Golf Digest Inc for *The Best of Henry Longhurst*

Hamlyn Publishing Group Ltd for *This Game of Golf* by Henry Cotton

A. M. Heath & Co. Ltd for extracts from pieces by Peter Dobereiner first published in the *Observer*

A. M. Heath & Co. Ltd for *The Bogey Man* by George Plimpton

Hodder & Stoughton for *The Long Green Fairway* by Pat Ward-Thomas

Hodder & Stoughton and Simon & Schuster for *The Greatest Game of All* by Jack Nicklaus with Herbert Warren Wind. Copyright © by Ohio Promotions, Inc

Hutchinson Publishing Ltd for *Martyrs of Golf* by Dick Aultman and Ken Bowden

Hutchinson Publishing Ltd for *On and Off the Fairway* by Jack Nicklaus

International Management Group for *Go for Broke* by Arnold Palmer

Hugh McIlvanney for extract from piece first published in the *Observer*, 10 July 1977

Pelham Books Ltd for *This Wonderful World of Golf* by Peter Thomson and Donald Zwar

A. D. Peters & Co. Ltd and The Sterling Lord Agency for *The Lure of Golf* by Herbert Warren Wind, Copyright © 1954 by Herbert Warren Wind

Prentice-Hall Inc for *Thirty Years of Championship Golf* by Gene Sarazen with Herbert Warren Wind, © 1950 by Prentice-Hall Inc

Sunday Times for extracts from pieces by John Ballantine, Dudley Doust, Henry Longhurst and Michael Parkinson first published in the *Sunday Times*

Foreword

by Henry Cotton

As the years go by and more and more people throughout the world become interested in golf, it is not surprising that an increasing number of books and articles are published to satisfy the golfing hunger of millions. The compiler of this book, Michael Hobbs, has taken endless trouble to find a way of telling much of golf's ever-growing history. Whilst there is a succession of new faces going up to receive the winners' prizes, only those who are repeat winners and winners of major events finally reach the list of 'golfing greats'. Striking a golf ball well is the aim of every golfer, but winning at golf is a thing apart, achieved by self-control and guts, though a good method, which leads to a 'repeating swing', certainly helps.

These pages contain insights into the lives of the greats of different generations. There will always be a desire to pick a definitive list of honour, containing the best players ever to walk a fairway and putt a green. The money list of honour is the most misleading guide, for obvious reasons; total money won in the course of a lifetime means so little – before the turn of this century a player will win more dollars in a single tournament than Sam Snead, one of the real greats and arguably the greatest, with 135 tournament wins to his name, won in nearly fifty years. Up to now Jack Nicklaus has won the most 'majors', all of them in the days of jet travel. Bobby Jones, who would be in second place, won his series in the days of the steamship and train; it took him five times as long to play in one event as today it takes Jack Nicklaus. No comparison is therefore possible, especially since Jones retired at twenty-eight years of age.

The smaller golf ball, 1.62 inches in diameter, was in general use until the USA adopted the 1.68-inch size. The low fast-flying 1.68-inch ball of today is the greatest ball ever made, so score comparisons are out. This ball sounds great off the club and its initial velocity is restricted to prevent it going too far. I have never enjoyed putting as much as I do today, for every putt sounds and feels perfectly struck and emits a satisfying 'click'. I often wonder how the great players of the generations up to only twenty years ago found their touch with a ball that sounded off the club face as dead and rubbery as a solid rubber ball dropped on a block of marble.

Roberto de Vicenzo, that great Argentinian pro, who has travelled the world for over thirty years competing everywhere he could and winning over 150 tournaments of all kinds, a record at this moment, has no world top-player ranking in terms of money, but the pros of his three playing decades know he is 'some' player: in many eyes without equal.

The ridiculous was enacted early this year, when just five pro players played a 72-hole medal, with amateur partners, for $1 million in prize-money. (Johnny Miller beat S. Ballesteros in a 9-hole sudden death for $500,000.) With inflation running wild, this $1 million will be a first prize before long! All this big money may suit the managers and the players, but is it good for the game? Time will tell, but in a world of uncertainty and unemployment such easy money can't be right. If the players' caddies on such occasions get their usual percentage (5–10 per cent) of the prize-money, they will be earning more than 90 per cent of the prize-money pros won just a couple of decades ago.

Michael Hobbs's *In Celebration of Golf* has produced some excellent reading to support the coverage of the TV cameras, which started showing golf in the home too late in my life for me to benefit directly, but, as golf has been – and still is – my life, I raise my glass with you all 'in celebration of golf'.

Introduction

An editor of a golf book is doubly fortunate: a great deal has been written about the game of golf and much of it is very good indeed. I believe that this is a result of the nature of the game, which is reflective and leisurely rather than instinctive and performed at high speed. It follows that comparatively little has emerged from football (any of the versions) because the charged moment is so soon over and a complete game impossible to remember.

Yet it is easy for the player or spectator to remember every stroke played in a round of golf and something of the manner, too. And during it all there is time in plenty for thought. These days a tournament round takes something like four-and-a-half hours, but the moments of action are compressed into little more than a minute per player. Only cricket can compare with golf, for quality and quantity of writing: perhaps for similar reasons, one of which is that both can last for days on end and resemble a campaign rather than a packed hour or so.

From its earliest popularity golf began to attract writing talents. Even now, no one has written more wittily about the game than Sir Walter Simpson well before the turn of the century; and another Victorian, Bernard Darwin, is arguably the best essayist to have written about any game.

In these pages you will find represented most of the best talents exercised in golf writing: Henry Longhurst, Herbert Warren Wind, R. T. Jones, Peter Dobereiner, Patrick Campbell, Dudley Doust, Charles Price, Michael Parkinson, Dick Aultman, George Plimpton. The list could go on but more interesting is the range of abilities expressed through golf writing. I hope that the reader will find this collection does them justice.

PART I
THE PLAYERS

The section that follows presents a selection of writings
about some two dozen of the best golfers of this century. The
aim has been to collect good writing, so that the exclusion
of this player or that is not intended to reflect on his or her
stature – indeed he may well appear in the second
section of this book.

Harry Vardon

Born 9 May 1870, Grouville, Jersey, Channel
Islands. Died 1937.

All a player can do is beat the greatest of his own time, and this, like
Young Tom Morris before him, Vardon undoubtedly did. What we
can judge of his swing today would suggest that he could not live with
later stars: his left arm really was *too* bent; his right leg *too* straight on
the backswing; he twisted his hips *too* much.

But there is another side to this particular coin. Vardon's method
evolved from playing with a gutty ball, thin-bladed irons and hickory
shafts, and in that period all his contemporaries without exception
gave him first place. Had he been born eighty years later I suspect that
we should be watching a Vardon with a very different kind of swing
and that he would still win the Open six times.

Two generations
Henry Cotton

I was too young to know Harry Vardon at his real best, and I was
then even too inexperienced really to appreciate his greatness, as when
I did know him his pathetic inability to bring the clubhead smoothly
to the ball on a two-foot putt startled me. Up to this distance from the
pin he still hit the ball with his lovely smooth swing, but the unbelievable jerking of the clubhead, in an effort to make contact with the ball
from two feet or less from the hole, had to be seen to be believed. I
believe he always had some difficulty in his life with the little putts,
but even that did not handicap him enough to prevent him, despite ill-
health at times, from winning the Open Championship six times.

I first played with Harry Vardon when I was a boy professional; he
would then be about fifty-seven I suppose, and he loved golf still. I was
most impressed then by his large, fleshy hands and by the narrow type
of stiff collar in which he had always played.

Harry's swing (I called him respectfully 'Mr Vardon' until one day he corrected me, then I felt I had won my spurs) looked demoded, with its bent left arm on the backswing, to the modern school – though Walter Hagen, another idol of mine, bent his left arm considerably too. This bent left arm did away with all tension going up and, in fact, kept it out of his swing altogether. One of Harry's classic remarks was, when asked, 'What do you think of the stiff left arm, Vardon?', his reply: 'I like playing against people with stiff left arms.'

His bent left arm and upright swing gave him much more time to hit early, and this he did; no player hit the ball as cleanly with all clubs. He could pick up a ball cleanly and hold it straight in its flight in a full shot with any iron club, which rather cut across my theory that a divot was absolutely essential for straight iron play.

Harry could play all the shots and, as he held his form for such a long time, it became more clear to me as I knew him better that he knew a lot about the game.

I was indebted to Harry for some lessons he gave to my wife, on condition that I 'did not interrupt', for Harry, although he loved to talk golf, disliked to be questioned. I was allowed to film these lessons, and found the sort of demonstrations and explanations he gave to his pupils were most interesting, and revealed how much he really knew about the game. He took the greatest interest in his pupils and bound them to give an account of their progress. I remember him demonstrating a pitch shot to a green sloping away from him, for which he used an old completely smooth-faced niblick. He put every ball within some three yards of the pin, and when we congratulated him on it, he said, 'Oh! I remember when I could back myself to put every one just within a few feet of the pin.' I then asked him why he had never written all he knew, and he replied, 'Henry, it all sounds so obvious when put on paper, that I always felt that anyone who did not know that much about golf should not be playing it.'

You may want to ask me straight away why I do not use the bent left arm or teach people to use it. The answer is because it is very difficult indeed to use. Like nearly everything else in golf I have tried it out! With a bent left arm I feel without power and find it difficult to keep a constant arc on the down-swing, for it is not easy to time the straightening of the arm and accompanying throw of the clubhead.

In America, Harry's visits are still remembered. Tales are told of his devastating accuracy. Here is one of the best, told by the older pros to the younger ones, who naturally are always anxious to visualize just how good the old master was in his heyday, so as to compare him with the modern players. 'He would not play any course twice in the same day, you know.' 'Why not?' 'Because he was so accurate, that in his second round his shots finished in the divot holes he had made in the morning, and that took the fun out of the game for him.'

This Game of Golf, Country Life, 1948

An ineffaceable mark
Bernard Darwin

Comparisons between players of different generations are, as a rule, futile, and particularly so in the case of golf, since the conditions under which it is played have so greatly changed; but no one who ever saw Vardon in his best days can doubt that his genius was unsurpassable. Those days are now rather distant because, although he won the last of his six Open championships in 1914, it was at the end of the nineteenth and the beginning of the twentieth century that he was in his most glorious prime. When he won the third of his championships in 1899 no one so much as dreamed that there could be another champion. He went up and down the country winning tournaments and breaking records, trampling down all opponents in his juggernaut stride. He did what only a very great player can do; he raised the general conception of what was possible in his game and forced his nearest rivals to attain a higher standard by attempting that which they would otherwise have deemed impossible. He had a great influence, too, on methods of playing. When he first appeared his notably upright swing, though so full of grace and rhythm, came as a shock to the orthodoxy of the time, but has now long since been accepted.

Three of his six championships were won after the introduction of the rubber-cored ball in 1902, but it was with the gutty, before his serious illness, that he was supreme. Had it not been for that breakdown in health his tally of victories would surely have been much longer; it was after his illness that his putting began to betray him. The modern golfer believes that Vardon was always a bad putter, but this is not so. He was not an outstanding putter, nor had he quite the same graceful ease on the green as elsewhere, but he was at least a very good approach putter and a competent holer-out. He could never otherwise have accomplished half of what he did.

7

Vardon's record is so long that it must be severely compressed. He was born on 9 May 1870, at Grouville in Jersey. He learnt the game there as a caddie and continued to play after starting work as a gardener at the age of thirteen. His younger brother, Tom, was the first to go out into the world, as assistant professional at St Anne's, and it was he who induced Harry to apply for a post at Ripon in 1890. In 1891 he moved to Bury in Lancashire and thence to Ganton in 1896. He had first played in the Open championship at Prestwick in 1893 (the year of Taylor's debut), but it was at Ganton that he became famous. In the spring of 1896 Taylor, who had been two years champion, came there to play Vardon a match and went home defeated by 8 and 6 and full of his conqueror's praises. A month or two later they tied for the Open championship at Muirfield, and Vardon won the play-off by three strokes. In 1897 he fell away slightly, but won again at Prestwick in 1898 and the following year won with perfect ease at Sandwich. These were his two supreme years. It was in 1899 that he beat Taylor, who was playing well, by 11 and 10 in the final of the tournament at Newcastle, County Down, and also beat Willie Park in one of the outstanding matches of his life.

In 1900 Vardon set out on what was practically a year's tour of the United States, though he broke it to come home to defend his title in the championship and finished second to Taylor at St Andrews. In America, where golf was still young, he travelled from end to end of the country playing an enormous number of matches and causing great enthusiasm; he hardly lost a match and won the American championship.

But the hard work of the tour took its toll, and it is doubtful if he was ever so brilliant again. After being twice runner-up in the championship to Braid and Herd respectively, he won at Prestwick in 1903 with a total of 300, and this he regarded as the best of all his achievements, since he was so unwell that he nearly fainted several times in his last round. Soon afterwards he had to spend some time in a sanatorium and made a more or less complete recovery. In 1905 came the second great match of his career, in which he and Taylor beat Braid and Herd over four greens by 11 and 10. Their play at Troon, where they won fourteen holes, was astonishingly fine, and so it was on the last links, Deal, though Vardon had had a haemorrhage the night before and was not really fit to play at all.

There followed a period of comparatively lean years and then, to the general joy, Vardon won again at Sandwich, in 1911, beating Massy so convincingly in playing off the tie that the great French player gave up at the 35th hole. The year 1913 saw Vardon tie for yet another Open championship, that of the United States, at The Country Club at Brookline. This was the historic occasion on which Mr Francis Ouimet, then little older than a schoolboy, beat Vardon and Ray after a triple tie and may be said to have founded the American golfing empire. It was unquestionably a disappointing blow for Vardon; yet he won his sixth championship next year at Prestwick, beating Taylor by three shots. The two were drawn together on the last day and took the whole of a rather obstreperous crowd with them so that it was a marvel that they could play as they did.

When the war was over Vardon was almost fifty and his victorious days were of necessity nearly over. Yet in 1920 he tied for second place in the American championship, one stroke behind Ray. In all human probability he would have won had not a fierce wind come up as he was playing the last few holes and was tiring fast. That was his final achievement, and during the later years of his life his health put golf to all intents and purposes out of the question. He bore the deprivation with philosophy and sweet temper, enjoying teaching when he could not play and always anxious to watch the younger players. This he did with an eye at once kindly and critical, being a staunch conservative and unshaken in his conviction that the greatest qualities of the game had departed with the gutty ball. From 1903 to the end of his life he was professional to the South Herts Golf Club at Totteridge, where he was an oracle and an institution. He has left a name affectionately regarded by everyone and an ineffaceable mark on the game of golf.

The Times, 22 March 1937

Abe Mitchell

Born 1887, East Grinstead, Sussex, England. Died 1947.

In the 1933 Open Abe Mitchell shared the lead after three rounds with Henry Cotton, Leo Diegel and Sid Easterbrook. In the afternoon he collapsed to a 79 and that was his last chance of winning an Open. Much the same had happened years before in 1920 when George Duncan began with a couple of 80s but Abe collapsed in the final round and was overhauled by him.

Yet Abe Mitchell was the best British player of the 1920s and the fact that he was still threatening to take the Open at the age of forty-six gives some indication of his quality and shows why he remains the best British player to fail to win the Open, though Dai Rees might dispute this.

A great player but . . .
Henry Cotton

No golf balls have ever been struck harder and truer than those struck by Abe Mitchell, during the years from about 1910 to 1933. If any criticism can be levelled at Abe as a professional golfer, it can be only that he was too kind. He had all the qualities of the great player, but somehow his gentlemanly, reserved disposition often prevented him from ruthlessly driving home an advantage.

Abe was beaten now and then by players who had no right to defeat him. He was accused of not being a fighter, but this is not true, as his record, both in match play and medal play, testifies.

I have always admired the crispness Abe put into his shots – a professional attack with a punch, as opposed to a swing, yet with rhythm all the same. Abe had a very personal swing which cannot be copied. His grip, though orthodox to look at, was again his own. His left thumb was outside his right hand and lay on the right-hand side of the shaft, and the club was allowed to slide in the right hand slightly during the stroke.

I always enjoyed watching Abe play. Long before I became a professional I used to be an Abe Mitchell fan, and I followed him round whenever I could. He was a most likeable fellow. In his heyday he gave the impression that he disliked teaching golf, and led people to believe even that he could not teach. Yet when you began to talk golf with him it was soon apparent what an experienced golfer he was and how much he knew about the game.

'The best golfer who has not won the Open Championship' is the much-used phrase of the golfing journalists describing Abe Mitchell when his name crops up, and how true it is! If the Open could have been awarded for skill and consistency, Abe would have been a multiple winner, but somehow things went wrong with him in championship week. He hated the waiting day after day, and the suspense used to tire him. Everyone knows when, and where, he should have won golf's major title, and it is history how he slipped up!

I loved to hear George Duncan and Abe Mitchell talking of their American trips. They visited the States in 1921, 1922 and 1924, as a team, and had three most successful tours. They made one of the most attractive golf combinations there has ever been, and George tells how he used to let Abe do all the playing, and he himself just tried to come in now and then, and do the talking, for in those days Abe could out-hit and out-play anybody all the time. You should hear George on this point!

Abe always used an aluminium-headed putter. He putted with his right thumb on top of the shaft, and his right hand completely overlapping his left hand. This is a very individual form of grip. He always was a beautiful putter, and gave the ball a decisive tap, again full of rhythm.

I have rarely seen Abe practise. He always was able to keep in form with a minimum amount of play, and when he did practise he hit the ball like a machine.

I regard Abe as one of the best spoon players I have ever seen; Joyce Wethered and George Duncan were in the same class. If ever I experienced trouble with my wooden shots through the green, the best cure I had was to go and watch Abe Mitchell hit a few shots at the pin. The last time I played with him was in a Red Cross match during the war. His spoon shots were really beautiful to watch that day.

I saw him play Archie Compston in 1925 in a 72-holes £400 match over St George's Hill and Wentworth, and win by 9 and 8. He gave Archie no chance.

Abe lost by 2 and 1 to Walter Hagen in a £1,000 match over 72 holes in 1926. It was in this match that Hagen kept Mitchell waiting on the first tee for over half an hour when Abe was four up at the end of the first 36 holes.

Abe never completely took to steel shafts. He used them successfully in his iron clubs, but kept changing from steel to hickory and then back again every now and again, as though he could not make up his mind. I think in his heart he preferred the shafts with which he first made his name.

Although he was an athletic type of man, and very strong physically, a delicate nervous system affected to some extent Abe's career as a professional. He died at St Albans in 1947, mourned and respected by the golfing world as one of the great players of all time.

This Game of Golf, Country Life, 1948

Walter Hagen

Born 21 December 1892, Rochester, New York, USA. Died October 1969.

It has been said of Jack Nicklaus that he is outstanding at no single department of the game – and bad at nothing either. With Walter Hagen matters were reversed. He was an inconsistent driver and lacked exceptional length; his fairway woods were unreliable enough for him to prefer using a long iron most of the time; his long irons were only modestly better. So Walter Hagen had to be outstanding at most of what is left in the game of golf – and he was. No one has ever excelled him in variety and accuracy of shots into the green from 140 yards or less; as a player of the delicate flick shot from greenside bunkers; or, most important of all, as a putter seemingly devoid of nerves.

Even so, I have omitted the most talked-about facet of the Hagen game – the recovery shot. Again and again match-play opponents were broken by seeing Hagen hook into woods or slice into rough with his tee shot (the sway was the prime defect in Walter's swing and produced hook and slice impartially) and shortly after appear unruffled on the green before sinking his putt for another birdie.

Possibly I exaggerate, for it's almost impossible to be as bad and as good as Hagen's contemporaries thought him, and this was a man who won more major professional championships (eleven) than any golfer except Jack Nicklaus. In the end, however, it is Hagen the man, not Hagen the golfer, that has gone down in golf lore and history.

The right man in the right place at the right time

Charles Price

Before Hagen racked up his clubs, he was to win eleven major national championships, capture sixty-odd other tournaments and play in more than fifteen hundred exhibitions. Like Francis Ouimet before him,

Hagen was the right man in the right place at the right time. It was the Jazz Age, an era best put into words by F. Scott Fitzgerald, best put into pictures by John Held, Jr, and best personified by the flat-chested flappers who drank instant gin and danced the Charleston with quick-buck Johnnies during the Saturday night dances at the thousands of new country clubs such an uninhibited age demanded. Into this gaudy period stepped The Haig, as he was called, with the *sang-froid* of a Valentino, his black hair pomaded to an iridescence, his handsome features browned by the sun and the wind until they had the hue of brierwood. At the time, when most golf pros were still dress-ing in sack coats and brogues, Hagen began wearing silk shirts, florid cravats, alpaca sweaters, screaming argyles and black and white shoes which he had custom-made at a hundred dollars a pair. When The Haig strolled past the verandas, he was enough to make the flappers choke on their gum.

If personality is an unbroken series of successful gestures, as Scott Fitzgerald wrote of another Jazz Age character, then there was something gorgeous about The Haig. It was impossible to tell what the man would do next, on or off the golf course, and most of what he did would have seemed absurd, even ludicrous, had it been done by anyone else. In an exhibition The Haig might have scrutinized the roll on a green before playing a brassie shot to it, and yet for a championship he might have holed a putt that had six breaks after only glancing at the line. At the peak of his career he once played eighteen holes in 58 strokes – and another eighteen in 93. One week after returning to San Francisco from a tour of the world which had netted him $23,000 in exhibition fees, a sum that somehow hadn't quite covered his expenses, The Haig was forced to sit in his hotel room for three days because he didn't have the cash to pay for his laundry.

The Haig handled his opponents as though they were yo-yos. While engaged in a tight 36-hole match for a national championship with Leo Diegel, a perfectionist who unfortunately had the nerves of a schoolgirl, The Haig invited him to have lunch at the end of the first eighteen holes. Diegel ordered tea and toast. The Haig ordered vichys-soise, roast duck and champagne. After forcing down his meal, Diegel became ill at the sight of Hagen gorging himself, bolted from the table and walked clear through a glass door. Hagen roared with laughter and then went out and won the match.

Walter Hagen was born on 21 December 1892, in Brighton, a suburb of Rochester, New York. His father, William, was a blacksmith in the car shops of East Rochester and made eighteen dollars a week. From him Walter inherited a pair of long, lean, surprisingly unmuscular hands, and for the rest of his life he was to be admired for how beautifully he made use of them. With his sleeves rolled up just a turn, a cigarette poised delicately between the forefinger and the middle finger, he used his hands later in life to dramatize practically everything he said, with the result that they were in a constant state of motion, flapping and darting about him like a couple of trained doves.

Young Hagen began to work as a caddie at The Country Club of Rochester, which was only a quarter of a mile from his house, when he was ten. He quit school when he was thirteen, literally by jumping out of a window, because he wanted to learn a trade. At no time in his teens did he ever conceive of himself as a professional golfer. His life's ambition was to be a big-league baseball player. Toward this end he tried without much success to support himself by working as a garage mechanic, a piano finisher, a taxidermist and an apprentice to a mandolin-maker. When all these jobs failed to pan out as expected, Hagen decided he would have to have something else to back up his projected career as a ballplayer. Golf seemed the logical answer.

For some years he had been carrying clubs for the members of the Thistle Club, a kind of club within The Country Club of Rochester. These men, who threw a good deal of weight, eventually fixed it so young Hagen could play the course, and by the time he was fifteen he had managed to break 80. That was a good score, Hagen knew, but since golf was such an unimportant game in those days he never really knew how good it was. Golf wasn't like baseball. That was different. There, he knew where he stood.

Anyway, young Hagen knew what he was doing with a golf club, and so did everybody else at The Country Club of Rochester know it. When Andrew Christy, the professional, needed a new assistant, it almost had to be Walter. He was in with The Thistle Club.

Walter had been playing with Christy when Walter first broke 70, and it was this occasion that led to his learning what he considered the biggest lesson of his life. Christy often played with Walter – at Christy's invitation – when they finished work at the end of the day. But they played with each other, not against each other. To himself, however, Walter always played Christy a match, and Walter usually won.

One day after work Walter took it upon himself to do the asking. With gigantic nonchalance he said, 'Come on, Mr Christy. Let's go out and see if you can beat me for nine holes.'

15

Christy didn't say a word for several minutes. Then slowly he said, 'Young man, when I want to play golf, I'll do the asking. Not you.' He turned round and walked away quietly. Walter was nonplussed. Man, he thought, did he carry it off big. From that day on, Walter decided, whatever he did, win or lose, he too would carry it off big.

Hagen was nineteen when he played in his first tournament. The Canadian Open was being conducted at the Rosedale Golf Club in Toronto; Hagen thought he ought to go and win it. He gathered his clubs and his suitcase together, took the day coach to Buffalo and the night boat across Lake Ontario from there to Toronto. This was the farthest he had ever been away from home. But most of it was over water, and for Hagen water never counted.

Hagen hit the ball like a fat lady and came in 36th. Then he took the night boat back to Buffalo and rode the train from there to Rochester. When he walked into the golf shop at The Country Club of Rochester, no one paid any attention to him.

'Well, I'm back,' he said, dropping his suitcase and his clubs to the floor with a bang.

'Where ya been?' someone asked.

'Toronto,' Hagen said.

'Yeah? What ya been doin' up there?' someone said.

'Playin' in the Canadian Open,' Hagen said.

'Yeah? How'd you make out?'

'I lost,' he said, and then he went back to being the assistant professional at The Country Club of Rochester – where he thought he belonged.

Later that year Hagen was made head pro when Andrew Christy left to become the professional at Equinox in Vermont. In addition to teaching golf, Hagen also gave lessons to the members in tennis, ice skating and even croquet. By the summer of 1913 he decided that it was about time he played in another golf tournament. Here he was at twenty, without a title to his name. The big tournament, the National Open, was scheduled for Brookline, so he thought it might as well be that one as any other. He threw some golf togs into his suitcase and then, because he was going to Boston, he dressed in what he considered to be the height of fashion: waxed-calf shoes with red rubber soles and a double-breasted suit that had three kinds of plaid superimposed on one another.

Hagen rode the coach all night to Boston. When he got there, he couldn't make up his mind whether to stay at the YMCA or at a hotel.

He had been warned about hotels back in Brighton. People said that you could have your money stolen and never know until it was too late, or that a woman might sneak into your room and claim she had been raped. Hagen decided that he wanted to look like a champion as well as be one when he got through at Brookline, so he went to the Copley-Plaza.

Hagen strode into the lobby with his suitcase in his hand and his golf bag slung over his shoulder. In those days it might just as well have been a bass horn. People stared. 'I'm here to play in a golf tournament,' he announced to the room clerk, with about twenty pounds of clubs on his back. 'Where's this place they're playin' the National Open?'

'At the country club,' the clerk said, eyeing Hagen suspiciously.

'You're kidding,' Hagen said. 'I thought it was going to be at the ball park.'

'No, at the country club,' the clerk said.

'*What* country club?' Hagen said. My god, Hagen thought, there had to be more than one in a town the size of Boston.

'*The* Country Club,' the clerk said. 'At Brookline. There'll be transportation in another hour.'

Hagen went to his room and dressed for his game. He put on a shirt with vertical red, white and blue stripes on it and a pair of white flannels. He turned up the trouser cuffs, just once. Two turns, in Walter's opinion, and he would have looked like a hick.

At the Country Club Hagen was astounded at what he saw and heard. Right in the middle of the golf course was a racetrack, and next to it was a polo field. There were red and yellow touring cars all over the place, the kind with spare tyres stuck into the fenders. All the members looked to Hagen as though they had bought their clothes in the same store and had been to the same barber. The women wore yards of silk and hats so big that when they took them off they had to have a bed to put them on. The men and women stood around in groups, as though it were against the law to be alone, and they spoke with slight accents. Everything seemed to be a surprise to them. It was 'You don't say?' and 'Not really?' and 'By George!' and 'I do believe.' Hagen was impressed.

At the half-way mark Hagen was leading Johnnie McDermott by a stroke. But twenty-four hours later he was back on the coach to Rochester, disgusted with himself. He had lost another tournament, having been beaten by Vardon and Ray and an amateur he had never heard of. That was the last tournament he ever would play in, he thought.

Yet when the National Open rolled around in August, Hagen put on his triple-plaided suit and his waxed-calf shoes with the red rubber soles. He packed his flannels with the cuff turned up just once and his red, white and blue shirt. Then he jumped on the day coach for Chicago, and he knew, win or lose, it was going to be golf from then on.

Hagen travelled to Chicago with a friend named Dutch Leonard. They checked into the Great Northern Hotel. On the night before the tournament, Hagen decided he wanted to go to one of the big hotels and eat with the cattle barons. Dutch reminded him that they were travelling on Mr Willard's money.* They found a side-street eatery with checked tablecloths and no carpets. Hagen ordered lobster.

After dinner the two of then took in a picture show, and then they went back to the Great Northern to go to bed.

At two o'clock in the morning Hagen woke up with a stomach ache. He felt as though he had swallowed an old boxing glove.

'What's the matter?' Dutch said excitedly when Hagen began to moan.

'I don't know!' Hagen said.

'You sick?' Dutch said.

''Course I'm sick.'

'I'll get a doctor.'

When the doctor came up to Hagen's room, he probed his stomach and then tossed some pink pills at him. 'Take these,' he said. 'I'll be back later this morning.'

'But he's got to play golf at nine-thirty,' Dutch said.

'I don't know much about golf,' the doctor said, 'but if he can play without exercise, he might make it.'

'Without exercise?' Dutch said. 'He's got to play thirty-six holes. That's almost eight miles!'

'He won't enjoy it much,' the doctor said. 'Can't he wait until next week?'

'Next week?' Dutch said. 'For heaven's sake, Doc! This is the championship of the world.' It was a pardonable exaggeration.

The doctor looked at Hagen and scratched his head. 'I'll be back at six o'clock,' he announced.

By six o'clock the boxing glove in Hagen's stomach had begun to

---

* Ernest Willard, editor of *The Rochester Democrat*, had agreed to pay all the expenses of Hagen and a friend – provided Hagen gave up any idea of pursuing a baseball career.

feel like a basketball. The doctor gave Hagen another going-over with his fingertips and then prescribed warm milk and toast, and aspirin every half hour. Pink pills, warm milk and toast, and aspirin tablets: Hagen figured this guy must have studied medicine by mail. He decided to hell with the National Open.

'But you gotta play,' Dutch argued. 'You gotta. What will Mr Willard think?'

'I'm sick,' Hagen said, and rolled over in bed.

'I know you're sick,' Dutch said. 'But how are you gonna explain that you didn't even try to play because you had a tummy ache?'

'I'll worry about that when it stops aching.'

'Look, Walter,' Dutch said. He was starting to plead. 'Why don't you ride out to Midlothian? See how you feel by starting time. If you're still sick, withdraw.'

Hagen realized Dutch was right. He had to make an effort at least. He got dressed and they grabbed the train to Midlothian. It was a hot day and the train windows were open. The soot flew in and got in Hagen's eyes and his mouth. He had cramps and his head ached. He was eating aspirin tablets as though they were salted peanuts.

At Midlothian Hagen went directly to the practice tee. After he had hit a few balls his headache surprisingly left. But the stomach cramps persisted, so Hagen decided to withdraw.

'Why don't you play a hole or two?' Dutch said. 'If you don't feel any better, you can walk in.'

The first fairway at Midlothian was cut in half by a stream two hundred yards from the tee. Hagen didn't think he could carry it. He flinched at the ball on his drive and sliced it deep into the rough. His recovery was surprisingly good, and he got down in two putts for his par. Dutch gave him an anxious look when he walked off the green. Hagen decided to play another hole.

He flinched at his drive again, but he made another sharp recovery and got his par. 'What the hell,' he said to Dutch. 'Might as well finish the round.'

Hagen shot a 68, a course record. No one in the gallery could have been as surprised at his score as Hagen, because, outside of Dutch Leonard, none of them knew how sick he was. Everybody made a big to-do about his score when he walked off the eighteenth green, so Hagen figured he must be leading by a mile.

To make sure, he walked over to the scoreboard. It was a sobering sight. He was leading, all right – by one stroke! Francis Ouimet, the defending champion, had shot a 69.

That afternoon, Hagen shot a 74. The next morning he shot a 73. He was still leading.

In the final round that afternoon, Hagen was busy trying to hang on to his lead. There was a pretty good-looking girl in the gallery, he had noticed, but he was too busy to pay much attention to her. Ordinarily, he would have made an effort to get acquainted, but he only had time to learn that her name was Mabel, that she was nineteen, had brown hair and hazel eyes, stood five-feet-four, weighed a hundred and ten pounds, had an ice-cream complexion and had never played golf before but was willing to learn. On the fifteenth hole – four holes away from capturing the National Open – Hagen stopped to ask Mabel if she would like him to give her a lesson. Mabel said yes, she would. They made a date for eight o'clock that evening.

Hagen then proceeded to three-putt both the sixteenth and seventeenth holes. On the eighteenth, worried about what those three-putt greens might have done to his chances, he got back to business and canned a twenty-two-foot putt for a total of 292. This score led the field.

Behind him there were still a few players who could beat him or tie him. There didn't seem to be much Walter could do about the situation, so he went back to the eighteenth green to watch the others finish. 'Aren't you nervous?' someone asked.

'No,' Hagen said honestly. 'Why should I be? I've *got* my score.'

The grapevine brought Walter the news that everyone who had a chance to beat or tie him had faltered, everyone except a local amateur named Chick Evans. Finally, Evans himself came up the last fairway, needing a three to tie. Evans hit his second shot to the front bank of the green, a good sixty-five feet away from the cup. To force a play-off, he would have to chip in. The prospect didn't bother Hagen a bit. He felt he could beat anyone head to head, particularly an amateur.

Evans played an almost perfect chip. It looked 'in' all the way. In the last few feet, however, it veered off to the left, stopping nine inches from the cup. Hagen had won.

People who had never before taken the trouble to speak to him slapped him on the back and wrung his hand. He peeled off his coat, rolled up his sleeves and tossed a cap on his head for the photographers. He didn't have to say 'cheese' to smile. Then the officials handed him the winner's cheque for three hundred dollars. Hagen thanked the

he jacket-and-tie era: the great triumvirate of J. H. Taylor (seated), James Braid and Harry Vardon.

Above left Harry Vardon, *circa* 1900. *Above right* Abe Mitchell as late as 1935. *Below* Walter Hagen always dressed the part and is credited with introducing two-tone golf shoes. Here he is en route to defeat at the hands of Archie Compston, Moor Park, 1928.

gallery and the officials, and then he ran off to find Mabel, his date.

The next morning Walter had breakfast in his hotel. Halfway through his grapefruit, he got a queasy feeling in his stomach. For the first time in his life he felt nervous. What he had done on the golf course the day before came over him all at once, and he had to stand up and make a pronouncement to Dutch Leonard and himself. 'Good *night!*' he said. 'I'm champion of the whole goddam country!'

The World of Golf, Random House, 1962, and Cassell, 1963

Who's going to be second?
Henry Longhurst

If I were cast upon a desert island, which the Lord defer, and were permitted to choose one man as my companion in exile, I sometimes think I should call for that great philosopher and good companion, Walter Hagen.

The prospect of being cast upon a desert island with a golfer is one to fill the mind with a horrid anticipation. But to Hagen, third greatest golf player of all time, golf was only a means to an end. He used it as Gene Tunney used prize-fighting, and as Henry Cotton, as I think you will find, will turn out to have used golf.

Hagen was bigger than the game by which he rose to fame. In any walk of life into which he might have drifted he'd have been a success. He probably stuck to golf because it brought him with the least trouble the things he most desired from life: wealth, luxury, travel, the limelight and the company of famous men – and women – on level terms.

That he made a million dollars from golf is certain. It was equally certain that he would not die a rich man. 'Easy come, easy go,' was Hagen's motto with money, and maybe he was right.

My own affection for Hagen bordered almost on hero-worship. What a character! Staggering self-assurance; wit and good humour; a bronzed, impudent countenance with a wide-open smile; inexhaustible zest for life; and a unique ability to combine wine, women and song with the serious business of winning golf championships – that was . Hagen. A fellow whose like you meet once in a lifetime.

His golf exactly matched his personality. Often brilliant; never, never dull. He won the Open Championship of my country four times and of his own United States twice, and he made more bad shots in doing so than the man who finished second would make in a month. He finished at the top because his powers of recovery were almost superhuman. When he won his first championship at Sandwich, he went through six rounds without taking a six, yet four times he was still in a bunker beside the green in three.

It was only natural that such a man should capture the imagination of the crowd. At first they resented his swagger and his multi-hued attire. On one regrettable occasion in the early days they even clapped when he missed a shot. But that soon passed when they came to understand the real Hagen, and long after he was past his prime they flocked round with him like sheep.

He took them through all the emotions. He would play a succession of holes as though divinely inspired, while they marvelled at his skill. Then from a clear sky would come a stroke of unbelievable inaccuracy – a wild slice, or a top, or a quick, semi-circular hook – and the heart of the duffer warmed to the god that could descend to the level of man. And then, when all was apparently lost, he would extricate himself with a recovery which to the faithful seemed nothing less than a miracle.

Where other men strove vainly for consistent perfection, it was part of Hagen's philosophy, typically enough, to expect his quota of downright bad shots in every round he played. He expected them, so they did not upset him, as they did the others, when they came.

He was, of course, the showman par excellence, the master golfer-entertainer. No matinée idol ever had a stronger hold on his audience. I recall a tournament at Porthcawl, when his days of winning championships were already over. Hagen, still in London, was informed that he was to be partnered next day with a certain British Ryder Cup player and that they were to start at 10.30 am.

'I'll start at three,' said Walter.

He is the only man in the game who would not have been disqualified. Instead, they meekly replied: 'Very well, you shall start at three.'

Word went round the little town, and no one bothered to watch the morning play. They stored their energy for the afternoon. The master arrived in a huge Daimler saloon – I can see him now – seated in the small space left by a number of cabin trunks. He had his feet up, and genially waved a large cigar. In the front seat sat his sixteen-year-old son Junior.

Hagen knew he had not the remotest chance of winning the tournament. So did everyone else. But did that make any difference? Not a bit. Every spectator on the course was there at three to see him drive off. They followed him eagerly to the end. He took 81.

Next day they were there again. Hagen by this time had no chance of even qualifying for the final day's play, but who cared? He played deplorably and again took 81. Everyone was happy. They had seen Hagen play golf.

Hagen was the dandy of the links. 'Sir Walter', they called him. His clothes were immaculate, if sometimes a trifle bizarre, according to Savile Row conceptions, and frequently he'd change his whole outfit at lunchtime. I think he'd as soon have scratched as appear in clothes that offended his sartorial eye.

Was it vanity? Twenty-five per cent of it, maybe. The rest was a part of his astute sense of publicity. He knew that making money from golf did not depend only on winning the titles. It depended on being noticed, talked about, quoted, criticized – anything, in fact, but ignored.

It wasn't only natural indolence that made him late wherever he went. He liked to set the world asking: 'Where's Hagen?' Had he arrived? Would he be disqualified? By the time he appeared, the stage was set for his entrance, his name on everyone's lips. 'Ah, there he is! Good old Walter!' In all the times I watched him play, I never knew him to reach the first tee before his opponents.

Hagen had an overwhelming confidence in his own powers. 'Waal, who's gonna be second?' he would drawl as he strolled out to the first tee. Then he would win – and win against the best competition the world could offer. His imitators cried: 'Who's going to be second?' – and then finished 20th.

Innumerable tales, some of them true, are told of his irrepressible self-assurance. Perhaps the most characteristic concerns the finish of his Hoylake Championship. He frittered the shots away in his last round and was out in 40 or 41. At any rate, he had to come home in 36, and knew it, to beat Ernest Whitcombe's total of 302 – and there is no tougher finish in the world than the last five holes at Hoylake.

He got by the tenth with a four and drove into a bunker at the Alps (the short eleventh). He blasted it out and holed the putt. Bunkered again at the twelfth, he holed a whopper for his four. Then his tee shot to the short thirteenth floated away into the sand, and that, surely, was the end. There were no strokes to be picked up on the last five holes, even by Hagen, and a four at the thirteenth must cost him the championship. He flipped the ball neatly out to within a few feet and got a three.

And so he came to the seventeenth needing two fours to win the Open. At the seventeenth he played what must stand as one of the greatest iron shots of all time, a long, low shot that ran nimbly through the narrow opening and lay eight feet from the hole. A three there would clinch it, but he rolled the ball casually along and missed it. Four to win! Every man in Hoylake, and half Liverpool, as it seemed, crowded round the last green. Watchers craned their necks from every window.

Hagen hit his second shot right over the back into the long grass. His approach, not bad in the circumstances, ran within eight or nine feet of the hole. One putt to win!

Where most men would have spent an age in preparation, Hagen strolled up to his putt and with scarcely a preliminary glance ran it into the hole.

As he walked from the green, having duly been embraced by his wife, a colleague of mine said to him: 'You seemed to treat that putt very casually, Hagen. Did you know you had it to win?'

'Sure, I knew I had it to win,' drawled Walter, 'but no man ever beat me in a playoff!'

Then again they'll tell you the tale of how Hagen was left with a long putt to tie with Leo Diegel for a tournament in America and insisted that Diegel should be summoned from the clubhouse to see him hole it – to be suitably impressed before the playoff on the following day. Of course, he holed it. The only trouble about this tale, which I have been told by several people who actually saw it happen, is that they saw it happen at several different clubs and the other man was not always Diegel.

All the same, I fancy that Hagen must have holed more crucial putts deliberately than any man who ever won a championship. Indeed, I recall no instance on which, in his prime, he missed one that he knew would win or lose him a title. Yet he was never a man to waste effort. The rich streak of idleness in his makeup saw to that. Thus when, at Muirfield in 1929, he was left with a putt of four feet to win the Open Championship, he missed it by inches. So great was his lead that he could have taken seven putts and still have won. But not a man doubted that he would have holed that putt if the title had hung on it.

They do say that Hagen that day played the greatest golf ever seen in the Open. On the previous day in calm weather he had gone round in 67, the lowest score hitherto recorded in a championship. (This prompted a friend of mine to send a wire to the green committee of the Honourable Company of Edinburgh Golfers, i.e. The Muirfield Club, saying: 'Suggest play off back tees for remainder of championship.')

On the final day there blew a mighty gale. Scores shot into the eighties and all day the best round was 74. But the gale only showed Hagen as the supreme artist, a man who could juggle with a golf ball as though it were tied to a string. He produced from somewhere a mallet-headed, deep-faced driver, and they say that for 36 holes he steered his ball along within twenty feet of the ground. Cannily, craftily, he was round twice in 75. Starting two strokes behind Diegel, he finished six shots ahead of the field.

As for the rules of training and physical fitness, Hagen defied the lot of them. He was the only man who could stay up till three in the morning playing bridge, smoking cigars and stoking up with whisky, and go out and win a championship in the morning. Others tried, and great was their downfall. His power of concentration, too, was exceptional. Even in the closing stages of a tournament, when a false step might cost £1,000 or more, he could converse with his friends as he walked along between shots, breaking off suddenly when he came to within a few yards of his ball and switching his mind completely over to the business in hand. The only thing I ever knew to put him off was when, at Sandwich, they told him the Prince of Wales had arrived to watch him. He topped his next shot forty yards. Then he pitched up and holed his putt for a four.

It was at Sandwich that he made perhaps the most famous of all Hagen gestures. Having won the Open Championship of Great Britain, he handed the first prize, then a meagre £50, straight to his caddie. He knew he could cash in on the title for thousands of dollars in America. As for the caddie, he died some years later, and his friends have told me that, following the celebration with Hagen's cheque, he was never the same man again.

Walter's first love, they tell me, was baseball, and he might have made a great pitcher. Later he became crazy on shooting and fishing, both of which sports he pursued with the eager enthusiasm of a boy with a catapult, and big game hunting, in which he indulged as a sideline during his golfing tours round the world. I remember sitting in the lounge of a Carnoustie hotel at half-past one in the morning during the 1937 Championship, when in walked Hagen with a basket under his arm. In it were half a dozen trout. He was lying well up in the championship, but that had not stopped him driving seventy miles for an evening's fishing. He took the fish down to the kitchen, gutted them and solemnly cooked them for his supper.

Two of his matches over here will never be forgotten. One will never be forgiven. It was in 1928 that he stepped off the boat and went straight to play Archie Compston over 72 holes for, it was said, £500. He was out of practice after the voyage, and was beaten by the staggering margin of 18 up and 17 to play, an all-time record. A lesser man would have struggled to keep the margin of defeat down to reasonable proportions. Hagen, I suspect, when he saw he could not win, saw to it that the margin was so colossal that the world would discount the result of the match. Be that as it may, the following week he went down to Sandwich and won the Open Championship. Compston was third.

The other match, against Abe Mitchell in 1926, brought all manner of abuse on his head and added a phrase to the English golfers' vocabulary – 'Doing a Hagen' – in other words, keeping a man waiting for the purpose of putting him off. In the first 36 holes at Wentworth Mitchell finished four up. The second was played at St George's Hill, and Hagen was half an hour late, a circumstance to which Mitchell's friends, though not so far as I know Mitchell himself, ascribed his ultimate defeat by 2 and 1. Hagen said his driver lost his way in the fog, and, indeed, St George's Hill is difficult enough to find on a clear day. Hagen's record for being habitually late makes it likely that, as usual, he had simply not bothered to get there in time. I doubt if he had any ulterior motive. In any case I always think the suggestion that Hagen won this match almost by cheating reflects at least as badly on Mitchell. It portrays him as a man of such meagre calibre as to lose six clear holes in a day for no better reason than that the match started half an hour after the advertised time. I don't believe it. Be that as it may, it took Hagen years to live the incident down.

Life has been very much the richer for having known Hagen. He was the most colourful, spectacular personality cast up by the game of golf, and will take his place in sporting history with the giants. Their statistical records may have been surpassed, but they stay on their pedestals, men who became legends in their lifetime.

The Best of Henry Longhurst, Mark Wilson and Ken Bowden (eds), Collins, 1979

The first chipper-and-putter
Henry Cotton

In 1933 I played a match with Hagen at Ashridge, which later became my home club, and got beaten 2 and 1 over 36 holes. Some months later I asked Hagen on behalf of the Waterloo Golf Club, where I was professional, if he would come and play there against me. He agreed and the golfers in Belgium were delighted.

As he had not arrived by the day preceding the match there was much anxiety manifest, and telephone calls were made to find out if he had forgotten the game. He was located and promised to leave by the 9 am plane from Croydon; this would give him time to reach the club shortly after 11 am. They telephoned from the club to the Savoy Hotel in London at 8.30 on the morning of the match to make sure he had left, and the call awakened him, for he had turned in late and had forgotten to leave a call in. Of course, he could not catch the plane, as it was a forty-minute journey to Croydon. The only way was to hire a private plane. No, he would not let me down, he'd be there! A private plane was hired and he calculated he had got away in time to reach the club by eleven something. It was foggy off the coast, so the pilot made for Antwerp and from there he telephoned to say, 'What do I do now?'

We found he could land at Brussels and so on came the little plane. Finally at about midday he arrived and greeted the crowd, which by this time was absolutely fuming at the delay, with a 'Howdy folks' and a big smile, whereupon he received a round of applause, had a quick drink and was soon on the tee.

Anyone who can do that sort of thing and get away with it 'has some-thing', and although I do not admire that kind of behaviour, for it is bad taste after all, Hagen somehow did it regularly and was always forgiven. Yet I do not think it was deliberate; he just had no sense of responsibility where time was concerned. It will be remembered how he kept Abe Mitchell waiting, and this cost Abe the match. This act went down badly at the time with the public over here, but Hagen soon outlived it.

On this occasion I played very well all day and beat him 6 and 5, but if I had not equalled the course competition record of 66 in the morning I should not have had a three-hole lead, for he did the course in 69 the first time round, and that is always a good round at Waterloo from the tiger tees.

Archie Compston beat him terribly on one occasion 18 and 17, but as he won the Open that same year, people said, 'Hagen couldn't have been trying' – rather unfair on Big Archie, but still, who could ever give Hagen any start?

Bernard Darwin tells the story of Hagen sitting up late playing cards at the Marine Hotel, Gullane, where he was staying for the 1929 Open at Muirfield. He was still enjoying himself at 3 or 4 am, and one of his admirers, wishing to drop him a hint that it was time he turned in, said that Leo Diegel, his nearest rival, had been in bed some hours. 'But,' replied Hagen, 'he won't be asleep,' and knowing Diegel's nervous temperament, how true that was!

Hagen had a good-to-watch swing, long and loose. He always had a sort of lurch, as if he was forcing his shots, and from a wide stance this sway was most marked. He had great control over his short shots, the stroke-savers round the pin, and yet I always felt his shots from fifty to one hundred yards were his 'strongest'. He holed many more doubtful putts than his contemporaries, but the pace has got so hot since his heyday that the winners hole the putts today for threes and fours where he was holing them for fours and fives, as the scores testify.

The first great American player of my day was Walter Hagen, my hero, and while no one ever claimed to copy his play, apart from his putting stance (for his long game, as I have said, was loose and consequently adventurous), he began the 'recovery era'. Hagen, now (1948) a bespectacled respected monument of a man, plays no golf to speak of. He never really did love it, he confessed to me in the train to Portland last year. He used his ability at the game to provide him with the necessary money to enjoy life, and his financial success and iron constitution enable him to keep right up to date with his programme, in a very important way. He was the first 'chipper and putter' winner, the first one I recall who made the world feel it was not the wrong thing to get a four with a one-putt green. He reminds me of a Japanese touring professional who aptly remarked one day, when asked why he did not win, 'I took too many two-putt greens.'

Hagen set a new professional golf style; he acted differently, not always beyond reproach, but always graciously, and his tongue never hurt anybody. He dressed well, expensively and with taste. He practised rarely. He made fast friends, and today his friends so love him that there are Hagen days everywhere in America, and there is even a movement on foot to make his birthday a national golfing holiday.

This Game of Golf, Country Life, 1948

A competitive genius
Gene Sarazen with H. W. Wind

Hagen was the poorest wooden-club player of all the great champions. He swayed on his tee-shots and fairway woods. It was the rare round on which he did not hook or slice at least three shots forty yards or more off line. After these chronic lapses, Hagen would have to walk into areas where Dr Livingstone would have feared to tread.

He made other errors. His long irons, which he played instead of fairway woods whenever he could, suffered from that same sway. In traps he had so little confidence in his ability to play explosion shots that he was forced to cut the ball out cleanly. How then was Hagen able to lead a very strong pro pack for over fifteen years and to win more major championships than any other modern golfer except Jones – two United States Opens, four British Opens and five PGAs?

To begin with, Hagen was the game's competitive genius. He could adjust himself to all conditions. He held his poise at crucial junctures, delivered his most telling blows when they really counted. He had an amazing reservoir of strength. He could write off his mistakes with no decrease in his confidence. His golf philosophy was, 'I'll miss shots and the other boys will miss them too, but I'll save them on the same hole and they won't be able to.' He did, too, because he was a masterful short-iron player – I can't think of anyone who could touch him from 140 yards in. Walter didn't sway on these short irons. He played them with a controlled brief pivot, and how he could feel that clubhead! There wasn't a type of pitch that he couldn't and didn't play, intentional draw shots, calculated fades, the high cut-shot, the low buzzer struck sharply on the downswing which bit like a bulldog, the sensitively gauged pitch-and-run – whatever shot was dictated by his lie, the speed of the green and the position of the flag. (He also hit more beautiful half-tops than any other golfer.) In the traps – as I say, he was shaky about explosions and there wasn't a one of us who wasn't, Jones included – you ought to have seen those hands work! Walter could nip that ball as cleanly off the sand as if it were resting on top of a three-inch tee, this when the faintest fraction of an inch too much of the ball or too much of the sand spelled instant calamity. Walter won the 1928 British Open with just such a daring recovery on the last round from the difficult trap on the fifteenth at Sandwich, and this was but one of the numerous instances when he displayed his majestic ability under fire. And on the greens – there you saw that marvellous temperament operating. He putted from a partial crouch, the ball lined up off his left toe. You could play four or five rounds with the old boy before you saw him stroke one putt off the line. I've yet to see his equal as a consistent birdie-holer from twelve to fifteen feet.

It was a cruel day for Walter, and indeed a sad one for all who love golf, when the years caught up with Hagen and he reluctantly retired. The British miss him as much as we do. The first question they still ask is, 'How's Walter Hagen?'

Thirty Years of Championship Golf, Prentice-Hall, 1950

Tommy Armour

Born 24 September 1896, Edinburgh, Scotland. Died
September 1968.

Perhaps the greatest Scottish golfer since James Braid, Armour was
best known for the quality of his iron play, though many judges felt
that his woods were not inferior.

Winner of three major titles – US Open, US PGA and the British
Open shortly described, he later became legendary as a teacher and
for his success in coming away with the money in four-ball matches –
this despite the fact that his putting was suspect.

He wrote a golf instruction book that I would guess has both sold
the most and remained the longest in print of the hosts that have been
produced (one per Open champion and many more besides).

Armour takes the breaks
Bernard Darwin

There is some judgement but a great deal of luck in seeing the important things at an Open championship, and it was wholly luck that
made me see the most crucial of all incidents in Armour's last and
victorious round at Carnoustie.

There is one point on the links where everyone forgathers. It is close
to the ominous wood of black firs into which luckless people may hook
the ball at the short eighth hole. Here the seventh, eighth, twelfth and
thirteenth holes all more or less converge, and here I was standing on
the last afternoon, rather dizzy in the midst of a whirlpool of rumours.
Along came Armour to the twelfth hole and hit a magnificent brassie
shot right onto the middle of the twelfth green, which very few players
could reach in two. Rumour, which turned out for once not to be
lying, said that his score was two under fours. That was just about
good enough to win, even though he had started five shots behind
Jurado, and clearly he must be watched.

He struck his long putt perfectly and the ball slipped past the edge
of the hole not more than two feet away. Then he took rather a long

while and missed the two-foot putt by a good two inches. To the next, the short thirteenth, he played a poor tee-shot and the ball ended off the green, rather fortunately not in heather or sand. Armour came up to play his chip and it was clear that his emotions had almost beaten him. He waggled and he looked up at the hole with a quick turn of the head, and he went on waggling and looking until no one else could bear to look at him. If he misses this one, I thought to myself, he is done; but he waited until he could settle down, he laid it nearly dead and he holed the putt. The crisis was past and he went on playing lovely golf to the end.

In the evening I told him that I had seen those two holes, and he agreed that they had settled the issue. No one could believe, he said, what a blow that short putt missed had been; there he was playing beautifully and then came this sudden, staggering shock. If, he added, his tee-shot to the thirteenth had found trouble, as it well might, he was 'gone', and, even when it did not, he felt he simply could not play the next shot because his brain was whirling like a mill-race, and he was thinking and thinking about everything in the whole world except the business in hand. Our Open championship was the one thing he wanted to win, and he felt himself on the verge of throwing it all away.

One could almost see him thinking all these things, and I have told the story at length both because I hope it is rather interesting and because it shows the kind of golfer the new champion is. He is full of imagination, a bundle of quivering nerves kept fiercely under control, and this is the kind of temperament that either breaks a player of games or makes him terribly formidable. As a striker of the ball, except sometimes when it is dead at the holeside, Armour is truly magnificent. I do not believe that Taylor or Vardon at their best ever gave themselves so many possible putts for three with their iron shots as he does, and his style is the perfection of rhythm and beauty. From the beginning of the week I bored all our small party at the hotel by telling them that Armour was the best player in the field, and I am not likely to recant now.

A man may be the best player and still he cannot win the championship unless the luck be with him. Armour unquestionably had the luck of the weather, and at the end of the first two days he said that, having had the luck, he had missed the chance of getting away with a substantial lead. The wind blew pretty hard on Wednesday morning and Thursday afternoon. It lulled on Wednesday afternoon and

Thursday morning. Sarazen and Farrell had to play their first round on Wednesday morning and their second on Thursday morning; Armour and Jurado had to do exactly the opposite, and while their advantage cannot be exactly computed in strokes it was a very real one. Had matters been the other way round, either Sarazen or Farrell might have won. As Gene said, 'You have to take the breaks,' and they did not have them.

The last three holes at Carnoustie with the wind blowing from the east (which is not the normal way or the best way for the course) make up just about the most testing and perilous finish in all golf. Consequently there were several tragedies enacted there. If Alliss could have done the last two in four and five he would have tied with Armour's score, and he took five and six with a dreadfully superfluous shot out of bounds at the last. Then there was Macdonald Smith. This was the supreme effort of a golfing lifetime on his own native heath; he had pulled round splendidly from a bad start in his first round and he was playing like clockwork in his last. He wanted 3, 4, 5, par golf, to beat Armour, and could afford to lose one stroke and yet tie with him. He lost four strokes in two holes and finished 5, 6, 5. I saw the six at the seventeenth, without his ball touching any form of hazard, and I felt rather as if I had gone to see a man hanged. Finally, and most poignant of all, was Jurado's tragedy, also at the seventeenth. He wanted a four and a five to win, and it seemed as if he could hardly fail to get the two fives to tie, for the seventeenth down the wind, though not an easy four, is quite an easy five. One thought of all sorts of mistakes he might make but one never dreamed of the one he did make, when he popped the ball into the burn off the tee, more or less in front of his nose. It was terribly sad, for he is a splendid little man (he does not weigh ten stone) and had played splendidly courageous golf, full of smiling excitement but always keeping control of himself. I wish these horrid things were not inevitable in championships.

Yet another tragedy, of course, had happened earlier in the day, and that was the breakdown of Cotton in his third round, when British hopes of his winning were very high. Cotton today is a great golfer, and I think his time will surely come, but a championship only comes once a year, and he that will not when he may, etc. The technical cause of his downfall was, as it seemed to me, that he was getting on the wrong side of the hole; he was sparing his approaches down the wind going out with the result that he left himself long down-wind putts. Continually to lay these dead is desperate work; he left himself too much to do, and when the ensuing five-foot putts went astray his game began to disintegrate. No doubt there was a more general cause, too, namely, that though Cotton has tried hard to school a naturally rebellious temperament, he has not yet wholly succeeded, and when things went wrong he could not quite stand the strain. It is this control that he has to practise now, for his hitting of the ball is just about good enough for anything or anybody.

Country Life, 13 June 1931

Joyce Wethered

Born 17 November 1901, Maldon, Surrey, England.

When the talk turns to who is the greatest golfer of all time, a surprising name is apt to turn up: Joyce Wethered. Few today have seen her play at her best, for her peak years occupied the 1920s, after which she mainly withdrew from competitive golf at the highest level.

In this decade she won the British Ladies four times and the English five. Perhaps as remarkable was that between 1922 and 1936 she won the Worplesdon mixed foursome eight times and it is said that more often than not she carried the male of the species to victory. Possibly she did not have quite the appetite for championships as others have had: her record is abbreviated by retirement rather than defeat.

In the mid-1930s she toured the USA playing exhibitions with the best players of the day, both male and female. All seem to have thought her their superior.

The greatest of golfers
R. T. Jones Jnr

Ordinarily I would never take advantage of a friendly round of golf by making the play of a person kind enough to go around with me the subject of an article. I realize that everyone likes to play occasionally a round of golf when reputations can be forgotten, with nothing more at stake than the outcome of the match and a little friendly bantering afterwards.

Just before the British Amateur Championship at St Andrews, Miss Joyce Wethered allowed herself to be led away from her favourite trout stream in order to play eighteen holes of golf over the Old Course in company with her brother, Roger, Dale Bourne, then recently crowned English Champion, and myself. At the time, I fully appreciated that Miss Wethered had not had a golf club in her hand for over a fortnight, and I certainly should have made no mention of the game had she not played so superbly.

We started out by arranging a four-ball match – Roger and Dale against Miss Wethered and myself – on a best and worst ball basis. I don't know why we didn't play an ordinary four-ball match, unless we fancied that the lady would be the weakest member of the four, and that in a best-ball match her ball would not count for very much. If any of us had any such idea at the start of the match, it is now quite immaterial, for there is not the slightest chance that we should admit it.

We played the Old Course from the very back, or the championship tees, and with a slight breeze blowing off the sea. Miss Wethered holed only one putt of more than five feet, took three putts rather half-heartedly from four yards at the seventeenth after the match was over, and yet she went round St Andrews in 75. She did not miss one shot; she did not even half miss one shot; and when we finished, I could not help saying that I had never played golf with anyone, man or woman, amateur or professional, who made me feel so utterly out-classed.

It was not so much the score she made as the way she made it. Diegel, Hagen, Smith, Von Elm and several other male experts would likely have made a better score, but one would all the while have been expecting them to miss shots. It was impossible to expect that Miss Wethered would ever miss a shot – and she never did.

To describe her manner of playing is almost impossible. She stands quite close to the ball, she places the club once behind, takes one look toward the objective and strikes. Her swing is not long – surprisingly short, indeed, when one considers the power she develops – but it is rhythmic in the last degree. She makes ample use of her wrists, and her left arm within the hitting area is firm and active. This, I think, distinguishes her swing from that of any other woman golfer, and it is the one thing that makes her the player she is.

Men are always interested in the distance which a first-class woman player can attain. Miss Wethered, of course, is not as long with any club as the good male player. Throughout the round, I found that when I hit a good one I was out in front by about twenty yards – by not so much when I failed to connect. It was surprising, though, how often on a fine championship course fine iron play by the lady could make up the difference. I kept no actual count, but I am certain that her ball was the nearest to the hole more often than any of the other three.

I have no hesitancy in saying that, accounting for the unavoidable handicap of a woman's lesser physical strength, she is the finest golfer I have ever seen.

The American Golfer, Charles Price, Random House.

The best player ever?
Henry Cotton

Whenever golfers gather and begin talking of one of the game's most popular topics, 'Who is the best player ever?' it is certain that before many minutes have passed the name of Joyce Wethered (now Lady Heathcoat-Amory) will be mentioned.

Lady Heathcoat-Amory, in the days when she was Joyce Wethered, was a great golfer, for she hit the ball as far as the average scratch player, and with feminine grace. She had the advantage of playing in her early days with her brother, also a wonderful golfer, and came to play at a much higher standard than any other woman has yet reached.

Lady Heathcoat-Amory hit the ball a long way from the tee, could play a spoon or brassie from the fairway as straight as most professionals could play a short iron shot and her chipping and putting were beautiful to watch.

Everybody has tried to form an exact comparison between this Queen of Golf and the men champions, but, despite the fact that Lady Heathcoat-Amory held Bobby Jones during one practice round, when she played in a four-ball match with him at St Andrews, there is no doubt in my mind that she would be the first to admit, modestly and seriously, that she could not be expected to play first-class male players on level terms.

On certain courses where, perhaps, length counts less than usual, Lady Heathcoat-Amory could keep up with the best men players on level terms, but from the back tees on the very big courses the carries are too long.

I do not think a golf ball has ever been hit, except perhaps by Harry Vardon, with such a straight flight by any other person. This feature alone made Lady Heathcoat-Amory's game unique to watch. Curiously enough, both she and the great Harry seemed to allow the shot to drift slightly to the right when it could not be described as dead straight.

In my opinion, the best feature of her game was her pitch-and-run shots. The rest were impressive, but it was these low-flying shots, played with a mashie more often than not, which intrigued me. They were played with such a beautiful touch, and had been well calculated beforehand. They were not just guesswork.

There are certain shots a weak golfer cannot play. Although Lady Heathcoat-Amory cannot be described as a weak player, she is the first to acknowledge that her brother, for example, always had an advantage over her in recovery shots, as she could not force the ball to the pin as effectively as he could from bad places. Then again, she was not required to play these shots very often!

One day I had a letter from Lady Heathcoat-Amory saying that she and her husband would like to come to Ashridge, at the time my home club, and talk golf with me. I was very pleased and honoured to have them visit me, and looked up the various golf books written by her, or about her, so that I had her old swing in mind. She had said in her letter that she had not played much lately, and was not hitting the ball as she used to do in the old days.

Lady Heathcoat-Amory had assisted so many men partners to win the Worplesdon Mixed Foursomes over a long period that she hoped to bring her husband through, although he was not quite up to the Worplesdon male standard, and having left big golf for some time she was not in her best form.

We all hit shots on the practice ground before lunch, and I timidly suggested that her 'perfect golf swing' of the old days was much narrower than usual. Lady Heathcoat-Amory widened her swing a little, and there followed a string of perfect golf shots which might have been poured out of a machine.

Then we began to hit shots with the left hand only. Although Lady Heathcoat-Amory had never before tried to strike the ball this way, she quickly adapted herself to swing with one hand. She hit the ball splendidly, which is always a good sign, as the left hand plays a great part in the swing.

After lunch I showed her some old photographs of herself, taken in her competitive days, and we discussed and analysed them together. We then played a round – a round I really enjoyed, for Lady Heathcoat-Amory gave a glorious display of hitting the golf ball, and perfect shot followed perfect shot.

Lady Heathcoat-Amory could play medal rounds and match-play golf; I believe every good player can, although there are still certain golfers who think a good medal player can be a bad match player.

In my time, no golfer has stood out so far ahead of his or her contemporaries as Lady Heathcoat-Amory. I am pleased to add to the world's acclamation my appreciation of this wonder golfer – a figure of modesty and concentration, and an example to everybody.

This Game of Golf, Country Life, 1948

Bobby Jones

Born 17 March 1902, Atlanta, Georgia, USA. Died 18 December 1971.

To me the most astounding feature of Robert Tyre Jones's record is that in only one year between 1922 and 1930 – 1927 – did he do worse than finish second in the US Open. In those other years he won four times, tied and lost play-offs twice and was second in the remaining years. His record in the British Open, with three wins and no other high placings, is at first sight less impressive. But Jones was an amateur and as a working man could infrequently afford the time for the long Atlantic crossing. So he won in 1926 and 1927 but did not compete during the two following Hagen years and his next appearance in 1930 was marked by another and final victory, followed a few months later by his retirement from competitive play.

Of course, the winning of the Grand Slam in 1930 – the US and British Opens and the US and British Amateurs – is the Jones achievement that is pre-eminently remembered and it is difficult to believe that it will ever be done again: in the fifty years since Jones's retirement just one amateur, Johnny Goodman, has won either Open, and even if another amateur of such ability were to appear in the year 2200 would he be able to reject the millions that the professional circuit offers? No, the modern Grand Slam has to be seen as the four major professional championships – the two Opens plus the US Masters and US PGA. To this, Hogan came close in 1953, his opportunity blocked by having to choose between the US PGA and the British Open. After that, only Jack Nicklaus has done enough to stir a little discussion of the possibility by winning the first two, the Masters and US Open, in 1972.

A genius for the game
Charles Price

The explanation for Bobby Jones's astounding golf is really quite simple. He had a genius for the game. Jones played in the 1916 National Amateur over the West Course at Merion when he was fourteen. Undisturbed by the fact that this was his first appearance in national competition, he led the field in the first round of the qualifying trials. When he was only twenty-four he became the first man to win both the United States and British Opens in a single season.

Then there was the Jones swing. This he put together by imitating Stewart Maiden, the pro at East Lake, his home course in Atlanta. It was flawless. 'There could be no more fascinating player to watch,' said Bernard Darwin, 'not only for the free and rhythmic character of his swing but for the swiftness with which he played. He had a brief preliminary address, but there was nothing hurried or slapdash about it and the swing itself, if not positively slow, had a certain drowsy beauty which gave the feeling of slowness. There was nothing that could conceivably be called a weak spot.'

As a putter, Jones was in a class with Walter J. Travis. In winning the 1927 British Open at St Andrews, Jones played the first round with twenty-eight putts – a not very remarkable total. However, in those twenty-eight putts Jones never missed one under twelve feet, and six of them were more than a hundred feet. On the fifth hole he sank a putt that was later paced off at forty yards.

The most charitable of men off the course, Jones on the course was absolutely without mercy to either his opponents or the course itself. He never once failed to qualify for a tournament he entered. In Chicago one year, he established the course record at Old Elm the first time he played it. A few days later he played the Chicago Golf Club and broke the course record there. The following day he broke that record and tied the old one on the day after. A few days later, while playing in a local invitation tournament, he broke the course record at Flossmoor, despite the fact that he played the first seven holes in two over par. He finished 3, 3, 3, 3, 3, 3, 3, 4, 3, 4, 4. After three more rounds, someone added up Jones's last dozen rounds. They came to this: 69, 71, 69, 68, 68, 68, 67, 68, 67, 70, 69, 67. Jones was then twenty-six, two years away from his best golf.

No amateur could hope to stand up to the way Jones assaulted par.

From the time Jones was fourteen to the time he was twenty-eight, no man ever beat him twice in championship match play. Among those who beat him once were Chick Evans, Bob Gardner and Francis Ouimet. Jones later beat Evans twice, Gardner twice and Ouimet three times. His defeats of these and other amateurs were sometimes so lopsided as to be embarrassing. In the quarter-finals, semi-finals and finals of the five National Amateurs he won, he stood a total of 136 holes up on his fifteen opponents, who, theoretically at least, were the best players in the field. In other words, he won these fifteen 36-hole matches by an average margin of 9 and 8. In still other words, he won one of every three holes he played. And Jones was not considered to be at his strongest at match play.

To depreciate Jones's record would be a little like saying the Civil War wasn't on the level. But the sad fact is, there are those who think Jones's record was too good to have been true. Jones, they say, played on easier courses and against weaker fields than exist today. Furthermore, they say, there is no telling how his record would have stood up had professionals such as Sam Snead, Ben Hogan and Byron Nelson been amateurs.

This last point is true; there is no way of knowing how many events Snead, Hogan or Nelson might have won had any of them been an amateur. But disregarding amateur events, it is without any disrespect whatever to Snead, Hogan and Nelson to point out that, when they reached the age at which Jones retired, Jones had won more open tournaments than any of them and more open championships than all of them. The notion that the men he defeated were not in a class with the players of today is, of course, ridiculous.

Furthermore, he won these championships on as fine an aggregation of courses as you will find anywhere in golfdom. At the time, artificial watering, of course, was unheard of. After a drought, greens would become so slick that a ball sounded like an egg frying and, drought or no drought, many of these courses were overrun with weeds, clover, couch grass and other fairway ailments that are all but unknown on championship layouts today. The scores he made on these courses were accomplished with wooden shafts and, with the exception of only one shot, without benefit of the sand iron.

Jones so devastated the opposition with his arrogance toward par and his disrespect for the record books that he could have been the most despised golfer of his day. Actually, he was the most admired and genuinely liked. No one before or since him has played the game with more modesty, thoughtfulness and integrity. On the night before his Sunday play-off with Al Espinosa for the National Open at Winged Foot, Jones, unknown to Espinosa, requested that the officials postpone the starting time for an hour so that Espinosa might have time to attend Mass. At four national championships, Jones called penalty strokes on himself for minor breaches of the Rules. In the 1925 National Open, at Worcester, he insisted on penalizing himself a stroke when his ball accidentally moved slightly in the rough when the blade of his iron touched the grass. No one else possibly could have seen the ball move, and the officials pooh-poohed the incident. But Jones insisted. That stroke cost him the title, which he lost in a play-off to Willie MacFarlane, and eventually prevented him from becoming the only man ever to win five National Opens. When Jones was praised for throwing the book at himself, he became indignant. 'There is only one way to play the game,' he said. 'You might as well praise a man for not robbing a bank.'

Jones was not just another athlete. He was an ultra-athlete, recognized as being better at his game than any other athlete was at his. Yet he remained unaffected at a time when flattering headlines were being made by athletes who had not a fraction of his talent, many of whom, if the public had had the stomach for the truth about them, would have been known to be a good deal more unsavoury than even the uninhibited journalism of that period cared to report. Perhaps no other section of American history has been more innocently recorded than the sports scene during the Roaring Twenties, yet Jones remained a man who was beyond the need of publicity when all about him odd characters by the dozen were being manufactured into public heroes. His public utterances were models of restraint and decorum, and so the image of him that was projected through the newspapers was impeccably true to life, not larger than life. With his personal fans – and golf remains the only game in the world where a spectator can touch his hero while he is playing – Jones's patience was monumental. He took them all in good-natured stride – backslappers, autograph hounds, favour seekers, story tellers, party crashers, name droppers, social opportunists, self-promoters, kissin' cousins, drunks and other assorted pests. 'He was the only celebrity I ever knew,' wrote Paul Gallico, who called athletes as he saw them, 'who was prepared to accept as gracefully as possible every penalty there is to be paid for fame and publicity in the United States.'

The remarkable thing about the way Jones could handle his public was that he was not the least bit calculating or priggish. He smoked to excess on the course, drank corn whisky off it, swore magnificently in either place and could listen to, or tell, an off-colour story in the locker-room afterward. He was spontaneous, affectionate and loyal to his friends, all of whom called him Bob, the name Bobby having been coined by British newspapers and then imported to the United States. Perhaps his closest friend was his father, Robert P. Jones, whom everybody called Colonel. (Bobby was named for his paternal grandfather, Robert T. Jones.) Jones's father was an eighty-shooter, but he always remained his son's favourite partner.

How well a man played made no difference at all to Jones when it came to choosing partners for a friendly round. He played with duffers and champions alike. While he did not like to lose to either, he knew how to lose. And when he won, he knew how to win. Indeed, when he had won everything there was to win, he had the incredibly good sense and grace to quit for good. 'With dignity,' said *The New York Times* of his retirement, 'he quit the memorable scene on which he nothing common did, or mean.'

The World of Golf, Random House, 1962, and Cassell, 1963

A close-up portrait
Grantland Rice

There are certain details connected with Bobby Jones's game that are beyond explaining. These include his complete co-ordination and his almost perfect smoothness that belong to genius. They are matters not to be defined in words. They can be seen and followed, but they cannot be taken apart for any casual inspection.

But there are also simpler details of his swing which can be more accurately hung up for public view. Where one might never understand just how any mere mortal can keep hitting the ball in exactly the same way and hitting it almost perfectly round after round, one can at least understand part of the physical accompaniment.

One of the first points to notice in Bobby Jones's play is the closeness with which he holds his feet together, even on full shots. Even on the drive I don't believe his feet are more than a foot apart, certainly not more than fourteen inches. Frequently on his pitch shots there is less than six inches separating the heels. On the short chip shots his heels are closer still, while in putting they are almost touching.

This matter of bringing the feet closer together than most golfers has two distinct values. In the first place it reduces tension throughout the body. It is more natural to stand with the feet fairly close than it is to spread them out in the braced attitude so many golfers use.

In the second place there is a feeling of better and easier balance. There is less tendency to hit with the body, a fault that has driven several million golfers into the borderland of melancholy depression, year after year. If you stand, for example, with your heels touching, you will find it practically impossible to use the body in the swing. If you attempt to do so you have the feeling of falling down. The closer stance where the feet are involved is a big factor in calling more upon the use of hands and wrists and arms.

There is still another aid to be obtained from this proximity of the feet. It makes the turn of the left hip a simpler, easier matter and this also applies to the transference of weight where there is less distance to be covered. Jones gets a world of leverage from this turn of the left hip. There is a greater tendency to keep the body locked and rigid with the feet spread too far apart for any comfortable body turn...

I watched him in practice at Brae Burn before his final match. For ten or fifteen minutes he hit almost every type of shot – drive, brassie, long-iron, full pitches and short pitches – and without exception he called on the straight left arm for every type of stroke. If there was the slightest kink in Jones's left elbow, it was not visible to the naked eye. It was not caught by the camera. The marvel of his swing was the way he could cock his left wrist at the top without bending the left arm. He had reduced his swing to two main hinges – the left shoulder and the left wrist. The hinge at the left elbow is eliminated. Naturally this leads to greater accuracy – the more hinges, the more chance for trouble.

Jones gives the impression of left shoulder power and left shoulder control. You can sense a feeling of strain or torsion in this left shoulder for any full swing. He also has a marvellous amount of leverage or punch in his cocked left wrist. There is firmness here, but no sign of stiffness. You get the impression that it is controlling the whip of the clubhead with the right hand coming in for the final flip or crack or blow.

There is still another feature of the Jones swing worth some study. This is the way he turns his chin slightly to the right as he addresses the ball. This was a trick that Jerry Travers always employed to make it easier and simpler to keep the head uplifted. Both seem to be looking at the ball with the left eye. When the chin is turned to the right it is more of an effort to look suddenly along the line of flight. It helps to keep the head fixed, a sort of subconscious suggestion to look away from the path of the ball where every human tendency is to see at once – often too quickly – just what has happened. This frequently takes place before anything has happened, before the clubhead has ever reached the ball.

Jones was badly bothered by his erratic putting up to 1922. I recall one round he had at Columbia in the 1921 Open where he took three putts on nine greens and still turned in a 77. He had every opportunity to break 70, but his putter blocked the road. At that time he was experimenting with various putting styles. A trifle later he went to a putting cleek and brought his feet close together, not quite, however, as closely as they are held today. In the United States Open of 1922 his feet were only a few inches apart, possibly two or three. Today the heels are almost touching. He has found again that this method helps him to a feeling of greater relaxation on the green and also to a slighter temptation to use the body in the putting stroke.

The Amateur Champion says he makes no direct effort to keep his body still, fearing a feeling of stiffness. But the fact is that his body seems to be completely still on all shorter putts from two to six or seven feet in length where the hands and wrists do practically all the work. So far as championship golf is concerned there has never been a surer putter from three, five or seven feet away than Jones.

He has a light, firm touch that is as smooth as velvet. It is his idea to get the ball just about to the cup, rather than ram for the back of the tin. For in the gentler putting system there is a wider target to hit – over four inches against a trifle more than two inches. A putt just getting up to the cup with only a slight run left will usually drop in from either side. But if hit too stoutly it must find the exact centre of the cup. This can be overdone by not getting the ball up to the cup, but it accounts for the fact that you almost never see one of Jones's putts from shorter ranges hit in and then hop out, one feature of golf that wrings raw agony from the most stoical of souls.

These features of Jones's play are mere segments, taken from a swing that is largely genius. One might as well attempt to describe the smoothness of the wind as to paint a clear picture of his complete swing.

The American Golfer, Charles Price, Random House.

A summary

Gene Sarazen with H. W. Wind

Jones was great because he had the finest mind of any competitive golfer. He was a brilliant student in college and is an extremely able lawyer and businessman. Bob had a natural genius for hitting a golf ball – he went to the third round of the Amateur at the age of fourteen – but there have been other youngsters with approximate if not equal aptitudes whose names do not appear on the championship cups. *Robert T. Jones, Jnr* is emblazoned on all the major trophies – once on the British Amateur, three times on the British Open, four times on the United States Open and five times on the United States Amateur – because he had, along with a great golf game and great fortitude, great intelligence. Jones was able to master his temper and every other problem that stood between him and consistent superlative performance. He knew exactly what he wanted to do. He set his sights on the four major championships each year. When he accomplished his incredible Grand Slam in 1930, Bob retired from competition.

Jones's long, rhythmical, truly spectacular swing was not the type of swing that could have stood up to continuous tournament stress. I think that if it had been necessary for Bob to play week-in and week-out tournament golf, he would have had to make some changes in his swing, and there is no doubt that Bob could have done so as successfully as Ezio Pinza switched from the less intensive schedule of opera to the grind of musical comedy. As it was, Bob's swing had a bravura quality to it. It took quite a bit of time to tune it delicately to tournament pitch, and it took a great deal of care to keep it on pitch. Near the end of Bob's career I thought I noticed that he had to keep watch against his swing's becoming too flat. It seemed to me that he exaggerated the pronation of his right wrist when he addressed the ball, as if he were consciously trying to open his clubhead a trifle. Jones's irons were better than good, but it was his driving and his putting that always impressed me most. He was remarkably straight off the tee in all kinds of weather and under all kinds of pressure, and when he wanted distance he could be as long as any of the boys. I don't think the present generation has any idea of how wonderful Bob was on the greens. His lovely smooth stroke on his long approach putts left him with little kick-ins time after time. He had a superb sense of distance.

Bob was a fine man to be partnered with in a tournament. Congenial and considerate, he made you feel that you were playing with a friend, and you were. At the same time, in a unique and wondrous way, Bob quietly unleashed the most furious concentration of any golfer, in those days when it was Jones versus the field. This arduous dedication to the job at hand left him spent and weary after each round. Bob never hung around the locker-room long after his day's play was over. Hagen – you could never get him out. The two great champions were completely dissimilar in their attitudes towards crowds. Jones was always polite toward his idolatrous galleries, but I think he regarded them as an element that could deter his concentration if he let it invade his thoughts. Hagen loved the crowd. He hated to have to leave his gallery at the conclusion of a match, and did everything he could to postpone that painful parting. In their one man-against-man meeting in Florida in 1926, Walter administered a decisive lacing to Bob, but it is notable that Walter never was able to win an Open championship in which Jones was entered. Walter had Jonesitis as bad as the rest of us.

Thirty Years of Championship Golf, Prentice-Hall, 1950

The last hole
R. T. Jones Jnr

When Gene Homans stroked that last putt on Saturday afternoon on the eleventh green and, before the ball had stopped rolling, came with a big smile to shake my hand, all at once I felt the wonderful feeling of release from tension and relaxation that I had wanted so badly for so long a time. I wasn't quite certain what had happened or what I had done. I only knew that I had completed a period of most strenuous effort, and that at this point nothing more remained to be done, and that on this particular project, at least, there could never at any time in the future be anything else to do. I am certain that many others have enjoyed this feeling – that the project, no matter what its importance, has been finished, and ahead, at least for a time, lies nothing but rest and cessation of worry.

Golf is My Game, Doubleday, 1960, and Chatto & Windus, 1961

Gene Sarazen

Born 22 February 1902, Harrison, New York, USA.

There is a legend that no overseas player can win the Open on first acquaintance with a British links course. It derives from the failure of Bobby Jones to qualify on his first visit to St Andrews, rapidly followed by a similar disaster to Sarazen at Troon in 1923. American golfers are used to firing their irons in high to the target and are mostly apt to hit all their shots high. They were therefore felt to be unsuited to the winds that usually blow and to playing irons that pitch short of the green and bumble along to the flag. The legend was more or less dispelled by Hogan, on his one and only appearance in 1953, Lema in 1964 and Watson in 1975, all in their first Opens. However, it is true enough that many American stars do very badly indeed on both first and later experience of links golf. Many come once and are happy never to return.

But Sarazen did, winning after many attempts, and he continued to return; eventually, fifty years after his first visit, it was Troon again and he was delighted to hole the Postage Stamp in one and then, in the following round, to hole out from a bunker for a two. Two attempts and the putter never left his bag...

In his career Sarazen won seven major championships, which puts him equal sixth on the all-time list, the last of these being in the second Masters in 1935.

The man from Titusville
Bernard Darwin

'"All right," said the Cat; and this time it vanished quite slowly, beginning with the end of the tail, and ending with the grin which remained some time after the rest of it had gone.'

When I read my *Alice in Wonderland* and come to that sentence about the Cheshire Cat, I think of Gene Sarazen. His grin is so very much an integral part of him, and even when he has dashed away after winning our Championship to win that of his own country, he leaves an agreeable appearance in the air, resembling a grin, to remind us of him.

It is by no means an unchanging grin, as was that of the Cat. It grows perceptibly broader as he holes a long putt at a crucial moment, seeming then to spread entirely across his pleasant olive face. It contracts into something of a wry smile when the putts just decline to drop and he has perhaps hard work to keep smiling at all. It is, however, impossible to think of him without it, because it is the outward and visible sign of the very charming and at the same time very strong and resolute personality that is Sarazen.

I first met that grin in a hotel in New York in the autumn of 1922. Its owner had leaped into sudden fame earlier in the year by winning the Open Championship at Skokie, a Chicago course. He then came from a course called Titusville. Nobody here had ever heard either of it or of him and even in his own country I do not think his fame was as yet very great. He soon proceeded to show that his win was no fluke, for he won the Professional championship of his country and beat Hagen in a set match over 72 holes, a thing that at that time no other golfer in the world was likely to do.

It was with the glory of his championship still upon him that he first came over here, in 1923, to play for our Open championship at Troon. His golf at once made a great impression on all who saw him. Arnaud Massy is capable of enthusiastic outbursts of hero-worship, and I remember his declaring that the championship was over before it had begun, since nothing could prevent Sarazen from winning by strokes and strokes. And then, by some astonishing accident, he failed to qualify. He had a bad first round, but played up gallantly in the second and was believed to have saved his bacon. I remember it well because after dispatching my telegram saying that he had qualified, I had departed far from Troon. Next morning I was horror-stricken to hear that someone had come in at the last moment and ousted him. Fortunately, there was a trusty person in London who had altered my message or furious editors would have had my head on a charger.

When we saw him after an interval of nine years at Prince's playing the sort of golf that seemed incapable of going wrong, it was almost impossible to believe in that earlier failure; but in the first place he was then nine years younger, and decidedly more 'temperamental', and in the second, allowance must always be made for the strangeness of a strange land. When Bobby Jones first played in our championship he tore up his card and drove his ball out to sea; when Hagen first played he finished in something like the fifteenth place. It is hard work to play a game in the other fellow's country, and it seems that a probationary visit is needed before even the greatest can give of their best. However it happened, Sarazen accepted his downfall very well and declared that he would come again if he had to swim across. He had to come again several times, but the long lane had a glorious turning at last.

Even in his own country Sarazen's golf suffered for a while a period of partial eclipse. I fancy that having at first played the game almost entirely by the light of nature he took to thinking about it. That is a thing that has almost got to happen to any good young golfer at some time and occasionally the young golfer is never so good again after-wards; the 'first fine careless rapture' of hitting, the splendid confidence are never satisfactorily replaced. If on the other hand he gets safely through this inevitable distemper he is a better golfer than ever he was, for he has knowledge to fall back on in evil days. Sarazen, I believe, tried experiments. He tried for instance the fashionable overlapping grip instead of the interlocking one that had come to him almost in-stinctively in his caddie days. I think in the end he did make some slight change, for I remember his asking me when we met again if I saw anything different; I had to confess that I did not and asked humbly to be told. At any rate the period of thoughtful sickness was safely passed and there emerged a Sarazen who, though he did not win another Open championship till this year, was yet a better golfer than before. He was always there or thereabouts, and I imagine that during the last few years no professional has equalled his record of earnings in the big tournaments for big prize money.

Today he is obviously a thoughtful person with plenty of decided and rather original notions as to the playing of the game. I remember for example his telling me that when he taught Mrs Sarazen to play golf he insisted on her learning with heavy clubs. I am afraid to say how heavy they were; they sounded to me almost cruelly so, but they had the right effect in making the pupil swing the club and let it do the work. It is probably on this principle that he himself is apt to practise swinging not with one club but with two or even three (it is a baseball player's trick) so that he looks like a lictor with a whole bundle of rods; but then he is as strong as a little bull and could doubtless swing a bundle of battle-axes.

Not only has he thought much about method but he is using his head all the time and plays the game strategically. At Prince's he several times took a spoon off the tee, so that he could reach the best place from which to play the second shot, without any fear of going just too far. It was particularly noticeable how he always took this spoon for his tee shot to the fifteenth. There was here no danger of the rough in going too far, but the pitch to that small plateau, cocked up amid all manner of perils, is perceptibly easier if it is not too short and so the ball can be hit the harder. How wise in him it was too to take his iron for the second at the seventeenth in the last round, when he was growing rather shaky and knew it. In the other rounds he had been hitting the most glorious seconds right home with the wood, but this time his ball lay a little more to the right, the danger of the bunker was a little greater and his confidence was a little on the wane; so he took his iron and played safely for a five. It is not everyone who would have had so much self-control at that moment, for the strokes had been slipping away, he knew all about Havers's 68 and, in short, things were not too comfortable.

That grin of his is the mark of a sunny and delightful nature, but not of an altogether placid one. He has had, unless I am much mistaken, to overcome something in his Latin blood that used to surge up untimely. Like Bobby Jones, he can boil inside and sometimes on rare occasions he used to boil over. When he was second to Hagen in the Open championship at Sandwich in 1928 he might have won or at least have tied but for one little ebullition. It was at the Suez Canal hole; his ball lay in the rough off the tee and his admirable caddie wanted him, I feel pretty sure, to take an iron. He took wood, missed the shot badly and then advanced on the ball again with the same club without giving himself time to think. Just for that moment he lost himself and that disastrous hole may well have lost him the championship. He would not have done that at Carnoustie last year when he fought on with a fine stoicism in the face of adverse fate. Twice in the course of the three days the wind changed between morning and afternoon, and each time it changed in favour of Armour and against Sarazen. That, to be sure, is one of those things that are 'all about the game' but it made a great difference. Sarazen's only comment was that in order to win 'you must have the breaks' – an undeniable truth but one hard to enunciate calmly in times of disappointment.

At Prince's he had no 'breaks' as far as the play or the weather were concerned. Indeed, in one respect he seemed rather unlucky, for he constantly hit the hole with his putts and the ball did not drop; but this misfortune is perhaps inherent in his method; he goes boldly for

wo key figures of between-the-wars golf: Gene Sarazen (left) and Bobby Jones. Sarazen won the US
pen in 1922 at the age of 20 – still to this day the youngest winner. Jones won in 1923 – at the age of 21.

Above Sarazen at Sandwich for the 1928 Open in which he finished second to Hagen. *Below* Bobby Jones on the first tee at St Andrews, 1927. He led all the way and set a new record.

ove Two expatriates who did well in the United States: (left) the 'Silver Scot', Tommy Armour, and *rnishman 'Long Jim' Barnes at Sandwich for the 1928 Open. *Below* Cotton in his prime, in action in a *38* charity match, playing the better ball of (left to right) Enid Wilson, Joyce Wethered and *me* Lacoste.

Above Sam Snead in play at Wentworth in the Canada Cup of 1956.
Below Henry Cotton in a wartime charity match.

the back of the tin and will have no truck with timorous trickling in at the side door. One bit of luck he did have in that he was drawn to start early on the last day, and so he could, just as in his original triumph at Skokie, set up a mark for his wretched pursuers to shoot at. He left Havers with a 68 to tie, and that was a task that seemed hopeless. I should have written 'was' instead of 'seemed' had it not been for Sarazen's own achievement in the American championship a fortnight later. Then he was left with a 69 to tie. He did a 66 and won by three strokes. If anybody likes to say that this was, in the circumstances, the greatest round of golf ever played, I do not see how anybody else can quarrel with him.

Finally in our Open champion we salute not merely one of the finest hitters of a golf ball that ever lived but also one worthy of the name of a good golfer, than which no man can look forward to a better epitaph. We may apply to him Hazlitt's famous words about Cavanagh the fives player, and I shall write them down yet again just for the pleasure of doing so. 'He had no affectation, no trifling. He did not throw away the game to show off an attitude, or try an experiment. He was a fine, sensible, manly player, who did what he could.' Of that last round at Fresh Meadow at any rate we may add Hazlitt's final sentence – 'but that was more than anyone else could even affect to do.'

Out of the Rough, Chapman and Hall, 1932

Henry Cotton

Born 26 January 1907, Holmes Chapel, Cheshire, England.

Until quite recent times the British preferred a certain degree of ama-
teurishness in their sporting idols. An amateur would always be chosen
to captain England at cricket even if he were seldom worth his place
on playing merit alone. We liked it that Chris Chataway, the 5,000
metre-runner, confessed to smoking even when he was in full training,
and we contrasted this with the humourless plodding of his contemporary Gordon Pirie and, even more so, the Russian Vladimir Kuts. In
golf the best parallel perhaps was Roger Wethered who, on tieing for
the first place in the 1921 Open, said that he had promised to play in a
village cricket match the next day and really didn't think he ought to
stay for the play-off against Jock Hutchinson. (He did.)

Cotton's career in the 1930s broke with this tradition. He was a man
who by birth ought to have been an amateur but who chose to turn
professional and then played the game in an entirely professional way.
What was more, the fellow practised until he couldn't stand up straight
for back cramps and he developed a permanent list to starboard because of the right-shoulder-down of his golf stance.

But if we can't have an amateur (in the sense not so much of money
but of someone who plays a game for fun) we do like a winner. That
Cotton certainly was. The best British golfer by about 1930, he held
that position for twenty years and in that period won three British
Opens. There would have been more if the war had not stopped the
championship for six years. His dedication to success would also have
brought him success in the USA if he had played in the days of quick
transatlantic travel.

Nevertheless, Cotton remains the greatest British golfer since Harry
Vardon.

The maestro

Henry Longhurst

When anyone asks me who is the greatest striker of a golf ball I ever saw, my answer is immediate. It is Henry Cotton. I am just old enough to have seen Harry Vardon play, but was not old enough at the time to make a fair assessment of his powers. Whatever they were, I cannot believe them to have been greater than Cotton's in the 'thirties. He lifted up the nation's golfing spirit after eleven long years of American domination and, with it, the status of his own profession.

For this the Americans themselves were largely responsible. In 1928, when he was twenty-one, he set sail for the United States under his own steam, buying his own ticket and taking with him a letter of credit for £300, which incidentally he brought home intact. He soon appreciated that the great sporting figures of the day were regarded in America almost as the aristocracy, whereas at home sport carried with it no special standing. When Walter Hagen came to England to win our championships, he stayed at the Savoy and drove up to the course in a hired Rolls-Royce. He was already 'one up' on the rest of the field. Cotton decided that what Hagen could do he could do.

I think it is fair to say that Cotton regarded himself, in his competitive days, as a kind of 'property', to be taken the greatest care of and kept in the best possible condition if it were to give the desired results. For this reason he took it to the best hotels and at lunch time, having no desire for the smoky air and, for the celebrated, the inevitable attachment of bores and sycophants to be found in the club-house, he changed his clothes in the car and retired to the hotel. Naturally enough, there were those who thought he regarded himself as too good for the common herd.

He developed an immense strength in his hands, and they became the focal point in his essentially simple swing. As the ball flew straight at the flag, you felt that, if you hit it in that fashion, it could hardly do anything else. He could do almost anything with a golf ball on purpose and would have made a great trick-shot artist. We often used to challenge him to take his driver from a bad lie on the fairway, simply for the aesthetic pleasure of seeing the ball fly away as though fired from a rifle, and I remember once at Bad Ems seeing him knock a shooting stick out of the ground with a 1-iron shot at a range of twenty yards. We christened him the Maestro, and he deserved it.

At the same time he developed a flair for getting himself into the news, sometimes, but not always, on purpose. With all this he was naturally the centre of attraction wherever he played, and became probably the first professional golfer to be recognizable at once to the man in the street.

In 1929, now aged twenty-two, Cotton played in his first Ryder Cup match at Leeds, where he beat Al Watrous by 4 and 2, and it now seemed only a matter of time before he won the championship. He had his chances, but on at least two occasions let them slip, mainly, as he now thinks, through listening to the rumours that used to fly about the course before the present walkie-talkie system came into use, and not appreciating what he needed to do.

It was against this background that the championship opened at Sandwich in 1934. Cotton had with him four sets of clubs – why, I do not know – and for once could not hit his hat with any of them. He practised on Saturday till darkness drove him in, and had never been in such discouraging form. He settled on a set of clubs, for better or for worse, and on Monday morning, in the first qualifying round, was drawn to go out first, accompanied by a marker. He played what remains in his own opinion the best round of his life. He hit every green in the right number – 33 shots, 33 putts; total 66. Such is golf.

The magic lasted. He opened the championship proper with a 67, and in such a way that one saw no reason why he should ever again take more. On the second day he arrived on the seventeenth tee needing only two par fours for another 67 and the then fantastic total of 134. At each hole he hit a tremendous drive. His second to the seventeenth ruled the flag and finished about twelve feet from the hole, and he holed the putt for a three. He hit another magnificent iron shot to the last hole, though he cannot have seen it finish, for he was at once enveloped by a stampeding multitude determined to see history being made on the last green.

I remember the shot perfectly. It bounced a couple of times and came quietly to rest about four feet from the stick. He made no mistake with the putt and history had indeed been made. Sixty-five! A total of 132 and the nearest man, Alfred Padgham, nine strokes behind.

On the morning of the final day Cotton turned in a 72 in harder conditions, a more than adequate score which was beaten by only three players, and now he was out on his own by twelve strokes. He returned to his hotel for lunch in the usual way, and I do not believe it entered the head of a single person present that they might be about to witness in the afternoon the most agonizing golfing spectacle any can remember to this day.

Things went instantly wrong. He timed his arrival for the start but found it postponed for a quarter of an hour owing to the immense crowd which had assembled to watch the triumphant formality of his final round. In his own words: 'Like a fool, I went and sat in a small tent all by myself. Lack of experience again. Today I should go out and hit balls, go for a walk, anything bar sit and brood. Already I had been undermined by people congratulating me before I had won. The editor of one of the golf magazines seemed to think he had appointed himself my official manager and kept popping in and out of lunch telling me not to sign anything without consulting him when I had won. I had been humbled by golf too often. I sat and thought how anyone could take 82 in a championship, and anyone else could do 69, and there is the whole thing gone. Why, it was only a mile or two away, at Deal, that poor Abe Mitchell took 83 to George Duncan's 71 and lost twelve strokes and the championship in a single round.'

The start was a foretaste of what was to come, and I hardly like to write of it even now. His first drive was skied and his second with a 2-iron hit a lady, standing at cover point, on the knee. Through the green it is no exaggeration to say that a competent twelve-handicap player would have given him a good game and, if he had not putted, considering the circumstances, miraculously, he might have taken 90.

There was much talk at the time of his having eaten something that disagreed with him or having failed to digest his modest lunch. The latter, I am sure, is true or he could not speak of it with such feeling to this day. 'I played in a cold sweat and wanted to be sick. I ought to have gone off and vomited in the nearest hedgerow, but I didn't, partly because I was too ashamed and partly because there aren't any hedgerows at St. George's anyway. I could not get anything but fives. I could not get a four even at drive-and-pitch holes where all the week I had been looking for threes.'

At the long thirteenth – 'another b—— 5 coming' – the course of the round, and with it, he now agrees, probably of his life, was changed. He holed a four-yard putt for four. It broke the spell and he coasted home to win by five shots from Sid Brews, of South Africa. He missed a short putt on the last green but it did not matter now. A British player had won the championship at last and they carried him shoulder high off the green.

The Sunday Times

Byron Nelson

Born 4 February 1912, Fort Worth, Texas, USA.

Although the winner of five major championships, Nelson is one of the few golfers whose fame derives more from his phenomenal achievements on the US tour (which are detailed in the passage which follows) and also because he is seen as a key figure in the development of the modern golf swing. It is probably true to say that his way of swinging a golf club has been more imitated in its essentials than anyone else's, with the exception of Harry Vardon.

The birth of the modern method
Dick Aultman

There is a fascinating similarity between how the golf swing has developed over the years and the evolutionary process in nature itself. In nature the plant or animal that is best suited to its environment is the one that dominates and survives. In golf, to a large extent, the player who has dominated his peers – survived the best – has been the one whose swing has best suited his environment, that being largely the clubs and balls of his day and the course and weather conditions under which he played. In nature the unusual strengths that allow the fittest to survive are passed on to their progeny. In golf the strongest swing characteristics of the dominant players are assimilated by those who watch them play.

During their respective heydays Vardon, Hagen, Jones, Snead, Hogan, Palmer, Nicklaus and others have all influenced the swings of their contemporaries, especially young people, who seem most capable of successful mimicry. This influence has naturally become stronger with the growth of golf books, magazines, movies and, finally, television. Palmer, for instance, has caused millions of viewers to realize that a slashing 'hit-it-hard' approach can be a successful alternative to the leisurely, flowing action that Vardon, Jones and Snead helped to make the vogue. Nicklaus no doubt has been influential in modifying, if not burying, the concept of a 'tight' right elbow and, in so doing, has probably raised the average swing plane of today's junior stars at least a few degrees.

It is fitting to air these thoughts about golf-swing evolution here because Byron Nelson for a short time dominated his peers as no one ever has or ever will and did it with a swing that departed dramatically from the norm. Nelson set a new standard of shotmaking excellence, and quite naturally some ingredients of his unusual technique became the model for those that followed. In fact, it can be safely said that if there is a watershed between the classical stroke spawned eighty some years ago by Harry Vardon and the swing method employed in large part by the top players of the world today, it was the one-piece, upright, left-side dominant, flex-kneed swing of John Byron Nelson.

Nelson's role as a pioneer of the golf stroke is most apparent when one studies movies of tournament professionals in the 1940s. Seemingly anyone who was anyone on the United States pro tour at that time paraded before the camera to make at least one swing for posterity. None of these 1940's swings was identical, of course, but one striking similarity soon becomes apparent. The finest players of that generation were all 'hitting against a firm left side', a phrase that was to remain a part of the golf-instruction lexicon for at least another quarter of a century. Just prior to impact these players' left legs would straighten and remain all but immobile while their arms continued swinging forward. Of the dozens of players filmed only Nelson retained some left-knee flex throughout his entire swing as he drove forward with both legs. Instead of hitting 'against' his left side, Nelson hit *with* his left side.

Nelson, like most of his peers, had started playing golf with wooden-shafted clubs. The few golfers of his era who hadn't were still highly influenced in their swing development by teachers and players who had. As a result, the vast majority of the swing techniques of the late 1930s and early 1940s had grown out of the need to accommodate very flexible shafts, which demanded a high degree of control, if not manipulation, with the hands and wrists to throw the twisting clubhead back to a square position by impact.

The metal shafts that began to appear around 1930 did not twist and bend as much, required less hand-wrist manipulation, and thus allowed players greater use of their legs as a source of power. While all great players, even as far back as Vardon, had used their legs to some

59

extent, none had done so to the degree that Nelson did. In short, the metal shafts created a new golfing 'environment'. Byron Nelson adjusted to it first and best.

Another environmental change that Nelson adjusted to supremely well was a larger golf ball. The United States Golf Association, concerned that extra distance resulting largely from the new shafts would render existing courses obsolete, had ruled that from 1 January 1931 no ball less than 1.68 inches in diameter would be legal for tournament play in America. The difference in size between the 1.62-inch ball that had been allowed prior to 1931 and the new 1.68-inch ball required thereafter may seem infinitesimal, but it dramatically affected the evolution of the golf swing in the United States.

The larger ball, for instance, would back-spin more readily. Thus it rose into the air more easily than did the small ball. Whereas the smaller ball had required throwing the clubhead under it with a wristy swing to flick it upward, the new ball would back-spin to adequate height even when hit with a definite downward clubhead motion. Good players found that they could contact ball first, turf second, thus minimizing the chance of 'fat' shots. The best downswing stroke for producing this ball-turf contact was one in which the legs led the way. Nelson, flex-kneed throughout, quickly proved that he had the fittest swing to survive in a world of stiffer shafts and larger balls.

In addition to using his legs dramatically, Nelson did several other things in his swing that departed from the styles of most of his contemporaries. These departures were really simplifications of the swing, and they led to superior shotmaking consistency. As we shall see, these departures also set the format for the swing pattern utilized by the vast majority of today's top professionals and amateurs, especially in the United States. Let's examine these departures as they occurred in Nelson's action.

The first alteration involved the way he swung the clubhead away from the ball. Early in his career Nelson's takeaway was similar to that of most of his fellow professionals and those who had excelled before him. His hands led everything else, moving a couple of inches or so to his right before the clubhead started to be dragged away. It was the 'drag and whip' technique, used by the hands-and-wrists players who for decades had flicked the smaller ball off the soft, short-bladed grasses of the great Scottish and English link courses, the technique that had been brought to the United States by the British professionals who first showed Americans how to play the game.

During the 1930s, however, Nelson worked on developing what has become known as a 'one-piece' takeaway. His hands, arms and club moved back together, with his left hand and straight left arm initiating the movement. He gradually eliminated the initial 'reverse cocking' during the takeaway that had led to so much wristiness among the old players and thus demanded such ultra-precise timing.

Nelson also avoided the habit of quickly fanning the clubface open during the takeaway, a technique employed by most of the early British professionals to help them flick the ball into the air. Nelson kept his clubface more or less square to its path of movement throughout his swing. He did so by establishing a straight-line relationship at the back of his left hand, wrist and forearm during his backswing and by maintaining it well into his follow-through.

Nelson's hip turn on his backswing was considerably less than that of most of his peers, including Bobby Jones, whose game and instructional writings and movies were still highly influential when Nelson first began to make an impact on the professional golf tour in 1935. Nelson's hip turn on full shots was less than 45 degrees, yet his shoulder turn was at least 90 degrees. When coupled with his one-piece takeaway and one of the straightest left arms in the history of the game, Nelson's minimal hip turn and full shoulder turn resulted in a highly compact backswing. His club never moved past horizontal at the top, even on his fullest swings.

His was also an upright backswing – perhaps the most upright of any great player except Nicklaus. By reducing his hip turn, Nelson was able to swing his arms and club more directly back and up than can the golfer who turns his torso on a shallow plane. As a consequence, Nelson's clubhead remained on the target line longer during his takeaway than anyone he competed against. He also swung his hands higher.

Most average golfers would find it difficult to copy successfully Nelson's high, upright swing plane and minimal hip turn. Less skilled golfers who swing on such an upright plane run the risk that any slight casting with the hands or shoving with the right shoulder from the top of the swing will move the clubhead outside the target line prior to impact, therefore forcing an outside-to-inside path during contact. The golfer with the upright swing plane must give himself plenty of time to change directions between backswing and downswing, time for his legs to lead his shoulders into the forward stroke to ensure that the clubhead will swing from inside to along the target line during impact.

'If the club does not come to a reasonable slow motion, almost a pause, at the top of the swing,' Nelson once told this writer, 'then it is hard to keep the downswing co-ordinated well enough to make any sort of solid contact.' Nelson, however, had the swing pace that gave his legs time to lead, just as does Jack Nicklaus, the current exemplar of the style that Nelson initiated.

Taken in sum, all the ingredients of Nelson's swing described thus far added up to an attractively simple method. He minimized moving parts and thus built a swing less likely to break down under pressure. His action was firm and positive, both starting back and at the top – the two most critical areas. His backswing was relatively short, his hip turn minimal, his leg action excellent even by modern standards. So was his ability to control the club with his left hand, arm and side. All in all, Nelson incorporated practically all of the swing factors that are part of what came to be called, more than a quarter century later, the 'square-to-square method'.

Perhaps the most graphic way to explain Nelson's amazing shot-making consistency is to look at his swing purely from a ballistic or geometrical point of view. Because his plane was relatively upright, his clubhead moved along the target line slightly longer, both going back and coming through, than does the clubhead of the player who swings more around his body. Thus, by his uprightness, Nelson increased his chances of contacting the ball while the clubhead was moving along his target line.

Because he did not fan his clubface open to its arc going back, Nelson also avoided the necessity of fanning it precisely back to square during his downswing in order to hit a straight shot. Thus he increased the odds that his clubface would be looking at his target during impact.

His pattern of swing also decreased the chance that his right hand, in an effort to throw the clubhead back to square, would break down the straight-line relationship at the back of his left wrist, a breakdown that could either close the clubface to the left of target or throw the clubhead too much upward instead of forward.

Finally, by retaining his knee flex well past impact, Nelson more or less 'flattened' the bottom of his swing arc, thereby lengthening the period that his clubhead moved through impact at ball level.

While these geometric or ballistic advantages may have been slight, they were sufficient to give him a considerable edge over the rest of the field. 'Even when Nelson is only halfway putting,' Tommy Armour once said, 'he can't be beaten. He plays golf shots like a virtuoso.

There is no problem he can't handle – high shots, low shots, with the wind or across it, hooks or fades, he has absolute control of the ball. He is the finest golfer I have ever seen.'

Several factors led to Nelson developing a 'virtuoso' swing. Certainly the conditions under which he played as a youngster had a lasting influence. Nelson grew up amid the winds and hardpan fairways of Ellis County, Texas, just south of Dallas–Fort Worth. The conditions demanded a wide variety of shots and precise striking. Wind is especially unforgiving of high shots, and Nelson sensed early on that lots of leg drive on the forward swing helped to produce shots that bore well into the breezes. He also found that a firm left arm and wrist through impact helped to drive the ball forward instead of upward.

Most good golfers suffer through a period of hooking. Nelson, with his exceptionally large, strong hands, was no exception. Leading with the legs – more or less dragging the clubhead toward the ball – helped him avoid prematurely closing the clubface and thus to avoid the duck hooks that ran seemingly forever in disastrous directions off those bonny Texas fairways. It was a lesson that years later another Texan, Lee Trevino, was to learn so well.

People as well as course conditions also influence a player's swing development. In 1927 the great Walter Hagen came to Dallas seeking his fourth straight PGA championship. Throughout his final match against Joe Turnesa, a fifteen-year-old youngster trailed at Hagen's heels every step of the way. At one point Hagen squinted into the sun and remarked that he wished he had a hat to wear for the next shot. The youth gladly proffered his tiny baseball cap, which Hagen, to the delight of the gallery, donned above one eye and somehow managed to keep in place during his swing. Twelve years later, in the same tournament, Byron Nelson's mother introduced herself to Walter Hagen as the mother of the boy whose cap he'd once borrowed. By that time the son himself had already won the Masters and the US Open.

It may seem ironic that a quiet and abstemious fellow like Byron Nelson would choose an outgoing, round-the-clock swinger like Hagen for an idol. What influenced Nelson, however, was Hagen's swinging on the course. Many players of Hagen's era – most notably Bobby Jones – swung the club well around their bodies early in the backswing, then up and slightly over, and finally down to the ball. As a result, the club moved on a slightly steeper plane during the downswing than it had early in the backswing.

Hagen was one of the first stars to reverse this process. By starting down with his hips sliding to the left, he pulled his club down to the ball on a slightly flatter plane than it had followed going back and up. This increased his chance of returning the clubhead from inside to along (rather than from outside to across) the target line at impact. Nelson, with his upright backswing and strong forward leg drive, produced an even greater lowering or flattening of plane on the downswing, much in keeping with the action of modern players like Nicklaus, Player, Miller, Weiskopf and Trevino.

An even stronger influence than Hagen on Nelson's game was George Jacobus, head professional at the Ridgewood Country Club in New Jersey, where Nelson assisted in the mid-30s. Jacobus encouraged Nelson to work on developing the ultrastraight left arm that became a hallmark of his technique and to eliminate exaggerated fanning open of the clubface during his takeaway.

'I had an idea to get the club higher and to keep the clubface square to the swing,' Nelson says. 'George was very helpful in developing my style of play.'

The fact that Nelson was not a great putter – he was more in a league with Vardon, Cotton and Hogan than with Hagen, Jones and Locke – does even more credit to his driving and iron play. Nelson's first round in the 1937 Masters more or less symbolizes his tee-to-green excellence. During that 18 holes at Augusta National, he hit every par-three green in one shot and all others, including the four par-fives, in two. He one-putted only two greens, yet shot 66. The two one-putts were from two and three feet.

Nelson, of course, is best remembered for his amazing feats in 1945, when he won nineteen of thirty tournaments he entered, eleven of them in a row, and averaged only 68.33 strokes per round. Even taking into account the 1974-5 exploits of Johnny Miller, it is difficult to conceive that any of these records will ever be broken.

There are those who tend to diminish Nelson's achievements because some of the better touring pros were still in the armed services for at least part of his supreme year. Perhaps these additional facts will put Byron Nelson's career in better perspective:

> He was a full-time touring pro only in 1945. He won twenty-six additional PGA tournaments while doubling more or less as a club professional.
> He won money in 111 straight events.
> He finished second in seven of the eleven tournaments he entered

in 1945 that he failed to win.

His stroke average in 1945 was almost a shot per round, or four per tournament, lower than anyone has ever recorded in a given year.

In the nine stroke-play tournaments he won in 1945, his average margin of victory was 6.3 strokes.

Most of the best players *did* compete in 1945: Hogan, Snead, McSpaden, Demaret, Harmon, Revolta, Shute, Mike Turnesa, Laffoon, Byrd, etc.

Nelson's fantastic success throughout his career, but especially in 1945, stemmed in large part from a basic character trait found in most great athletes. Nelson was and still is a perfectionist. Throughout his ten-year career he had tried to 'play each shot for what it was worth', but in 1944 he actually charted every shot he made, hoping through this analysis to find some means of reducing his scoring average.

In reviewing his little black book, Nelson realized that despite his efforts to concentrate fully on all shots, he was still blowing an occasional stroke because of carelessness. 'I recall once I had the ball an inch from the cup,' he later revealed. 'I just pushed at it. The putter hit the grass behind the ball – never reached it.' Thus Nelson went into 1945 vowing to reduce his stroke average by one shot per round. Actually, he chopped off almost 1.5 strokes, having averaged 69.67 in 1944.

Perhaps none of Nelson's fellow competitors felt the sting of his precise shotmaking more than Mike Turnesa, his second-round foe in the 1945 PGA championship. Nelson went into that major event with eight straight tournament victories, but it appeared that the string would end when Turnesa led 2-up with four holes remaining at the Moraine Country Club in Dayton, Ohio. Turnesa played those last four holes well, scoring three pars and a birdie. Nelson, however, shot birdie, birdie, eagle, par, to win 1-up. 'Nelson chews you up and spits you out,' said Turnesa, seven under par for the round. 'How can anyone beat him?'

Nelson himself solved that puzzle early the next year when, after winning the first two tournaments, he announced his retirement from the pro tour. He had decided to settle down with his wife, Louise, on the Texas ranch he'd always wanted, away from all the off-course demands that were increasingly sapping his time and energy. He was only thirty-three at the time. Contrary to popular belief, his nerves were not shot. Much ado has been made about Nelson's inability to retain food before an important round when, in fact, he'd played with a nervous stomach all his life and welcomed it as a sign of being 'up' for the competition. Recently, of course, he has been well known as a television golf commentator, whose main characteristic is modesty, exemplified by the unstinting praise and admiration he offers his successors.

It is difficult to imagine the heights that Nelson could have achieved with his 1975-model golf swing had he not retired in 1946. Perhaps our best appraisal of his prowess should come from another who also retired at the peak of his career:

'At my best I never came close to the golf Nelson shoots,' said Bobby Jones.

Masters of Golf, Stanley Paul, 1976

Ben Hogan

Born 13 August 1912, Texas, USA.

After turning professional in 1929, Ben Hogan endured many years of failure, not winning his first tournament until 1938. From this point he became a consistent winner although his first major title did not come until 1946, when he took the US PGA and also twelve tournament victories. After continuing successes Hogan was involved in a temporarily crippling road crash in 1949 which at the time seemed to have ended his career. Indeed it is now clear enough that he would have recorded many more successes than he did but for an earlier failing of his powers brought on by the after-effects of his accident.

But this was not at all apparent when Hogan returned to tournament golf in January 1950 and tied with Sam Snead, then in the next four years won three more US Open titles, a British and two US Masters. In 1953, his best year, he became the only player to have won the Masters and US and British Opens in the same year, a record that has since only rarely been distantly threatened and never equalled.

Overall, he lies fourth, behind Nicklaus, Jones and Hagen as a winner of major championships, and joint third, with Arnold Palmer at sixty-two, behind Sam Snead and Jack Nicklaus, as a tournament winner on the US circuit.

However, his status among all-time golfers is higher even than this indicates and Hogan is usually bracketed with Vardon, Jones and Nicklaus whenever discussion turns to 'Mirror, mirror on the wall, who was the greatest of them all...'

A stairway of compensations
H. W. Wind

Depending on how you look at it, everybody knows or nobody knows the change Ben Hogan mastered in his method of striking a golf ball in 1948, the season he won his first Open. If one means the exact key to his method of imparting a controlled fade to his shots – the exact key being what is referred to as Hogan's Secret, since he has no desire to reveal it to the rest of the trade – then no one knows. If one means more generally doing everything to retain his power and yet everything to guard against a hook, then everyone knows what Hogan does. The swing he compounded and learned so well that he could execute it flawlessly under fire has varied somewhat in its details from season to season, but it had, and has, as its features (bypassing Hogan's true fundamentals of perfect balance and his wide 'forward' arc) such anti-hook staples as the left thumb down the shaft and the right hand riding high, the slightly opened stance, the club taken back a shade outside, the outward thrust of the right forearm at the beginning of the downswing that produces what the pros call the triangulation action, and the maintenance of an anything-but-shut clubface as he biffs through the ball.

Hogan lost some roll as the result of 'the slight fade' but what he gained was ten times as valuable. His approaches became a softer kind of shot. They coasted over the flag and dropped gently onto the green. More important, when he failed to meet his drives just right, the ball did not hook into trouble, it merely veered a few yards to the right in a far safer and 'slower' parabola than a hook describes. Before effecting this change, when Ben had played an unbroken competitive stretch, he had been prone to tire near the end of a tournament. When he was tired, he hooked. When he hooked, he incurred rough lies and sometimes penalty strokes. When he incurred these extra strokes, it defeated him. His revised swing gave him margin for unpenalized error and proved to be the difference between Ben's becoming a great champion and not remaining just a great golfer.

Contrasted with a swing like Snead's, which is natural and (because of Sam's exceptional leverage) naturally powerful, the swing Hogan built was not a picture-postcard lyric. It was constructed, as its critics pointed out, too much like a stairway of compensations. When these broke down – and they did to some degree in the Masters in 1952 and 1954 and in the last two rounds of the '52 Open – Hogan had his problems. But Hogan's swing, when he had the time to tune it up properly and the physical reserve to maintain it as he wanted it, was so functional and assertive that it had a smooth, efficient beauty of its own.

The Lure of Golf, Heinemann, 1971

Return from the dead
Charles Price

Driving east from Phoenix to their home in Fort Worth on the foggy morning of 2 February 1949, Ben Hogan and his wife, Valerie, collided grille to grille with a Greyhound bus that was attempting to pass a truck on a lonely stretch of Texas highway near the town of Van Horn. Had he not instinctively thrown himself across Valerie to protect her, the steering wheel would have impaled him against the front seat. After the crash, Hogan was picked carefully from his demolished car and laid by the road. Because everybody involved in the accident assumed somebody else had called for help, Hogan lay there for an hour and a half before an ambulance arrived on the scene. He then faced an agonizing trip of almost a hundred and fifty miles to the Hotel Dieu Hospital back in El Paso. There it was discovered that Hogan had fractured his pelvis, a shoulder, a rib and an ankle. He was also suffering from severe shock. After his bones were set, his body was wrapped in a cast from his chest to his knees. It was removed thirty days later when his condition took a turn for the worse. A blood clot had formed and, to prevent it from reaching his heart, a surgeon performed a major operation known as a ligation of the inferior vena cava; that is, one of the large veins through which blood is returned to the heart was tied off.

If anyone doubted that something as seemingly inconsequential as golf could assume proportions as large as life to man, he could have had dramatic evidence at Hogan's bedside. In those moments of delirium which followed his accident, he went through the motions of gripping his clubs, squeezing and twisting his hands in an effort to place them firmly on a club that existed only in his imagination. At other moments he would toss a hand in the air as though he were throwing strands of grass to the wind to test its direction. Sometimes he would call for the galleries to move by waving his arm at them. 'Back on the left!' he would yell. 'Back on the left!' Then, satisfied that they were out of his way, he would take his stance with life.

Hogan was discharged from the hospital a month after his operation. Back home in Fort Worth, he went about regaining his health with the intense concentration and disciplined patience with which he prepared for a golf tournament. One look at his emaciated body in a bedroom mirror was proof that he was a definite longshot. He weighed ninety-five pounds, less than seven stone.

Hogan's first efforts to walk were three laps around his living room. After increasing the number of laps as the weeks wore on, he took to walking up and down stairs. Then he ventured out to the yard where he would trot about on the lawn. The process of recovery was like hitting ball after ball on the practice tee, and, characteristically, he often overdid it, paying the penalty with nightmares. By June his doctors were amazed with his recovery and so permitted him to make a trip to England as the nonplaying Captain of the 1949 Ryder Cup Team.

Back home that summer, Hogan gave little or no thought to golf. His shoulder was still too weak to swing a club and his knitting pelvis made long walks inadvisable. But his main trouble was from that operation. It had detoured his blood system, with the result that his muscles tired easily and cramped. As fall wore on, he took to wandering out to the Colonial Country Club, where he would putt a little and maybe walk a hole or two with friends. Sometimes he would ride around the course on a motor-scooter, but playing still seemed remote and he refused to think about it. By early December, he had attempted a few shots and on a few occasions had played a hole or two. Heartened by this, he one day unwisely attempted a full round, and spent the next day in bed from exhaustion.

The first intimation that Hogan had returned to something resembling himself came in a wire-service dispatch from Fort Worth just before Christmas. Bob Harlow, Hagen's old tour manager, who was then editing a weekly newspaper in Pinehurst, was so surprised by this report that Hogan was playing golf and shooting respectable scores that he immediately called Hogan long-distance to verify it. Hogan denied that he had been playing full rounds at all, much less playing them well. Harlow printed the denial but a few days later was astonished to hear that Hogan had filed an entry for the Los Angeles Open, to be played the first week in January. To Hogan, the decision to play was an 'experiment' to see if he could stand the exertion of seventy-two holes. If it failed, it would be at worst a vacation in one of his favourite cities.

Hogan claimed that he had played only four full rounds of golf previous to departing for Los Angeles. But if the number had been forty, the golf he played at Riviera would still have been impressive. The one truly definitive characteristic of a champion is the ability to get up off the floor and win, and Hogan was doing exactly that when he stepped to the first tee at Riviera. With rounds of 73–69–69–69 for a total of 280, the effort didn't quite come off because Sam Snead made one of those spectacular finishes for which he will always strangely be forgotten. He tied Hogan by scoring birdies on the last two holes, both of which are long and treacherous.

That Hogan was able to tie for first on his initial jump out of the gate flabbergasted the press. The local newspapers had assigned 'city-side' photographers to cover Hogan's every gesture in the event he collapsed or, possibly, dropped dead. There were so many of them buzzing around him on the course that Hogan insisted the tournament committee post a sign banning all cameras from his gallery.

Hogan's play at Riviera was not discernibly different from its pre-accident magnificence. Not even Snead, who eventually won the play-off, played better from tee to green. Since Hogan three-putted eleven greens, it stands to reason he outshot the field. The public, golfers and nongolfers alike, were enthralled by the news of his comeback, but Hogan himself exhibited remarkable indifference to the melodrama of it. When informed that Snead had a remote chance to tie him after he had finished his round, he said, 'I'm tired. I hope Sam wins so I won't have to play off.' His attitude toward his score was 'complete surprise'.

After the Los Angeles Open, Hogan played in two more tournaments, winning neither, and then went home to rest. While he was there, letters began arriving from strangers who, inspired by his comeback, asked advice on unheralded problems of their own. It was then that Hogan began to feel the frustration of his near victory at Los Angeles. He became determined to win a top tournament, which he felt would be the best blanket answer he could give to their problem. He set his sights on the Masters Tournament, which was scheduled, as usual, for early April.

But this attempt fell short of success also when he soared to a 76 on the final day, pulling up lame with an attack of cramp. Since he did not think it expedient to play in the PGA Championship, with its gruelling matches that last almost a week, he began preparations for the National Open, scheduled for Merion in early June. For a tune-up, he went to the annual party for socialites and golf pros at the Greenbrier in White Sulphur Springs, where he shot the grass off the course with a record 259, winning the event by a clear fourteen strokes.

All the smart money at Merion rode on Hogan. The only reason he was not the overwhelming favourite was that the newspaper choice was, as usual, the long-overdue Snead. Hogan gave Merion his usual prechampionship scrutiny and came to the conclusion that, with its abundance of 'drive-and-kick' holes, it was an anachronism, engineered for the wooden shaft and less explosive tee shot of twenty-five years before. Preferring a course where the emphasis is more on power and variety of shots and less on putting, a department of the game he had always considered foreign to the rest of it, he nevertheless decided that a score of about 286, six over par, would win the championship.

Always thinking in terms of seventy-two holes, Hogan paid little heed to his opening round of 72, which was seven strokes off the record pace being set by an unemployed driving-range instructor from Alabama, and then broke par on the second day with a 69. That afternoon the tournament began to tell on him. Driving back to his hotel in Philadelphia with his wife and his lawyer, Hogan was overcome with nausea. He had the car stopped and got out to fight off an attack of retching. After pulling himself together, he climbed back in and proceeded to his hotel. In his room he peeled off the elastic bandages with which he had taken to wrapping his calves and climbed into a hot bath in order to draw the cramp out of his legs.

On the third and final day of the championship, Hogan managed the first round with a 72 and suffered no ill effects. As a precautionary measure during the afternoon round, he had his caddie pick the ball out of the cup for him so that he would not have to aggravate his legs by bending over. He made the turn in 36, which meant that par on the back nine would give him a winning score of 282, four less than his anticipated 286.

As Hogan started the final nine, he was seized by an extreme cramp in his left leg. By the time he reached the thirteenth green, which lies near the clubhouse, the pain had become so acute that he contemplated withdrawing, not because he didn't think he could win, but because he didn't think he could walk, much less play.

The fact that he didn't withdraw is now, of course, history, and he stumbled home with a total of 287, tying George Fazio and Lloyd Mangrum. His winning the play-off the next day was strictly an anticlimax, the denouement taking place on the sixteenth green when Mangrum was penalized two strokes for blowing a bug off his ball. Hogan then rang down the curtain by scoring a birdie-two on the seventeenth hole to give himself an insurmountable lead on the last hole. The nation's press was considerably less ghoulish than it had been at Los Angeles five months before. The *New York Times* gave his win front-page treatment, the first time this had happened since the Grand Slam twenty years before, and it also ran an unprecedented editorial.

The Ben Hogan that appeared at Merion was somehow an even more efficient machine than had appeared before his accident. He still addressed his shots in the boxer fashion that was slightly reminiscent of Jerry Travers – his weight planted solidly on the balls of his feet, his knees flexed, his spine arched to the point where his posterior protruded. But he had lopped off half a foot from his old, exaggerated backswing, and he now finished his follow-through in a more balanced, stand-up position instead of at the point where his back was all but facing the hole, as he had often done. He still looked uneasy sometimes while standing over the ball with his putter, but he had developed the knack, like Guldahl, of not drawing back that blade until he had out-stared the ball. Claude Harmon, who had won the 1948 Masters and was one of the few pros in whom Hogan confided his theories, was of the opinion that Hogan had made himself into the best putter in the business, a point of view that, like so many you could get from the pros if you took the trouble to ask them, was in direct contradiction to what the public thought. The really obvious change in the Hogan machine, however, was in his style of swinging. There was something not quite so slashing about it. Perhaps it was the solidity which twenty extra pounds over his pre-accident weight had given his frame, but he seemed to move into and through the ball with a rhythm that was almost Sneadian. Whatever it was, it produced a shot that was more predictable in its outcome. Hogan wasn't nearly as long off the tee as he had once been, but, by intentionally fading the ball, he had all but eliminated the hook which had so often flown off the face of his driver like a frightened quail.

In the spring of 1951 Hogan again won the Masters Tournament, which meant that he had won every major title in golf, except the British Open, at least twice. He was then as doubtful of crossing the Atlantic to win it as he was of crossing the street to get to the other side. The National Open that year was played at Oakland Hills, which had been revamped so severely by architect Robert Trent Jones that everyone considered it to be the sternest test on which the championship had ever been played. Hogan started with a wobbly 76, a score that left him forty places from the lead despite the fact nobody else broke the par of 70. He then got down to work. In the second round he scored a 73, and he improved on this with a 71 in the third round. At lunchtime, Hogan stood two strokes off the lead being established by

Locke and Demaret, but he played his fourth round as though he didn't know they were in the championship. He wasn't trying to beat them, he was trying to beat that course, as though he were caged, whip in hand, with a recalcitrant lion. Hogan made the turn in par and then birdied the tenth, 448 yards long, by poling a 3-iron shot four feet from the hole on the terraced green. A good putt put him two under on the par-three thirteenth, but he lost a stroke to par with a bogey-five on fourteen. On sixteen, a par-four, he drilled a drive and a 6-iron four feet from the hole and got down the putt to go back to two-under, where he stayed until he reached the eighteenth, a dog-leg to the right. Hogan crashed his drive here and carried the dog-leg. He hit a soaring 6-iron about fifteen feet from the hole and then carefully dropped the putt for his 67 and the championship. The round was, he later said, the finest of his life. 'I am glad,' he said, referring to the course at the presentation ceremonies, 'to have brought this monster to its knees.'

The year 1952 was an indifferent one for Hogan. He was then only interested in titles and the only titles he was interested in were The Masters and the National Open. In both he started strongly but finished in a way that made many people suspect that, verging on forty, he had finally reached the point of no return. In high winds at Augusta he played the last round in 79, one of the worst scores of his professional life, and in a siroccan heat at Dallas he faded on the last day after leading the event for the first two rounds.

Underestimating Hogan, of course, had always been dangerous thinking, but nothing had been more deceiving than the tired, faltering golf he played in 1952. Hogan not only came back in 1953, but improved to the extent where he seemed almost to have satisfied even his severest critic, Ben Hogan. At Augusta for The Masters, Hogan played so impeccably that in the four rounds, during which he broke the old scoring record by a margin of five strokes, no one could remember a single shot that was not brought off almost precisely as he had planned it. 'I think,' said Hogan in the most generous words he had ever allowed himself, 'that's the best I've ever played for four rounds.'

Hogan won two tournaments between The Masters and the National Open, which, almost as though it had been preordained for his big year, was scheduled for Oakmont, a course as formidable as Hogan himself. With no respect whatsoever for the reputation of the course, he opened with a five-under-par 67 and never looked back. In the last round, he hit a spoon to the sixteenth green and got down in two putts for his par. On the par-four seventeenth, he drove the green and took two putts for another three. On the long eighteenth, he crushed his tee shot and then threw a 5-iron to the back of the green six feet to the right of the hole. He addressed the putt as though the championship depended on it and then slid the ball across the marble green directly into the cup. He won by six strokes over Snead.

There now remained only one major championship in the world of golf Hogan hadn't won – the British Open. That year it was scheduled for Carnoustie, a course whose 7,200 yards of length would appeal to him. For months Hogan had been beseeched by his friends to enter the event; Walter Hagen had made an eloquent plea by long-distance phone only hours after Hogan had won the Masters in April. Under this pressure, Hogan had wired an entry before the National Open, but had held off his final decision until after the event. Now, having won it, he decided to take a crack at the British title.

The World of Golf, Random House, 1962, and Cassell, 1963

That small colossus: Hogan at Carnoustie
Bernard Darwin

As long as golfers talk championship golf, 1953 will be recalled as Hogan's year. Indeed, I think it would have been even if he had not won, so entirely did that small colossus bestride and dominate the tournament.

It was Hogan that sold the tickets in their thousands to the great joy of the authorities and filled the huge park with row upon serried row of shining cars; it was Hogan that produced what was, I think, the greatest crowd of spectators that I ever saw at a championship; and it was Hogan that every single one of them wanted to watch. Hardly anyone there had seen him play before, since when he was here in 1949 he was still too ill to play, and in less than no time anyone with any knowledge of golf came back overawed and abashed by the splendour of his game.

There were to begin with certain local patriots disposed to speak of him as 'Your man Hogan', and to murmur that he might do all manner of things on American inland courses, but let him wait till he comes to play over the great Carnoustie course in a Carnoustie wind. Yet even those more parochial critics were soon convinced, for they knew golf and were too honest not to admit that here was such a player as occurs only once in a generation or indeed once in a lifetime. As soon as the one Scottish hope, Eric Brown, had faded away I think the whole of that vast crowd wanted Hogan to win. This is not to say that Dai Rees, the ultimate British hope, who had played most gallantly, would not have been a most popular winner. He certainly would, but the feeling that the best man ought to win – there was no earthly doubt who that was – overrode all other sentiments.

And what a wonderful win it was! He did what Bobby Jones, Hagen and Sarazen had all failed to do at the first attempt. He came here weighed down by his immense reputation, and for the first two rounds his putting was unworthy of him and he seemed to have got the slowness of the greens a little on his nerves so far as he has any nerves. Yet when he once began to take some of the chances which his magnificent iron play gave him, when the putts began to drop so that we said 'Now he's off!' and it was almost a case of in the one class Hogan and in the other class all the other golfers, it was a measure of his quality that having been hard pressed for three rounds, sharing the lead with one very fine player and having all sorts of others hard on his very heels, he yet managed to win with something like ease.

It is an impossible task to give anything like an impression of the player to those who have not seen him, but one can perhaps pick out one or two points. Hogan stands decidedly upright with his weight rather forward on the left foot and the right foot drawn a little back. He holds his hands decidedly high, the right hand notably far over and the right wrist almost arched. The swing is rhythmic and easy and not as long as I had expected from the photographs. The club at the top of the swing may in fact go a little past the horizontal, but if so the eye – or my eye – cannot detect it. The impressive part of the swing comes in what the books call the hitting area. Then the clubhead appears to travel with such irresistible speed that it goes right through the ball and far past it before it begins to come up again. He has, incidentally, a good deal of power in reserve, and when he really means to hit out, as he did with his two wooden clubs at the long sixth hole, his length is very great indeed. I suppose, however, it is his iron play – particularly his long-iron – which is most striking. It is that which gives him so many chances of threes because he hits so appallingly straight. When we were all waiting behind the home green for his iron shot to the seventy-second hole and Hogan, no doubt giving the out-of-bounds on the left a wisely wide berth, finished up eight or nine yards to the right of the pin, somebody remarked: 'He's dreadfully crooked, isn't he?' It was a true word spoken in jest. Eight yards to the left or right of the pin was definitely crooked for Hogan.

Country Life, 16 July 1953

Sam Snead

Born 27 May 1912, Hot Springs, Virginia, USA.

In my remarks in this book I may seem to over-emphasize the importance of winning major championships. If this is so, consider the case of Samuel Jackson Snead.

He has won more tournaments world-wide than any other golfer, though Roberto de Vicenzo and Gary Player are close rivals, and more, emphatically, on the US circuit: eighty-four. He also won seven major championships: the Open, three Masters and three US PGAs. He remained a golfer of the highest class incomparably longer than anyone else: forty years. He is considered by most to have the smoothest and most effective swing yet seen in golf.

But he never won the US Open. To make matters worse, he was second no less than four times, losing 70 to 69 in a play-off for the 1947 Open while in another, the 1939, he stood on the last tee needing just a six to win. But no one told him and Sam thought a par five was required. He went for prodigious recovery shots that were not needed and in the end took eight.

Only this failure to win a US Open has meant that Snead is now considered a very great golfer rather than one of the three or four best of them all.

A swing for all ages
Dick Aultman

It is the year 2000. The 100th United States Open championship has just been completed. The winner accepts the first-place cheque for $200,000. He studies it a moment to make sure it's certified, and then he looks up at the gallery, his bright eyes twinkling under the brim of his straw hat.

'Ah figured ah was about due,' says eighty-eight-year-old Sam Snead.

As this chapter is being written, in August 1974, Sam Snead is sixty-two. It's an age when pro golfers sit back in the soft chairs on the clubhouse verandas at major tournaments, recalling the days of Hagen, Jones and Sarazen and accepting warm handshakes from members of the Hospitality Committee.

Not Snead. Last weekend he finished third in the PGA championship behind Trevino and Nicklaus and in front of Player, all of whom were just out of diapers when he first won the event thirty-two years ago. A few months previously he was placed second in the Los Angeles Open, six shots under par on the demanding Riviera Country Club course. All told, he has averaged over $4,000 per tournament entered in 1974. In short, Sam Snead is playing golf just about as well today as he did thirty-seven years ago when he made the United States Ryder Cup team as a rookie touring professional.

There are many reasons for Snead's amazing longevity. Largely they fall within one or more of the following broad categories:

The way he learned to play
The way he swings the club
His unusual suppleness
His enthusiasm for the game.

Within each of these categories the reader will find not only explanations of why Snead has played so well so long but also some clues to how he or she can also minimize the toll of advancing years. Legend would have us believe that Sam Snead climbed down from the trees just shortly after Neanderthal man, ripped off a limb, and with it started winning golf tournaments – barefooted. Actually, Snead did grow up in the Back Creek Mountains of Virginia. He did carve clubs out of swamp maple limbs, leaving some bark on for better gripping. And he's always found it easier to make a balanced swing when bereft of shoes.

While fact and legend often become inseparable in Snead's case, there are two things that are certainly true about his formative years in golf. First, he learned to play more or less by trial and error. Second, he learned to play largely by feel.

There were far more amateur whisky distillers than professional golf instructors around Ashwood, Virginia during the 1920s. Snead learned golf by watching his oldest brother, Homer, wallop 300-yard drives across the back pasture of their small cow-and-chicken farm. With his swamp maple, Snead imitated Homer's roundhouse swing by the hour. If he sliced the ball, it fell into some mucky bottomland. Therefore he experimented with different grips and stances until he found one that would keep his limited ball supply intact. (Perhaps the fact that Harry

Snead's pasture lacked sufficient drainage on the right side is a major reason why his fifth son, Sam, has always preferred to draw his shots from right to left.)

As Snead experimented with his swing, he gradually learned what would work for him and what would not. He found, for instance, that he could overcome his tendency to smother-hook his drives by positioning both hands a bit more to his left on the shaft (counterclockwise). He also discovered that he could hit the ball much farther and straighter if he held the club more lightly, especially in his right hand, than he did when swinging a baseball bat.

To this day Sam Snead has seldom looked elsewhere than into himself for counsel about his golf game. Learning by trial and error has given him the wherewithal to find a cure somehow for any problem that might occur, whether it be smothered drives or putting 'yips', the bugaboo that has stifled so many fine players in middle age, including Vardon, Cotton and Hogan. Snead knows exactly what works for Snead, and that is a big reason why he has played so well so long.

Another reason is that what works for Snead is usually what feels right for Snead, apart from what some textbook on golf advocates as being proper. This is not to say that Sam doesn't understand textbook fundamentals. He can talk technique as perceptively as any man I have met. The point is that he has always made a conscious effort to avoid too much conscious thought while swinging. 'Thinking instead of acting is the number one golf disease,' he says in his excellent autobiography, *The Education of a Golfer*. 'If I'd become tangled up in the mechanics of the swing when I first hit shots, chances are I'd have been only an average player.'

Snead certainly doesn't knock golf instruction, either written or oral, but he does feel strongly that information about the swing is in itself of little value to a pupil until he or she can learn to apply it in a way that feels comfortable. He also points out that some things simply don't feel comfortable until you've done them over and over again, perhaps thousands of times, on the practice tee.

Once the editors of *Golf Digest* magazine asked some playing and teaching professionals what each did or advocated to achieve proper swing tempo. Various pros described various swing mechanics to produce a smooth swing pace. Snead closed the subject when he said simply: 'I try to feel oily.'

As golfers advance in years, they generally find it more difficult successfully to direct themselves mentally to make a given move physically. A common complaint is: 'I keep telling myself to slow down my backswing but nothing happens.' Wouldn't it be so much simpler to play good golf longer if, like Snead, we'd simply learned to 'feel oily'?

Playing by feel makes it simpler to think simply. The student of the game who continually absorbs swing theories may find six or seven different ideas running through his head between the time he steps up to the ball and actually starts his takeaway. Three or four other thoughts may creep in while he swings. Too often the result is an inhibited swing that breeds inconsistency from shot to shot.

Snead has reduced his thinking to a few simple 'keys', as he calls them. The result is a free-flowing stroke that has remained amazingly consistent over the years. It is a simple swing. It has no unnecessary moving parts that might cause variation from shot to shot.

One of Snead's keys is merely to set the club in 'the slot' during his backswing. No one knows better than Sam that the main purpose of the backswing is simply to put the club into such a position that a freewheeling forward swing will deliver its head along the target line at great speed through impact. His slot at the top of the backswing is the space between his right shoulder and his head. He merely swings the club around and up so that at the top it lays in this slot and points more or less in the direction he wants to strike the ball. To set the club in this same slot time after time, Snead has said that he imagines his swing as being a wheel, with his head as the hub and his straight left arm as a spoke. By swinging this spoke around and up so that his hands finish in the slot, his clubshaft automatically becomes properly positioned.

Most golfers do not swing back and up on the same plane that they swing down and forward. Some, in changing directions from backswing to forward swing, loop the club more inside, behind themselves, and thus swing back to the ball on a flatter plane. More commonly, others loop the club in the opposite direction, forward or outside, so that the downswing plane becomes steeper than that of the backswing. The inside loop is preferable because it is more likely to return the clubhead from inside to along the target line during impact instead of from outside to across the line. The flatter downswing plane also keeps the clubhead moving at ball level longer through impact, on a shallower arc than does the steeper plane that results from the outside loop. The force of the blow thus becomes directed more forward, toward the target, rather than downward into the ground.

Snead's swing, however, has remained consistent over the years largely because he, more so than any other great players, swings back and up and down and forward on practically the same plane. He sets the club into a position at the top – in the slot – from which it becomes unnecessary to swing into either a flatter or a steeper downswing plane. Thus he eliminates the inconsistencies that can result from looping.

Most golfers, even the best, need a slightly flatter downswing plane to assure swinging the clubhead back to the ball from inside to along the target line. They need this flatter downswing plane for insurance against the deadly outside loop that must inevitably swing the clubhead across the line – outside to inside – during impact. Snead, however, does not need this insurance for several reasons.

The first deals with the alignment of his body at address, especially his shoulders. Snead has always aligned himself in a slightly 'closed' position, one in which a line across his shoulders would point at the target or even a bit to the right of it rather than parallel to the target line in the so-called square alignment. By setting up slightly closed, he can be sure that he will always swing the clubhead into the ball from inside to along the target line – even on those few occasions when he happens to loop a bit outside onto a slightly steeper plane than he adopted going back.

Snead seldom loops to the outside, however, because of his excellent rhythm and tempo. He has always stressed starting both his backswing and his downswing slowly. This gives him sufficient time in changing directions from backswing to downswing to allow his feet and legs to initiate his forward stroke. With legs leading, his shoulders and hands are relegated to being followers. They do not have an opportunity to shove or throw the club into the outside loop.

Snead's unhurried swing-pace results largely from his second key, that being always to swing at less than full power. He has estimated that on a normal stroke he uses only eighty to ninety percent of the power that is actually available to him. On those occasions when he needs extra distance, he relies on what he calls his 'supercharger', which is nothing more than a somewhat more aggressive forward driving of his feet and legs at the start of the downswing. Most golfers, in attempting to add extra yardage, unconsciously use their hands and/or shoulders too soon too aggressively, from the top of their backswings, which invariably forces the club onto an outside loop and thus into a too-steep downswing plane. Leading with the feet and legs in Snead-like fashion increases leverage while maintaining a proper downswing plan.

A third Snead key is simply to think of returning his arms and the clubshaft back to the same position at impact that they were in at address. Purists will find that actually there is a slight variance between Snead's overall body position at address and impact. By contact his legs have shifted farther toward the target and his head and shoulders a bit farther away from it. There is a close, if not identical, similarity, however, between his arm-club relationship at the two stages.

This writer believes that it is Snead's thought of returning his arms to their address relationship that helps him swing his arms so freely on his forward stroke. The outstanding British instructor, John Jacobs, has noted a feature of all great golf swings, especially true in the case of Snead's. That feature is a rapid and dramatic increase in the space between the hands and the right shoulder during the downswing. Golfers who shove with the shoulders and thus do not swing their arms freely forward will not get nearly the separation that we see in those, such as Snead, who swish their arms freely down and through as they drive their knees smoothly forward and their hips around. The golfer who fails to achieve this separation will tend to top his or her shots and would be much helped by Snead's key.

Another Snead key thought is to finish with his hands high. This is the thought he uses when he finds his shots are pulling to the left. Thinking 'hands high' helps him avoid the too-steep downswing plane that causes the relatively low finish position. It helps him to return the clubhead from inside to along the target line.

Snead's swing is probably best known for its unhurried, flowing grace. It gives this appearance largely because it is so unified. When he came on the scene in the 1930s, the emphasis was still on 'hand action'. While Sam certainly does nothing to stifle normal use of his hands, his swing exemplifies the 'one-piece' unification of body, legs and arms. His arms swing back and up in direct conjunction with the turning of his body. There is absolutely no independent lifting or turning of the club with his hands and wrists, no flippiness at the top, no casting with the hands at the start of the downswing. In short, his hands are 'quiet' throughout his swing. It is this lack of wristy jerking above all else that makes Snead's swing look so smooth. It is also a major reason for his remarkable consistency over the years.

No discussion of Snead's longevity as a winner would be complete without mention of his remarkable physical assets, most notably his unusual suppleness. On request he will demonstrate his flexibility by high kicking, cancan style, a normal eight-foot-high ceiling. He will also bend forward, with legs stiff, and pluck golf balls out of the cup. Even today, although his equator has broadened considerably, he still makes a fuller shoulder turn on his backswing than do most of the youngsters he competes against.

Beyond inheriting some exceptional genes, however, Snead also employs certain techniques in swinging a golf club that enhance suppleness. These are techniques that less well-endowed golfers could also adopt to help themselves play better longer:

He holds the club lightly, thus avoiding arm and shoulder tension. He controls the club largely in the last two fingers of his left hand, but with a pressure he has likened to holding a fork or a billiard cue.

He waggles the club freely at address, all the while shifting his feet and legs, trying to feel 'oily'.

He cocks his chin toward his right shoulder just before swinging, thus moving it out of the way for a free turning of his shoulder.

He starts his swing with a definite forward press, easing his right knee and his hands slightly toward the target before swinging immediately thereafter into his backswing.

He addresses the ball with a slightly closed shoulder alignment. For average golfers this minimizes the degree of shoulder turn required to place the club in proper position at the top.

He starts the club back low and slow, thus encouraging a full left-arm extension and a full shoulder coiling. Starting back slowly minimizes any involuntary grabbing with the right hand in order to control the club – grabbing that will tense the right arm and shoulder and abbreviate the backswing.

He keeps his swing thoughts to a minimum. As he's said, too much analysis causes paralysis.

No golfer can play golf so well so long as Snead unless he has a tremendous love for the game and a great pride in his ability to excel. Once, at a *Golf Digest* seminar, Bob Toski, the outstanding American golf teacher, asked Sam why he has been able to strike the ball better and score better for longer than any player who ever lived. For answer, Snead revealed that during the forty-odd years he had played golf for a living, he had never gone more than two weeks without somehow playing a few holes or hitting balls.

'The only time I came close was when I went to Africa on safari,' Sam said. 'We were right out there in the bush, shooting elephant and buffalo and all that stuff. But somehow a couple of golf clubs came

ove left Byron Nelson at the Masters, Augusta, Georgia in 1981.
ove right Tommy Bolt at the 1980 Benson and Hedges International.
ow left Ben Hogan at the 1956 Canada Cup at Wentworth, Surrey. Hogan won the individual title to
ke his record in Britain – played twice, won twice. *Below right* Bobby Locke and his highly individual
sition at the top of the backswing: Worthing, 1951.

Above Palmer in one of his finest
hours: winning the 1962 Open
at Royal Troon. *Below* You can
see why he is said to have the
toughest forearms in the
business: aged over 50, he
performs in the 1980 US Open.

ck Nicklaus, who has small hands, is one of the few great players to use the interlocking grip.

Below Jack Nicklaus two holes away from victory in the 1980 Open at Baltusrol and *right* putting in the US Masters from a fringe: his long putting has always been a feature of his play.

along and the next thing you know a guy called Gordon Fawcett and me have got a little game going.

'We've got a hole from here over to the wall and we're using elephant droppings for balls. Only trouble was you couldn't hit 'em too hard, 'cause they'd explode. Seem to remember I beat this guy. I'd hit my ball on its hard side and it'd stay in one piece and I'd make five. His kept falling apart.

'The point is I couldn't keep away from golf. I'd been gone two weeks and here I was playing again. I reckon if I'd ever taken a year off, I wouldn't have been able to play at all when I started again.'

It is the year 2001. The 101st United States Open championship has just been completed. The winner accepts the first-place cheque for $210,000. He studies it a moment to make sure it's certified, and then he looks up at the gallery, his bright eyes twinkling under the brim of his straw hat. 'Ah figured it was so much fun ah'd try it again,' says eighty-nine-year-old Sam Snead.

Masters of Golf, Stanley Paul, 1976

How it ought to look
Patrick Campbell

In January 1961 an exhibition match took place between Sam Snead and Harry Weetman, to celebrate the opening of Israel's first golf-course at Caesarea.

It also marked the first occasion upon which a match was followed by a gallery of two thousand people only twelve of whom – by my own personal estimate – had ever seen the game played before.

A brisk breeze was blowing up the first fairway, touching at times, I should say, fifty miles an hour, as Snead and Weetman tossed for the honour. Snead won, teed up his ball and then stood looking at the audience with an appearance of patience which anyone knowing him would not have trusted an inch.

What the audience was doing was commenting in Hebrew, German, Polish, French, Spanish and a variety of Scandinavian languages upon the force of the wind, the magnificence of the new club-house, the political situation vis-à-vis Jordan, Colonel Nasser and half a hundred other matters including Snead's Palm Beach straw hat. The babel of sound was tremendous, and only partially dissipated by the gale.

None of those present, of course, could have been expected to know that death-like silence should have been their portion, that Snead had been known to threaten legal action against people dropping pins half a mile away while he was trying to hole a four-foot putt.

As the Master continued to remain inactive, save for an ominous tapping of the right foot, the noise became even greater. I was able to identify enquiries in English, French and German as to whether he had already, perhaps, done it and if so where had it gone, and if he hadn't what was he waiting for and would it be possible for him to get on with it now?

Snead then made a suggestion which some of the stewards carried out in part, waving their arms and asking politely for silence. This had the immediate effect of redoubling the noise, people asking one another in genuine bewilderment how silence on their part could possibly contribute to whatever Snead was trying to do. In the end a comparative hush was achieved, Snead stepped up to his ball and with that long, beautifully timed, power-packed swing slashed one straight down the middle, quail high into the wind and all of 280 yards.

Deathlike silence fell upon the gallery, for the first time. They'd seen him hit it, but no one was prepared for the result. No one, in fact, had seen where the ball had gone. It had simply passed out of their ken and so they remained silent, rather than to appear at a disadvantage by applauding where, perhaps, no applause had been earned.

They were more ready for Weetman, as he stood up to it. Word had gone round that perhaps the ball went rather farther than anyone could have a right to expect. They saw every inch of Harry's tee-shot, an obviously apprehensive right-handed bash that took off like a bullet, turned sharp left and finished on the far side of the ninth fairway, about 150 yards off the line.

A great roar of applause went up, a thunderous clapping of hands. Snead's expression, never too sunny in action – or even in repose – would have frightened the lives out of a platoon of armed Algerian terrorists in broad daylight.

Subsequently, there was even worse to come. Many of the stewards got tired of the labour of lugging ropes around, seeing that the gallery paid little attention to them, and knocked off, leaving the ropes where they lay. At one moment, round about the seventh, Snead found himself trying to play a wedge shot over or around three splendid bearded old gentlemen who stood directly in front of him, watching whatever he was trying to do with lively interest. Later, a pretty girl in khaki shorts picked

Harry Weetman's ball out of a bush and helpfully placed it in his hand.

But how, as I say, could anyone who had never seen golf played before know any better? And how can anyone who has never seen Snead hit a golf ball guess that that is the way it ought to be done?

How to Become a Scratch Golfer, Blond, 1963

Bobby Locke

Born 20 November 1917, Germiston, Transvaal, South
Africa.

Bobby Locke was a dominant force on the British circuit and on his
home ground between the end of World War II and the mid-1950s, his
greatest achievements being his four British Open titles and fourteen
wins on the US circuit at a time when foreign players were almost
unknown there and, if they won, like Locke, were resented. In the
last thirty-five years only Player has surpassed Locke's successes as a
foreigner in America while Jacklin and Ballesteros have gone one
better in winning a major championship. Neither, however, has had
comparable successes in tournament play, where the Australian Bruce
Crampton is his nearest rival.

Of all the great players, Locke's swing is the least imitated, because
of the oddities which are described in the passages that follow. Many,
however, would like to have imitated his success with the putter. He is
acknowledged to be one of the best two or three putters of all time –
many would say the best.

The gentleman in a necktie
Charles Price

The 1947 National Open was not a Hogan story in any sense. The
year had not been one of his best, mainly because he was in the process
of revamping his swing for the umpteenth time, and so the headlines
fell to one of the most incongruous professionals the game has known:
Bobby Locke, of South Africa. The only thing that Locke did the least
bit like any other professional in the world was win tournaments, and
even here he differed from the others in the way he won them. At a
time when alligator shoes, canary-yellow slacks and fuchsia sport shirts
were practically the uniform of the day for the American professional,
Locke dressed in grey flannel knickerbockers, white buckskin shoes
and linen shirts complete with necktie. His swing was put together by

exaggerating everything which the American pros had come to regard as anathema. He employed a long, meandering backswing, at the top of which he collapsed his left side. By the time he had gone into his downswing, the clubhead had described an almost perfect figure-of-eight. He slapped the ball into a long, sweeping parabola that started far to the right and then, as though guided by some personal radar, hooked unerringly back to the target. Locke hooked every shot in the bag, including his *putts*, and his method here had some purists among the pros kicking lockers in frustration. At a time when almost every pro on the circuit putted with a mallethead, Locke used a hickory-shafted blade that might well have once belonged to Tom Morris. He addressed his putts with a closed stance, opened the blade on the backswing and then jabbed the ball, sometimes so abruptly that some bug-eyed pros contended he took divots. The ball crept toward the hole and then, just when it was about to stop on the lip, it took one more turn and fell in. To most of his competitors the harrowing thing about this technique was the uncanny way his putts had of almost always dropping in on the right-hand side of the cup. Un-American though his methods were, Locke won fourteen tournaments in the United States, seven of them in 1947 alone, and he became the most serious foreign threat to the National Open since Ted Ray.

The World of Golf, Random House, 1962, and Cassell, 1963

Tommy Bolt

Born 31 March 1918, Haworth, Oklahoma, USA.

Besides the temper exemplified in the passage that follows, Bolt could also talk rather directly. Before his singles in the 1957 Ryder Cup against the Scotsman Eric Brown he is supposed to have invited Brown to take first tee shot by saying: 'Your beat, sucker.' Brown retorted by winning 4 and 3. Such was the animosity supposed to exist between them that they were said at one time to be settling their differences on the practice ground 'throwing clubs at each other from fifty paces'.

Bolt was US Open Champion in 1958 and won a tournament or so annually throughout that decade. He had, and has, one of the most rhythmic swings in golf, which lasted well enough for him to win the US Seniors Championship for five consecutive years, and he can still play a sub-par round today.

Ol' Tom

George Plimpton

Tommy Bolt is the contemporary golfer spoken of when temper tantrums are the topic, particularly fits of club throwing, though he has kept them under control in recent years. I have always liked the following exchange:

CADDIE: Mr Bolt, you'll be using either a two- or a three-iron for this shot.

BOLT (*incredulously*): Hell, man, that's 350 yards out there. Ol' Tom can't begin to reach the green with a two, much less a *three*, iron.

CADDIE: Mr Bolt, all you got left in your bag are those two clubs. Unless you want to use your putter.

BOLT: Oh.

CADDIE: And your putter's missin' its handle. You snapped it off on the first nine.

BOLT: Oh.

One of Bolt's most famous outbursts occurred on the Cherry Hills course in Denver during the 1960 Open. He was playing well until the twelfth hole, when he suddenly got himself in trouble by dropping a shot into a pond. He had a heated argument with a USGA official as to exactly where he should drop his ball for the penalty shot. His concentration upset, what he refers to as his 'tempo' gone askew, he proceeded to three-putt the next hole, bogey the next and then on the eighteenth hole he hooked two drives into the lake. He strode down off the tee up to the edge of the lake, peered in, abruptly reared back, and then, with his left foot far advanced and planted to get leverage and power, he sailed his driver into the water. What happened next surprised everyone, Bolt included. A small boy, marking the splash, waded into the lake, belly-flopped down and disappeared. He surfaced with the club. The crowd, a considerable one around that last green, which had given an odd grunt of dismay and surprise at Bolt's temper, now cheered as the boy worked his way to the bank. Bolt himself stepped forward, his rage eclipsed quite completely by the ferocity of his club throw, a smile, if a somewhat grim one, working at his lips as if he had in mind to say, 'Ol' Tom sure appreciates this, son...thanks,' or some such pleasantry since the driver was a favourite. The boy hauled himself up the bank and, giving a startled look at Bolt advancing on him, took a few quick steps this way, then that, dodging him, and then lit out across the fairway, the club still in hand and the crowd roaring. Someone in the gallery, which was not particularly sensitive to Bolt's dismay after watching his display of temper, gave the kid a leg up over the fence, and he was gone.

Bolt kept his sense of humour about this incident, as he generally does about his rages. I have always liked his dictum about club throwing: 'If you are going to throw a club, it is important to throw it ahead of you, down the fairway, so you don't waste energy going back to pick it up.'

The Bogey Man, Deutsch, 1969

Arnold Palmer

Born 10 September 1929, Latrobe, Pennsylvania, USA.

Palmer has won eight major championships, lies third in the list of all-time tournament winners and has won well over $2 million. These are rather threadbare statistics and they tell very little indeed about what Palmer has been to the game of golf.

In the 1920s and 1930s Walter Hagen, by his engaging personality, and Bobby Jones, by his excellence, sweepingly increased public interest in the game. When they departed the scene, interest plummeted. While it revived after the war with the excellence of Nelson, Snead and Hogan, the arrival of Palmer and particularly his spectacular win from behind in the 1960 US Open, made golf a major spectator sport and everyone, above all, wanted to follow the daring deeds of Arnold Palmer.

The spin-offs were many and varied: money to be won on the tour increased dramatically, from about $600,000 in the year that Palmer turned professional to $3 million in 1966, $5 million in 1968 and $7 million in 1972. In the same period the number of tour events went from twenty-six to the mid-forties. Even more substantial was the effect of Palmer's popularity on the earnings of a world-class golfer outside his basic golf winnings. He can take between £5,000 and £10,000 for giving a golf clinic or turning up to play at a company outing and in Palmer's case particularly the millions rolled in from the use of his name in promoting products that had no direct connection with golf.

All this in essence derived from the drama of the man's play: the fact that he swung a driver with such patent violence; that his recoveries from rough and woodland caused both turf and bushes to fly; and not least, that he was an *aggressive* putter – in watching most players, one is aware that putting is a matter of some delicacy, of coasting the ball up to the hole. Palmer almost gave it a bang, confident that if he went a few feet past, there would be no problem in getting the return putt in.

The passages that follow centre more on the way Palmer played the game – alas, he has changed a lot – than accounts of this event and that.

Arnie's Army
George Plimpton

I found this experience – being in his Army – one of the most exhilarating experiences a sports enthusiast can have: I found myself transfixed by the excitement of it, scarcely believing that it would be possible to walk around a golf course and watch a golfer – if one was lucky enough to crane over the ranks and actually see him swing – hit a golf shot and wax enthusiastic over it. Of sporting spectacles a golf stroke is surely the one least adaptable to exhilaration. And yet Palmer made it an art of such excitement.

The Bogey Man, Deutsch, 1969

The prize-fighter
Charles Price

Palmer usually walks to the first tee quite unlike any other pro on the circuit. He doesn't walk onto it so much as climb into it, almost as though it were a prize ring, and then he looks around at the gallery as though he is trying to count the house. As usual, this was the air with which he approached the first tee of the last round of the 1960 National Open. When it was his turn to shoot, he again gambled on a shot with his driver.

Palmer's address, particularly with a driver, is a semi-circle, his shoulders rounded and his knees knocked. Crouching over the ball that day at Cherry Hills, he gave the general impression of tenseness, as though he were about to dive into a pool of sharks. When he swung, it was with all the abandon of a drunk at a driving range. The ball hung in the air so long it looked as though it had been painted there. When it finally came down, it tore through the rough in front of the green; bounded through the grass bunker and came to rest on the putting surface about twenty feet from the hole.

Palmer's first putt just missed the cup, but his second gave him the birdie. He was on his way. He finished the front nine in thirty, a record nine-hole score for the National Open. He played the back nine in 35 and won the championship by two strokes with a 72-hole total of 280, just as he had predicted.

The World of Golf, Random House, 1962, and Cassell, 1963

A change of technique

Arnold Palmer with W. B. Furlong

I put perhaps a quarter of a century into developing a style that brought me to success. When I finally had it honed to the best that I could do, Henry Cotton, one of the finest golf stylists in Great Britain, analysed it this way:

'Palmer has little style...
'He often hits with no follow-through at all...
'He rarely finishes two swings the same way...
'Sometimes he finishes almost on his knees...
'Even with his crouching putting stance, he stands rather oddly: very knock-kneed...'

And when you stop to think of how many years it took me to get *that* good...

Actually, Henry was not being malicious. He was being analytical and balanced. ('Palmer drives as far and straight as anyone playing...Arnold hits his iron shots to the pin like Sam Snead and putts as well as, if not better than, Bobby Locke.' That was quite a compliment: Bobby Locke was perhaps one of the two or three greatest putters in golfing history.)

The reason I bring it up is to suggest that perhaps it's not so different. It's not necessarily that I've got better. It's that I've got different.

And the difference was harder to achieve than some of the boldest shots in my inventory. For it defines the difference between challenge and change. Challenge involves only one person – me. Nobody else needs face the hard shot, nobody else can be hurt by it. But change – any kind of change – involves many people. And some of them can be hurt – or puzzled or chagrined – by my change.

And so the way I think about change is different in degree, but not kind, from the way you think about challenge. Which is to say: it is done more slowly. And cautiously.

94

To understand all this, you must understand that boldness is a philosophy of play, not a style of play. There are a good many styles that can fit within the philosophy; I've used several different ones myself.

Yet you find people who feel that a 'bold' player is, by definition, a power hitter. That's not quite true. A very modest hitter can be quite bold as a player. The fact is that some of the boldest shots in the game are the putts, the chip shots, the short approach shots. For they determine the skills and attitudes of the player. Is he willing to go for the pin, to get a birdie or an eagle, instead of going for the fat part of the green and taking, safely, a par? Is he willing to go boldly for the cup on his first putt – a long putt, let's say – with all the risks involved in putting past the cup and into disaster? Or will he nudge the ball up to the cup, in an effort to protect his par?

Boldness is a matter of attitude, not of power. It is a matter of shaping the tools you have to your philosophy of the game, rather than shaping your philosophy to your tools – boldness to power, caution to lack of power.

My own feeling is that boldness should be a liberating philosophy, not a confining one. I certainly haven't felt compelled to stick with one style of golf, even though I've stuck with one attitude toward it.

When I first went out on the tournament trail, I heard a lot of criticism that all I could hit was the low, hard-punched shot. It was true – but then there were a lot of golfers who couldn't do that. It had its drawbacks, of course. For one thing it gave me a lot of roll on the ball after it hit the ground. That added yardage to the drive – but I never could be sure where the ball would roll to. There are a lot of golf courses where added roll means added trouble, because the fairway grass is so thin that the ball never quite stops where you want it to stop. It rolls on and on into a sand trap or water hazard or skips into the rough. There are other courses where you don't get the added roll. The grass is so verdant and strong that the low line drive with high momentum tends to come quickly to a stop. Augusta National is an example. The grass is so rich, even in the spring, that you get very little roll on it. You get greater distance by keeping the ball in the air as long and as far as possible – i.e. with a high-trajectory drive – because you can't expect any longer distance from a ball that flies low and hits early; the grass just won't let it get that extra roll. Yet I won two Masters tournaments at Augusta with the low, hard-punched shot. And I won two British Opens. And I won the US Open.

For six or seven years after I joined the pro tour, I stayed with that shot. But bit by bit, as I came to understand the magnificent vagaries of the golf courses on the pro tour, I came to feel that this shot was not enough. I had to face the hard fact that the world out there on the pro tour was different from the world in which I'd learned the game of golf.

Not all the tournament courses were so deliciously free of fairway bunkers as the one at home. I sometimes found, on the tour, that a low, hard-punched shot would hit safely short of a bunker and then roll and roll and roll until it nestled in the sand. Nor were all the greens as soft as the ones at home, where I'd learned to hit a low, hard-punched shot with a 1-iron, knowing that the green would slow the roll. When you get to a course with small and sometimes elevated greens – like Merion, the site of the 1971 US Open – you're really in trouble if you've got an approach shot that has a lot of roll. For each time they cut the grass they do it three times on those greens – and from three different directions – and any way you hit a low-punched shot onto those greens, you've got a good chance not only of rolling past the cut but of rolling over and off the green and down into some deep trouble.

The lessons were sometimes learned hard – through experience – but the alternative was so difficult that I came very slowly to the conclusion that I was going to have to make a basic change in my game.

It would be a change in style, not in philosophy. I would not play less boldly than before. Nor would I hit the ball less hard. But I would hit it high as well as hard.

It was a long and slow process: it took the better part of an off-season and a spring to gain any credence with it. Until then, I was teeing up my ball about a quarter of an inch. And I was placing it slightly more to the right, as I faced it, thus making contact with it while the clubhead was still descending. Sometimes I hit the ball and the ground at virtually the same instant; sometimes – because of the trajectory of my swing – I was hitting the ground first. The ball did not go high but it went far, and it got a roll that carried it farther. In short, it had greater impetus than height; it had considerable momentum after it hit the ground, which gave it that extraordinary roll.

Would more accuracy be worth the loss in distance?

I thought so. And I knew how to go about seeking it.

I began teeing up the ball a little higher – about an inch higher. Then I began planting it a little farther forward, closer to the line of my left heel. So instead of hitting it while I was still in the downswing I'd be hitting it exactly at the bottom of the swing, or even a shade beyond it. The idea was that by moving the ball to the left a little, I'd be lengthening the distance over which the clubhead was travelling in a straight line – not much, perhaps only an inch. But that, I felt, would give me a little more accuracy – just as you get more accuracy from a rifle than a pistol.

By raising the ball on the tee, I'd get more loft into the drive, which would cost some distance. It would reduce the roll – but it was the roll after hitting that ground that was getting me into deep trouble. The loss in distance was not what would make most men weep; I could still average 275 yards off the tee. But there was a distinct advantage to it all: I'd avoid hitting the ground with the club at the instant that I hit the ball, as I had under the old system. By teeing the ball up higher, I'd avoid that jarring dislocation of the clubhead that could alter the whole flight of the ball.

But if I raised the ball, what happened to the impact-point on the clubhead?

Wouldn't it – the 'sweet spot' on the clubhead – now be coming through the impact area lower than the centre of the ball?

Possibly.

To compensate for that, I went to a driver with a deeper clubface. It was thicker from top to bottom. My drivers now measure about $1\frac{3}{4}$ inches in depth at the 'sweet spot'. In that way, I felt that I'd get solid, continuing contact with a ball teed an inch off the ground.

It was not an immediate success. I had a great deal of trouble with it in the winter tour of 1962, notably at the Bing Crosby Pro-Am and the San Diego Open. It seemed to come around during the Lucky International at San Francisco that year and then it sustained itself well during my victory at the 90-hole tournament at Palm Springs.

I was aiming to get it into shape for the Masters; the Augusta National course places a considerable premium on accuracy off the tee. The fairways are wide enough so that you don't get into rough often but accuracy is needed so that you can get position on fairway shots that will open up the green for you. I was relaxed about it all; I figured to have ten weeks to get everything into shape. But I got a message at the Phoenix Open in 1962 at the Phoenix Country Club. (It alternates between there and the Arizona Country Club.) In the past, this had been a difficult course for me, if only because it had narrow, tree-lined fairways that tended to inhibit my long game. This time I found myself curiously eager to attack the course, to try out my new driving procedure on it.

The eagerness was well founded. Everything I hit stayed in the fairway, and I went on to win the tournament by twelve strokes – the biggest margin of victory by anybody anywhere that year.

Later on, I was to go on to win the Tournament of Champions at a course heavily edged by rough that somehow had kept me from winning before. And I would win at the Colonial Invitational, and at the Texas Open and at the British Open – at nine different tournaments. The most delicious of them all: my third victory at the Masters in Augusta.

Go for Broke, Kimber, 1974

A $5,000 Nassau
George Plimpton

Frank Gifford, the football player, told me about a dinner at P. J. Clarke's restaurant in New York, a big pleasant hangout which many athletes frequent. He was sitting with Arnold Palmer and their wives, and behind them, at another table, a man kept leaning across and touching Palmer on the shoulder, pushing a question or two, perhaps a comment, trying to insinuate himself into their circle. Gifford was more annoyed, he said, than Palmer. It was a farewell dinner for Palmer, who was leaving for a trip abroad – Cairo, or some such place – early the next morning. The man's efforts seemed impertinent. Then to Gifford's astonishment he realized the man was trying to hustle Palmer. He was trying to goad him into a match. 'I'd seen the guy around before,' Gifford said. 'I knew he was a damn good golfer – a country-club player – but it was hard to believe: I mean, he was telling Palmer that he didn't think that there was that much difference between a crack amateur and a pro, and he was willing to prove it.'

He wanted to tee off the next morning; he offered Palmer his choice of golf courses in the vicinity; the only concession he wanted was a handicap of one stroke a side. The two would play $500 Nassau – that is to say, a bet of five hundred a side and five hundred more on the final outcome of the match. Palmer was very polite in refusing. He half-turned in his chair and said that he was flying for the Middle East the next morning, it really wasn't something he could fit in.

The amateur put on a smug expression and he hitched his chair around to turn back to the people at his table. His voice rose as he explained how the great golfer, the *pro-fession-al*, had backed down. He was pretty exuberant. He clicked his fingers and ordered a beer.

Suddenly Palmer swung his chair around. He tapped the man on the shoulder. He said: 'All right, I'll tell you what I'll do. I'll postpone my trip to Cairo. We'll tee off at Winged Foot at nine o'clock tomorrow morning. OK?' The man was staring at him, astonished. 'Except I'm not giving you one stroke a side. I'm giving you two strokes. And we're not playing $500 Nassau. We'll play $5,000 Nassau.'

Gifford said you could hear the man gulp. He looked down at the table top, and he never said another word. Palmer looked at him a bit, and then swung back to his table, disgusted. Palmer really would have stayed, Gifford felt. He wasn't trying to scare the man off by increasing the size of the bet, he had just been trying to make it worth his own while to postpone the trip. As a competitor he was interested in the challenge, perhaps even in the man who had made it. But then he had swung the chair around and leaned half out of his chair and confronted him, so that the man was suddenly looking into that familiar face with the eyes full-blast on him, and that had folded the amateur up: he had gulped and felt foolish.

The Bogey Man, Deutsch, 1969

A matter of the mind
Dick Aultman

Anyone who has played serious competitive golf realizes that the fine line between success and failure depends more on the mind than it does on the body. This is true because in golf, perhaps more than in any other sport, the player's personal psychology determines how his physical self will perform.

There may come a distant day when some progressive university offers a course called something like Golf Psychotherapy E3, an advanced study requirement leading to a Doctorate of Mind Control, DMC. If so, perhaps the professor would include at least one lecture analysing the case history of one Arnold Daniel Palmer, that great American player of the twentieth century.

Between April 1958 and April 1964, Arnold Palmer won seven of the twenty-five major championships held, finished second or third in six others, and leaped tall buildings at a single bound, without ever having to dress up like Superman. He could seemingly *will* the ball into the cup from any distance, especially if a major title were at stake and the TV cameras were beaming in. 'If I ever needed an eight-foot putt and everything I owned depended on it,' Bobby Jones once said, 'I would want Arnold Palmer to putt it for me.'

In the decade since April 1964, Palmer has won no major championships, seriously challenged in them only about six times, and recently found it more and more difficult to survive the 36-hole cutoff.

Perhaps we should admit that when a golfer approaches and passes forty, the odds against his winning prestige tournaments increase rather rapidly. Palmer, however, was only thirty-four when he won his last major title, the 1964 Masters, an age, for example, when Ben Hogan had yet to win eight of his nine majors. What is even more puzzling is the fact that even today (1974), at forty-five, Palmer, as we shall see, seems to be swinging as well – some say better – than ever before. Over the years it has been said that Palmer's biggest weakness was his golf swing and his great strength his inner ability to generate a great shot – often a putt – whenever it was needed most. In this chapter we shall first discuss Palmer's swing, pro and con, yesterday and today, as well as his personal psychology, in hopes of ascertaining what has happened to him as a total golfer.

A few years ago *Golf Digest* magazine ran an article in which twenty-five touring professionals each selected the fellow pro he felt had the best swing. Not surprisingly, Sam Snead won the most votes. Gene Littler, though inactive at the time of the polling, received several mentions. Tommy Bolt, himself playing only infrequently, finished fifth behind Snead, Nicklaus, Trevino and Weiskopf. Palmer, then the winner of more PGA tour events than any other player in history except Snead and Hogan, received only one vote – from Trevino.

Probably Palmer would have fared even worse in a similar poll of the generally less-informed golfing public. We tend to ascribe greatness to those swings that look smooth, graceful and effortless – Bobby Jones, for sure, Snead, Littler, Bolt, Boros. A Palmer would never make the list. His swing is too fast, too violent, too lacking aesthetically. This is unfortunate because, while Arnold's swing will never be regarded as a model worthy of emulation by the masses, a look behind its facade of unruly vigour reveals many admirable qualities.

Palmer's grip, for instance, deserves top marks. Throughout his years as a junior golfer Arnold held the club with his left hand in a so-called strong position: turned well to his right, wrapped across the top of the club-shaft, so that at address he could look down and see the top knuckles on all four fingers, with his left thumb resting on the right side of the shaft.

In 1948 Lew Worsham, former US Open champion and head pro at Oakmont Country Club near Arnold's Pennsylvania home, encouraged Palmer to adopt a more reliable 'neutral' grip, one in which the left thumb sat on top of the shaft so that the back of this hand faced down the target line. Some 500,000 practice shots later, Arnold emerged with the excellent grip he uses today, the palms more or less facing each other and aligning with the clubface itself. His hands are firmly melded together and to the shaft itself in a standard overlap grip. He talks about using firm grip pressure instead of the light pressure advocated by many modern teachers, but if he does hold tighter than most, it's simply because he swings faster than most; he needs the extra control. Partly because of his firm hold, Arnold has never been flippy-wristed. He swings with jackhammer firmness.

Palmer made a second major improvement in his technique about 1962 when he began gradually playing the ball farther forward in his stance, more toward his left foot. No doubt this modification forced him to use more leg action in his downswing, which in turn increased the duration his clubhead moved on line and at ball level through impact.

His firm-wristed, 'one-piece' takeaway, with the clubhead moving straight back from the ball for at least a few inches, gives Palmer one of the game's wider swing arcs. His straight left arm and full shoulder turn give him a tremendous coiling of back and shoulder muscles without necessitating an overlong backswing.

Palmer's swing tempo is faster than most people could handle successfully. It works for him, however, largely for three reasons: first, though Palmer's overall pace is fast, there remains a definite 'beat' to his swing, a specific 'one-two' count with sufficient time between the numbers to let him shift gears and change directions from backswing into forward swing. Second, his unusually strong hands and forearms let Palmer retain control of the club while swinging shorter and faster than most. Thus he avoids the sudden increase in grip pressure – the grabbing – that ruins the rhythm of so many weekend swings. Third, Palmer plays well with a fast swing because of his steady head position.

While his head does swivel during his swing, in conjunction with the turning of his shoulders, it remains free of any up-down or left-to-right swaying. In short, it serves as a highly effective anchor that helps to keep him in balance despite the fury of his action.

Another commendable feature of Palmer's swing is his outstanding left-hand, left-side control. At impact the back of his left wrist and his left arm are about as firm as they could possibly be. Byron Nelson has described Palmer's impact position as being 'absolutely perfect'. There is no indication whatsoever of right-hand takeover, no breakdown at the back of the left wrist, no bending of the left arm, any of which would reduce both distance and accuracy.

Palmer's excellent left-side control stems in part from his emphasis on pulling with the last three fingers of this hand during the early stages of his downswing. This left-hand pulling effort is aided in large part by his legs. They act as leaders in his downswing, making the first move to his left side. Were his extremely powerful shoulders to lead, his right side and right arm would force his left arm and wrist to break down either before, during or shortly after impact.

Palmer's legwork is unusual and worthy of mention in any discussion of his game. Arnold's right leg actually stiffens during the middle stages of his backswing. Such stiffening would inhibit most golf swings, making it all but impossible to drive with the legs during the forward stroke. Palmer, however, recovers from this right-leg stiffening before he completes his backswing, by re-flexing the leg once again well before his club has finished moving back and up. Thus, by the time he's ready to move into his downswing, Arnold's legs are both flexed and ready to lead the action. Thereafter he retains this flex throughout his forward swing.

It has been this writer's observation that in recent years Palmer's leg actions and footwork on the forward swing have become, if anything, freer. In this respect his swing has improved with age. Another improvement noted by various Palmer watchers is that his swing plane, which has always been on the flat side because of the distance he stands from the ball, is now more upright, at least in terms of the plane on which he swings his left arm. This arm, which he once swung back and up on the same plane as his shoulders turned, now swings higher – less around and more skyward.

Arnold's more upright arm swing sets his club into a better position at the top of his backswing, by placing it less behind his body and more above his shoulders, not quite so far away from the target line. Therefore, in returning the clubhead back to that line, he is less likely to shove, push or throw with his right shoulder, arm or hand. With his hands higher and the club set more 'above' the line, all he must do is pull it down and forward with his legs, left side and left arm and hand. The increased left-side control that results helps decrease his chance of hooking or pulling shots to the left.

Thus it would appear that whatever flaw or flaws might be working to undermine Palmer's once-glorious game, they do not originate or manifest themselves in his full swing.

In Palmer's heyday the bigger the challenge, the better he seemed to play. He often performed relatively poorly when he had a big lead – witness his loss of seven strokes over the last nine holes against Billy Casper in the 1966 US Open. He played good golf when he was battling more or less level with other contenders. He played outstanding golf when he was behind – witness his final-round 65 to pick up nine shots and win the 1960 US Open. The need to attack the course when trailing brought out the boldest and the best in Palmer, just as it had in the case of Hagen.

During the four-year period 1960–3 Palmer went into the final round of thirty-eight tournaments on the PGA tour with a reasonable chance of winning. He finished on top in twenty-nine of those events – over seventy-six per cent. During the next three-year period, however, he challenged in twenty-two tournaments and won only six – about twenty-six per cent success.

It was during much of this drought that Palmer self-admittedly shed some of his boldness. Instead of attacking with what always seemed to others reckless abandon, he tried, as he said, to 'Hogan it'. Instead of banging away with the driver and charging the flagstick on approach shots, he became more cautious, more strategic. He began manoeuvring his tee shots with a 3-wood; he tried to cut shots into safe parts of the greens. It was not Palmer golf and it didn't work for him. Whereas as a challenger in the thirty-eight events of 1960–3 he had shot final rounds of 68 or better seventeen times – over forty-four percent of the time – in the aforementioned twenty-two tournaments that followed he bettered 69 only three times.

Only after he was able to recover his normal, bold, attacking style did the Palmer charge come forth once again. In 1967 he challenged in twelve tournaments and averaged 69.17 strokes in fourth-round play, a full shot and a half less per round than in the preceding years.

Today Palmer still plays boldly from tee to green, but there it stops. While his full swing remains intact, the same cannot be said for his putting. There was a time when Arnold continually amazed his adversaries, notably Nicklaus and Player, with his ability to clang the ball into the hole off the back of the cup from any distance or angle, but expecially from ten feet in. He'd do it on any type of green, from the slick roller coasters of Augusta to the slow platforms of Las Vegas. And it didn't seem to matter a whit to him if a missed first putt rolled well past the hole – what was a mere five-footer coming back?

Today Palmer is an inconsistent putter. He has the occasional good day or good two or three days, but then his touch seems to disappear. His short putts don't dive into the centre of the cup quite so frequently, but rather slide by to one side. The curling sidehillers often fall below the cup, too cautiously stroked, or skin the high side, slightly pushed or pulled.

When a golfer's putts stop dropping, the normal tendency is to try a new technique. The new method may work in practice but not on the course under pressure. Or it may work for a few holes or a few days and then crumble. Then the search must start again.

Experimenting with one's basic putting style is a hazardous enterprise. It can start a vicious cycle. Too much experimentation leads to overconcern about the 'mechanics' of the stroke, which inevitably causes a lessened sense of feel, which leads to bad stroking, which causes a loss of confidence, which necessitates yet more experimentation.

The loss of putting confidence also puts extra burden on the rest of one's game, especially those parts that are weakest. Palmer, for instance, has never been outstandingly skilful with the wedges. Gary Player (though admittedly prone to occasional exaggeration) once told him, 'Arnold, your wedge and bunker play has lost you at least eighteen tournaments. In fact, I have personally watched you lose twelve of them.'

Ten years ago Palmer could miss a green, make a half-decent wedge shot, and still expect, with reasonable certainty, to save a par with his putter. Today, when putting badly, he must putt the same wedge shot even closer in order to approach the putt with a similar expectation of success.

Loss of confidence on the greens is something that has struck down many mighty golfers. Vardon, Hagen, Cotton, even Jones after he had retired are just four who admitted to the disease. Perhaps Palmer, like the venerable Snead, can find a way to regain putting confidence before its absence totally erodes the rest of his game. To do so represents the biggest challenge of his golfing life. To beat the challenge, to make at least one last charge, will be largely an issue of mind over matter.

Masters of Golf, Stanley Paul, 1976

Jack Nicklaus

Born 21 January 1940, Columbus, Ohio, USA.

So many words have been written and spoken about Jack Nicklaus that in the passages that follow I decided to select mainly from fairly early writing about him, pieces about championships that have dimmed in memory as the Nicklaus phenomenon carried on through the years.

How much longer that phenomenon will last has been the subject of speculation for many years. He was 'burnt out' in 1967, 'not as good as Miller' in the mid-1970s, number two behind Watson late the same decade, and definitely the great days were gone as the 1980 season opened. It is very recent history that two more major championship victories raised his total to nineteen, six clear of Bobby Jones, his closest rival. It is highly unlikely that any of today's superstars will equal that near impossible total. True, Ballesteros has begun well with two majors and could be at the beginning of a dominant career. Equally he might be burnt out in a few more years. Watson certainly rivals Nicklaus as a tournament winner on the US circuit and his record in the British Open (entered seven times, three wins) is superior, but to that there are only two Masters to add. In the majors, Nicklaus had done much more by the time he reached thirty.

The majors apart, what are Nicklaus's other vital statistics? In money won on the US circuit he is comfortably past $3\frac{3}{4}$ million and will almost certainly – partly the result of inflation – be caught eventually by Watson. On the same circuit he lies second, with sixty-eight wins to Sam Snead's eighty-five, and Watson, just past twenty-five, is unlikely to match that. Since turning professional in 1961 Nicklaus has been leading money-winner on the US circuit eight times, despite the fact that his sights have always been set on major championships and he has progressively played less on the US circuit.

At the beginning of his professional career Nicklaus said that his aim was 'to be the greatest golfer the world has ever seen'. There can be few to argue that he has failed to achieve that ambition.

An irresistible force
Pat Ward-Thomas

Mention was made in an article from Pebble Beach of Nicklaus at practice, and of how drive after drive flew down the precise line to a caddie in the remote distance, with an unwavering regard for the shortest distance between two points. The impression was not so much of a ball driven by a swing, which certainly is true of Palmer for all that he hits so hard, but rather as if it had been propelled by a hammer blow from some mechanical device.

Nicklaus is so strong that he does not require a full swing, and at the top of it the club never reaches the horizontal. The backlift is simple with no break in the wrists until the widest possible arc away from the ball has been achieved. Then, from a stance which makes clearance of the left side after impact as easy as possible, and an anchorage so solid that it might well be cast in concrete, so massive are his legs, Nicklaus lets fly. There is no suggestion of a slash. Considering the force involved, the whole method is remarkably balanced and controlled.

The same strength is revealed in his long irons, and, like Palmer, Snead and J. Hebert, among the few leading golfers who do, Nicklaus carries a number 1. In one round he was green high in two at the eighteenth, well over five hundred yards, using this club for the second shot in still air.

It was interesting to examine his clubs, for their comparative lightness, and to see how low on the blade the beautifully compact mark of impact was, compared to that made by most other golfers. This was evidence of an abnormal precision and purity of striking but, all these considerations of strength aside, much more is required to have reached the peak of achievement already attained by Jack Nicklaus.

On the second hole after lunch in the final, his ball lay on sandy grass. A wide bunker was between him and the pin, which was placed just beyond, and yet, with a swing so delicate in rhythm that it concealed the firmness beneath, he played the shot perfectly to within two feet of the hole. He has a remarkable sensitivity of touch in the short game, and his pitching with wedge or short irons is wonderfully exact. Time after time he would finish within a few feet of the hole, invariably leaving himself with a putt for a birdie. This standard is unapproached by the British, which is one of the principal causes for their failure in competition against Americans. Nicklaus always attacks with this shot to the pin, and with the putt that follows. Never has one seen a golfer whose whole appearance on the greens suggested a greater degree of determined concentration.

His putting method is similar to Palmer's except that the knees are not locked inwards to the same extent. The body is crouched over the ball, with the head well down; and the stroke is the usual crisp American tap, the right hand pushing the club through low along the line. The sight of Nicklaus on the green, the chunky body absolutely motionless save for the quick turns of the head as he checks the line with those clear blue eyes of his, the ash-blond hair peeping from beneath his white cap, and the set lines of his face, remain an enduring picture, but there is another besides.

Nicklaus is intensely deliberate in the playing of his shots. He takes a while to rock into his stance and has several waggles before swinging, but otherwise he moves briskly. I can see him now, alert, confident, striding down the fairways, far ahead of his caddie, Gonzales, a quaint figure, round, swarthy, Portuguese, with cigar in holder, who carried for H. R. Johnston when he won the Championship at Pebble Beach in 1929.

The Long, Green Fairway, Hodder & Stoughton, 1966

Flat and upright swinging
Jack Nicklaus with H. W. Wind

This is perhaps the logical spot to voice my thoughts on that old controversial topic, the flat swing versus the upright swing, and on one other aspect of technique: how hard should you swing at the ball?

A golfer's build determines the plane of his swing. The shorter he is, the flatter his plane will be, since the ball will be proportionately farther away from him. The taller he is, the better his chances of approximating what is theoretically the perfect arc for the golf swing: the arc of a pendulum on which the clubhead would always be square to the line of flight. Byron Nelson is usually recognized as the man who pioneered the modern upright swing. Some of the present players who belong to the upright school are Billy Casper, Allan Geiberger, Terry Dill and young Bob Dickson. I am a decidedly upright swinger. The more upright a golfer can swing the club without artificially forcing it, the simpler it is for him to keep the club on the right line. One of these days a very tall player with excellent co-ordination will come along who will hit the ball straighter than anyone before him. It is just one of these unexplainable things that a towering, talented golfer-athlete hasn't appeared up to now. Down through the years medium-sized men have generally been the game's finest exponents, but there's no real reason why a very tall man should not be just as well co-ordinated for golf.

How hard should you swing at the ball? For myself, the only club I hit full force is the driver. With all the others, I try to swing well within myself. If I am, say, 160 yards from a green and another fellow about the same distance out elects to play an 8-iron, I'll still stay with a 6-iron. I'm not interested in how far I can press a club; I'm interested in playing the club that will get the job done best. However, after I get to the driver, there ain't no more. If I need every yard of distance I can muster, I've got to go after it with that club. I will only go all out for distance, however, when I believe it won't hurt to sacrifice a degree of accuracy. I might do that, for illustration, on the long fifteenth at Augusta where the fairway in the driving area is a good seventy-five yards wide. When I shoot the works for distance, I concentrate on taking the club back slower than usual to give myself the time to complete the fullest backswing I can make. The wider my arc, the farther I should be able to hit the ball. Then, on the downswing I try to move my hips as fast as I can.

To repeat, except for certain situations where I have ample margin for error on the tee-shot, I never hit the ball with everything I have. It's too risky – you can lose your balance and your timing so easily if you try to hit the ball too hard. As a matter of fact, I would class myself as an only moderately long iron-player. Here, in any event, is how I chart my range with the various clubs under normal playing conditions:

sand wedge: up to 80 yards
pitching wedge: 80 to 105 yards
9-iron: 105 to 135 yards
8-iron: 130 to 145 yards
7-iron: 140 to 155 yards
6-iron: 155 to 170 yards
5-iron: 170 to 185 yards
4-iron: 185 to 200 yards

3-iron: 195 to 210 yards
2-iron: 205 to 220 yards
1-iron: 215 to 235 yards
3-wood: 235 yards and up
driver: 250 yards and up

The Greatest Game of All, Hodder & Stoughton, 1969

The spinster
Peter Dobereiner

The record books say that Jack Nicklaus is the best golfer who ever drew breath. A few voices may be raised to dispute that judgement but sound insulation of padded cells being what it is, they are pretty muted.

Nicklaus is not the longest hitter, nor the straightest, nor the best sand player. He is not the best chipper and pitcher. He is not the best chipper and pitcher, a statement I repeat to thwart those who are about to respond, 'You can say that again.'

However, his marks are high enough in all these departments to average out well ahead of his rivals. Probably his strongest attribute is his golfing brain, and his knowledge of golf courses, nourished by an obsessional interest in design, gives him a distinct edge over his challengers.

Only a fool, and a reckless one at that, would take issue with him on the playing qualities of a course. He has a withering line in repartee at times and could always end the discussion by asking: 'How many Open championships have you won?' Well, speaking as a golfer whose collection of precious metal trophies would not excite comment alongside the gold fillings in the front teeth of any self-respecting Armenian pimp, let me climb into the motley and assert that on the subject of Carnoustie Jack Nicklaus is talking through his ear.

You will recall that Nicklaus described Carnoustie as the toughest course in the world. My view is that Carnoustie can be the easiest course on the Open championship roster. Note well the 'can be'. Of course, when it is played in a gale, with rain and sleet driving horizontally across that bleak wasteland, then it is difficult. Such conditions prevail at Carnoustie about 364 days a year, on average.

However the world's weather has gone quite mad. Who knows but that two weeks of heatwave may not be followed by two more? The only indication we have that Carnoustie will probably produce its usual rough stuff is the forecast of the met men that the fair, dry spell will continue.

If they should be right – and, like clocks which strike thirteen, we cannot rely on them being wrong – then Carnoustie will surely be ripe for plunder. It is a basically fair course with only two follies, the fairway bunker on the second hole and the screening dune in front of the fourteenth. The greens are superb and, thanks to the Royal and Ancient's agronomist, the conditions underfoot will be impeccable.

That last statement requires some qualification. The spirit of proud independence which once made Britain great is kept alive today by only one section of the community, the greenkeepers of Scotland. No one born south of Auchtermuchty can hope to pronounce the word agronomist with the same growling contempt as these men. Those rolling R's like a battle cry in their whisky-roughened throats.

So when the R and A offered expert advice on the preparation of Carnoustie the locals reached for their cylinder mowers, and hollow tine drills, and dreaded two-handed scythes, and declared that they would turn any fancy agronomist into a fine mulch for top dressing. After that, they just had to get the course into good nick.

As to the winner, if only Nicklaus would do as I tell him there would be no doubt about the outcome. He would win by twenty shots. But he is stubborn. He gets his kicks like a teenager playing chicken in his first jalopy, pulling away at the last minute to win by a shot. The last Carnoustie Open (1968) he put the wind up himself by driving out of bounds at the sixth. That gave him a real challenge and his golf for the rest of the round was the finest I have ever seen.

Most of the time he plays with the timidity of a middle-aged spinster walking home through a town full of drunken sailors, always choosing the safe side of the street. Sometimes he gets home safely. But more often he gets grabbed. In the recent US Open (1975) at Medinah he was molested three times in the last three holes and bang went the Grand Slam.

The Observer, 6 July 1975

Nicklaus the swinger
Hugh McIlvanney

The sight of Jack Nicklaus at the head of the Open field was so familiar that few people at Turnberry took time to notice the profound change of swing that helped to put him there. Tuesday of last week should be seen as a momentous day in the history of golf because during that day Nicklaus did no less than rearrange the method that had won him sixteen major titles and made him the most acclaimed master of the game since Bobby Jones.

All his life until these past few days Nicklaus has used a technique which is not so much a golf swing as a sequence of independent movements. It goes something like this: Left hand grip on club. Clubhead to ball. Right hand to club. Feet into position. Minor shakedown adjustments to address position. Scrutiny of target. Check alignment of blade. Scrutiny of a spot to front of ball on target line. Recheck alignment. Hypnotic stare at ball. Slow tilt of head, pointing chin at right foot. Backswing at the measured pace of a drawbridge being raised. Hint of a pause. All hell breaks out. Earth shakes. Women swoon. Men spectators exhale the word 'jeeze' or another that more earthily expresses awe. Ball departs like a shell to distant places, usually those marked by a flag.

All of that added up over the years to one of the most intimidating declarations of power in sport. Bobby Jones did not recognize it as golf but it was undeniably effective. Here at Turnberry Nicklaus has undoubtedly been playing golf as Jones knew it, with a real swing and rhythm. And, more remarkably, he has been doing so to almost irresistible effect.

When the *Observer*'s golf correspondent, Peter Dobereiner, asked Nicklaus about the transformation, the great man explained that he had fallen into the habit of standing to the ball slightly open, with the hips turned toward the target and the hands too far forward. As a consequence he had tended to block out the action of his arms with his body, producing a push shot. In making adjustments to correct this fault he had arrived at a new address position from which he could make an unrestricted swing with the arms and so achieve what the professionals call working the hands inside the line.

Thus defined, these seem to be tiny changes but in total they represent a new swing, one that completely altered the appearance of Jack Nicklaus as a golfer. For nine holes of the first round he was uneasy with the method. Even at his level the temptation to revert to habit under stress is intense, but for the remainder of the championship he was a golfer in control of his technique, in control of the ball, and as he entered the last round just about in control of the 1977 Open.

He had taken extraordinary pains to accomplish such mastery long before he left his home in Florida. As usual he arrived in plenty of time to familiarize himself with the course and, as usual, he was disappointed with what he found. Drought had shrivelled the vaunted Turnberry rough to the point of virtually eliminating any premium on accurate driving; the greens, although good by recent Open standards, were mosaics of different varieties of grass and had not been trimmed down to championship length. It was obvious that they would not provide their truest putting surface until the third round.

At his own expense Nicklaus had sent his agronomist to Britain and had submitted to the Royal and Ancient Club a report listing recommendations on preparing a championship course. So far as he could discern not one of these suggestions had been adopted. His reaction stopped short of anger. He has learnt that extreme emotions are bad for his golf. His attitude was rather that of a patient schoolmaster whose favourite pupil tries hard but simply cannot get the hang of quadratic equations. There was nothing to be done about the conditions at that stage, anyway, so he concentrated on observing how the roll and pace of a putt was affected by a patch of bent grass on the greens compared with fescues and *poa annua*, concentrated on putting himself in the right physical and psychological shape for an occasion that he considers one of the four great challenges of his season. He made quite a good job of it, new swing and all. Ask Tom Watson or Ben Crenshaw.

The Observer, 10 July 1977

How my game has changed
Jack Nicklaus

As this book was being completed, I had just concluded my twenty-fifth straight year of tournament golf and was coming on my thirty-eighth birthday. How did my game stand at that time, and what did I see for it in the future?

As an amateur, I was essentially a one-dimensional golfer: a left-to-right player. I was also mostly a one-style golfer; hit it hard, find it, and hit it hard again. Strength was, of course, a big factor in both those characteristics. I was so strong that I almost had to play from left to right to be able to control the ball, and I could certainly well afford to give up whatever distance I lost by fading rather than drawing shots in return for that greater control. Also, the amount of raw strength I had at my disposal tended to make me somewhat cavalier about the sorts of problems that less powerful players usually rely upon finesse to overcome. Frequently I could simply whale the ball over obstacles that others would prefer to finesse their way around with artfully flighted shots. So far as rough was concerned, with all that strength and an upright swing plane, and being generally a good way out from the tee, I encountered very little from which I couldn't bulldoze the ball either onto the green or very close to it. The 'explosive' method, I guess you could call it. Distance first and worry about everything else after that. It was an effective way to play at the time, but hardly the most graceful approach to the game.

For several years, I played basically the same way as a professional, but eventually I realized the need for some improvements and refinements and gradually began to make them. A variety of factors contributed to these changes, but the primary one was my own personal golfing ambition. I wanted to be the best, and I increasingly recognized from studies of the great golfers – not to mention my day-to-day observations of them as tour adversaries – that the absolute basic requirement in achieving such a goal was the ability to play any given shot at any given time, including those moments involving extreme tension and stress. Another factor was pride. Simply to satisfy myself, I wanted to make myself as good a golfer technically as it was possible for me to become.

The improvement process has been going on now for some twelve years or more, and I expect it to continue for as long as I remain competitive at the game. Basically, I've learned as I've gone along, rarely more than one thing at a time, always working within the framework of the fundamentals imparted to me as a teenager by Jack Grout and always using essentially the same golf swing. My initial improvements were primarily in the long game: learning first to control the height of shots and then to draw the ball as easily and reliably as I have always been able to fade it. Bunker techniques have been re-modelled or revised on a number of occasions, as have basic approaches

to pitching and chipping. Being so largely a matter of feel and inspira-
tion, putting has always undergone almost daily fine tuning, and sometimes drastic surgery, from one green to the next – but, again, always
within the framework of what I believe to be the sound stroking mechanics I learned as a youngster.

And the sum of this long effort? Well, the first thing I have learned
is that you never stop learning about golf, which is probably the single
greatest source of the game's enormous appeal to so many disparate
people around the world. Beyond that, although I am not as powerful
a golfer as I was in my twenties, it seems to me that I more than make
up for whatever I have lost in distance and bulldozing capacity with
greatly improved shotmaking versatility. I wouldn't say there aren't
golf shots I can't hit to order these days, but I would say they are fairly
few in number. That wasn't true of my amateur days or my first few
years on tour.

The greatest improvement, however, hasn't been in shotmaking but
in the area of the game that I have always believed finally sorts out the
wheat from the chaff – and the one, incidentally, most neglected by
most amateurs of more than a six-handicap. This is the art, craft or
science of scoring. Hitting the ball is really only half the game of golf.
Once you become reasonably adept at that, how well you play – how
often you win and lose – depends almost entirely on how effectively
you learn to manage the game's two ultimate adversaries: the course
and yourself. Managing the course takes patience, the discipline to
train yourself to be habitually observant and analytic, and the kind of
knowledge that can be gained only by study and experience. Managing
yourself requires intelligence and emotional control. Both, like learning
to hit shots, require perseverance. In theory, maturity builds all the
resources, and in my case I believe it has done so now, to the point
where I can consider these aspects of my game to be my strongest
competitive weapons.

So, in short, I think I'm a better golfer today than I have ever been.
And the future? God willing, I intend to get better yet.

On and Off the Fairway, Stanley Paul, 1979

Tony Lema

Born 25 February 1934, Oakland, California, USA. Died
July 1966.

In these days when golfers travel more than they play golf it is perhaps
a statistical surprise that just one great player has been killed in the
process and sad that he was one full of grace who had quite recently
taken his place at the top of the game.

Most of our sportsmen today are dour fellows, and who can blame
them? Its difficult to relax when there is so much gold and glory at
stake. But Tony Lema was an exception in the golf world, and when
his private plane crashed more than a champion was lost to golf.

A case of champagne
Henry Longhurst

Anthony David Lema, the new (1964) Open champion, is really rather
a splendid fellow, absolutely in the Hagen tradition of not wanting to
be a millionaire but possessed of a strong determination to live like
one. Gay, debonair, handsome and, at the age of thirty, something of a
reformed character, he now has the world before him.

In the past few weeks he has won four tournaments and $20,000.
The advertised prize for winning the Open is a mere £1,500 but in
effect it ranges between £3,000 and £19,500 since the winner is entitled
to a place in the four-man television World Series, for which the first
prize is £18,000 and the last £1,800. In addition, with the aid of an
old friend of mine, Fred Corcoran, who is one of the most experienced
managers and organizers in the game, he should 'cash in' on his victory
to the tune of many thousands of pounds.

Lema's father, a labourer of Portuguese descent, died when the boy
was three, leaving his mother, widowed and penniless, to bring up four
children 'on the wrong side of the tracks' in an industrial area of Oakland. Lema's boyhood was marked by playing truant from school,
getting into fights and picking up the odd dollar when and where he could.

Soon, like so many American pros, he started caddying at the local municipal course and golf became the abiding passion of his life. On the spur of the moment, when he was 'just batting around', he enlisted in the Marines and with them spent two years in Korea, gaining twenty pounds in weight and becoming a fine athletic figure of a man.

After this he became an assistant at a club in San Francisco, then a teaching pro and finally secured a businessman backer – to whom, on account of his liking for first-class travel and the good things of life, he was soon owing some $11,000. In the whole of 1959 he won only $6,000 and in 1960 it sank to $3,000.

At this period there was no doubt about his being a fine swinger of the club, with the beautiful and natural rhythm that characterizes his style today, but he was temperamentally immature. The unlucky breaks inseparable from golf got on his nerves and he became convinced that the world was against him. To win his first tournament became such an obsession as to make it all the more difficult.

Nor perhaps did the sort of party to which he invited a number of fellow professionals to his suite in a St Paul hotel, and eventually finished by opening the window and driving balls down Market Street, add greatly to his prospects on the following day.

Suddenly, according to Lema's own words, everything in his life fell into place. He still liked, as did Hagen, to travel through life first class, but the days of the wild parties were over. His golf rapidly improved; he learnt that 'missing a short putt doesn't mean that I have to hit my next drive out-of-bounds'; he became, as all successful professionals must, a good 'bad player' – in other words, on the inevitable off days he became able to squeeze his score down to 72 instead of 78, and above all, in 1962, he won his first big tournament, on the third extra hole of the playoff.

It was on this occasion that he earned his nickname of 'Champagne Tony' by celebrating his victory in the press tent – an agreeable custom which he continued at St Andrews last Friday evening, though I am afraid I was too occupied in other directions to go and draw my ration.

At St Andrews he did everything well and really it was impossible to fault him. He drove exactly where 'Tip' Anderson, the best caddie in the town, directed him; his iron shots flew like rifle bullets, and his putting was a joy to watch. He is a tremendous 'birdie putter', as they call it. One after the other, when he had a chance of a three – and sometimes when he had not – he knocked them in. As for the short

ve Tony Lema drives during the most famous match ever of the World Matchplay against Gary
yer (1965). Lema was seven up with 17 to play – and lost. *Below* Player is bunkered at Sunningdale,
6.

Left Severiano Ballesteros hurries to congratulate Player as a putt drops for a last-round 64 and victory in the 1978 US Masters. *Below* Player goes for the green in the 1978 Dunlop Masters.

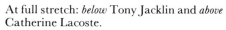

At full stretch: *below* Tony Jacklin and *above* Catherine Lacoste.

Above left Johnny Miller. *Above right* Tom Watson studies the line of a putt, and *below* is watched by his mentor, Byron Nelson, during a practice round of the 1981 US Masters, which he won.

putts, Nicklaus, though he holes them, makes them look difficult. Lema was putting them in without giving the spectator the slightest twinge of sympathetic anxiety.

Above all, though, must rank his temperament, which carried him through one of the most dramatic moments in championship history. Going into the third round, he was nine ahead of Nicklaus. He opened with 4, 5, 4, 5, 5, 4 – three over fours, though admittedly with the Loop, where you hope to pick up shots, to come. The sixth green adjoins the twelfth, indeed they are all in one, and on the twelfth at this moment was Nicklaus, five under fours. Eight shots gone!

It must have been a ghastly moment for Lema. Perhaps the greatest tribute that I can pay him is simply to record his figures for the remaining twelve holes: 3, 3, 3, 3, 3, 4, 4, 4, 3, 4, 4, 3. It that is not worth a case or two of champagne, I do not know what is.

The Best of Henry Longhurst, Mark Wilson and Ken Bowden (eds), Collins, 1979

Gary Player

Born 1 November 1936, Johannesburg, South Africa.

It is a truism of golf that few of the great players have been able to remain great for much more than a decade. For some, there has been a brief glimpse of the peaks, and here Weiskopf, Jacklin and Miller are clear examples, while others have not maintained their highest standards year after year after year. Amongst these might be grouped Palmer, Hogan, Guldahl; and indeed one wonders how long Jones would have continued a winner after 1930 – he had lost the knack of it when he returned to compete in his own US Masters from 1934 onwards.

For sheer longevity we are left with three players: Snead as a great player but not a likely championship winner after the later 1950s; Nicklaus, a major champion over almost twenty years; and Gary Player, who won his first major in 1959 and what was probably his last in 1978. As a tournament winner his career is about six years longer.

The passages which follow examine what has made Player such an achiever in golf; certainly one factor has been his dedication to practice – even Ben Hogan has declared that Player equals him in this respect – but there have been others – Hagen springs to mind –who have practised little. Perhaps what singles Gary Player out is determination. Once in the lead he singlemindedly seeks to increase it, and very few have kept trying as does Player when apparently not in contention. Hagen just enjoyed the walk if he felt he was too far back to win; Gary keeps hammering away and sometimes, as most notably in the 1978 US Masters, things begin to happen and he wins. But I'd dearly love to overhear a conversation between Hagen and Player on what makes a great competitor: it would be whisky versus wheatgerm; indolence v dedication; late to bed v early; sexual promiscuity v moral rectitude – the list could go on.

To be the greatest, you need an edge
Dick Aultman

Some say that you can tell a great deal about a man by the books he reads. Four books in particular have, at various times, strongly influenced Gary Player's life-style: the Bible, *The Power of Positive Thinking*, *Imitations of Christ* and *Yoga and Health*.

These books reflect Player's intensive efforts over many years to improve himself as both a human being and, as a direct result, as a golfer. Gary is a man looking for an edge on life, especially if it puts him one up on those with whom he competes for his daily bread. Chances are that Player would have become a purist even if he had followed his father's footsteps into the gold mines of South Africa, but his avowed goal from the start – to become the greatest golfer in the history of the game – has made his regimen of hard work and self-denial even more rewarding.

Any discussion of Gary Player the golfer must begin and end with a clear understanding of his unflagging determination – almost compulsion – to become the best. In this chapter we shall thus first look closely at his golf swing and then discuss the nonswing factors that have brought him at least in sight of his ambition.

As it is true of so many golfers, the evolution of Player's overall swing is directly related to the evolution of his grip. He started with a 'hooker's grip', in which both hands were turned well to his right on the clubshaft. The fact that he is short in stature and thus stands farther from the ball than most further accentuated his tendency to hook badly on occasion.

Shortly after first visiting England as a teenager, and noting the comparatively 'weak' grip of the British star Dai Rees, Player went to the other extreme and adopted a slicer's grip. Instead of showing all four knuckles of his left hand at address, he turned this hand so far to the left that no knuckles were visible. As might be expected, the shape of his shots reversed. In comparing Gary's game with that of his fellow countryman Bobby Locke, the ultimate right-to-left player, one British writer observed in 1956: 'When Locke's on the tee the cry is "fore on the right!" When Player shoots it's "fore on the left!"'

Player's slice grip eventually forced him to find some compensation that would allow him to draw the ball or at least hit it fairly straight.

This compensation was to swing on a very flat plane and bow the back of his left wrist outward slightly at the top of the backswing, thus setting the clubface into a somewhat closed position.

It was Ben Hogan who detected the cause of Gary's flat swing and suggested he again modify his grip slightly by placing his left thumb down the top of the shaft at address instead of down the top-left side. This change made it easier for Player to draw the ball and thus eliminated the need for him to swing so flat going back and to close the clubface by bowing his left wrist.

Today Gary positions his right hand a bit farther to the left than most, as an antihook measure, but still sets his left thumb down the top of the shaft as prescribed by Hogan. His swing is still flatter than most, but more upright than it was in the late 1950s. The back of his left hand, wrist and forearm align straight, not only at the top of his swing but thereon all the way through impact and, on most shots, to the finish. His ability to maintain this straight-line relationship throughout his forward swing, with no inward collapsing at the back of the wrist, attests to his ability to lead with his legs, pull with his left arm and hand, and accelerate both arms freely down and forward as he moves into and through impact. Any right-hand takeover (casting from the top) or slowing down of his arms would force the back of his left wrist to collapse inward. He would then not achieve the excellent extension beyond impact that he now enjoys. His clubhead would, instead, swing upward and inward too abruptly.

Gary still complains of occasional hooking, and seems to come up with a new remedy about once every three months. The hooking occurs when he fails to clear his left hip – turn it to the left – fully during his downswing. Instead of turning his hips, he sometimes slides them too far to the left laterally – 'blocks out', as they say – a move that forces his hands and wrists to release a shade too soon and throw the clubface into a closed position during impact.

The need to clear the left hip is particularly important in Player's case because of the way he turns his shoulders on a relatively flat plane during his backswing, largely because his lack of height necessitates his standing a goodly distance from the ball. Then, however, instead of returning the shoulders on a similar plane on his downswing, Gary drops his right shoulder dramatically downward. With this shoulder and his arms thus swinging from so far inside the target line – from 'behind himself', if you will – extreme suppleness is required for his left hip to turn freely to the left.

To carry the matter one step further, in this writer's opinion it is Player's head position that dictates the extreme lowering of his right shoulder during his downswing. At address a line running across his eyes would more or less parallel his target line. A similar study of Player's head position just prior to impact clearly shows that by that point in the swing, a line across his eyes would extend far to the right of target. If one accepts the premise that what we see tells our subconscious what path we should swing along, it becomes apparent that Player has turned his head into a position from which his eyes are telling him to swing back to the ball along a path from far inside his target line. For normal humans such a swing path would push shots far to the right until an involuntary reaction set in of throwing the clubface closed to the left. Gary, however, is supple enough to clear his left hip soon enough to swing the clubhead back on line by impact – at least most of the time. When he fails, to avoid pushing to the right, he overreacts with his hands and hooks to the left.

This is not to imply that Player has a bad golf swing, but is merely an explanation of what basically causes the problems on those rare occasions when he gets into big trouble. His swing is otherwise magnificent in most respects, especially as an example of how to generate absolute maximum distance while maintaining outstanding accuracy. Player not only drives the ball farther than most physically bigger professionals but probably – when in peak form – misses fewer greens than anyone since Hogan.

Player's distance stems largely from his unusual suppleness, born of constant physical conditioning. This allows him to make an extremely wide and longish backswing – note especially the full extension of his straight left arm and the unusually full coiling of his shoulders – while resisting with his legs; note that his left heel never leaves the ground. The result is a tremendous buildup of leverage during the backswing that is even further increased – rather than released – early in his downswing.

Gary sets the stage for his left-arm extension – his swing's width – by pushing the clubhead straight back from the ball, along the target line, an extremely long way. He maintains this extension throughout his backswing by turning his chin slightly to his right, a move that makes it easier for his shoulders to coil fully. Meanwhile his legs remain rather immobile, his right knee remains slightly flexed, and his weight remains largely on the instep of his right foot. This lower-body resistance effectively restricts his hip turn and thus further accentuates the stretching of muscles across his back and down his left side resulting from his full shoulder turn.

Player's muscle stretching increases early in his downswing as his left knee shifts to the left while his arms and club are still swinging back and up. Then he actually increases his wrist-cock by slowly pulling with his left hand – instead of throwing with his right – as he starts the forward swinging of his arms. Thereafter his arms continue to accelerate forward freely with no apparent effort either to inhibit or to help the free lowering and squaring of the clubhead through the ball. Again, while his arms freely swing the clubhead forward and gradually turn the clubface to the left after impact, the back of his left wrist remains straight and firm throughout the follow-through.

'I feel I swing as hard as I can,' Gary has frequently said. 'Some say they don't, but I think all the players on the pro tours hit the ball as hard as they can and still keep it in play.

'I would advise a young boy or girl starting out to do the same,' he adds. 'It's simple to go from a hard swing to an easy one, but if you've been an easy swinger it's difficult to start hitting the ball hard. More often it goes the other way – an easy swinger develops a lazy stroke as he gets older.'

Gary's ability to swing the golf club has been directly affected by his lifelong determination to become the world's greatest golfer. In his particular case the factors spawned by this tremendous drive to excel overshadow even his actual swing technique and thus merit discussion here.

Practice. Player doubts that any golfer in history, except perhaps Ben Hogan, worked harder on his game. Hogan himself was quoted in 1958 as saying 'I know how hard he (Player) has worked. He's doing what I've been advocating for a long time. That is working hard on fundamentals, and then working the fundamentals into his game.'

George Blumberg, a close friend of Gary's from South Africa, recalls once seeing him as a teenager practising bunker shots at the Virginia Park course in Johannesburg. It was six o'clock in the morning. About noon that same day Blumberg happened to pass the same bunker. Gary was still blasting away.

'I'd hit shots into the sand,' Player recalls, 'and then I'd play them to the green. I wouldn't let myself quit until I'd sunk three shots. Sometimes I'd be in there until it got dark.'

At other times Player would practise chipping until he'd holed ten times. If he wanted to work on hitting the ball low, he'd punch shots under a tree limb until he could do so ten times in a row. If the tenth shot clipped the branch, he started again.

'A golfer should never stop using a certain club because he believes he cannot use it well,' Player once told this writer. 'It's best to practise with that club until you can master it. If you ignore your inability, chances are the swing errors that are causing the trouble with that club will creep into the rest of your game.'

Gary played his first round of golf at the age of fourteen (he parred the first three holes) and turned professional at seventeen. Three years later he beat the best British professionals in winning the highly regarded Dunlop Masters tournament in England. His swing in 1956 was too flat, his stance too wide, and his head position downright dangerous – turned toward the target well before impact – but he'd learned enough shots to score 70-64-64-72–270 (plus 68 in the play-off with host pro Arthur Lees) at Sunningdale. He'd even learned how to play in the rain, having purposely practised through downpours in South Africa in preparation for conditions in Britain.

Attention to detail. Few top-level golfers in history have been as meticulous about their games as Gary Player. Readers may recall the scene in the 1974 British Open when his ball became lost on the seventy-first hole. With a six-shot lead and less than two holes to play, the possibility of his blowing the title seemed highly remote. Even if the ball were not discovered he could all but wedge his way home and still win. But Gary knew, of course, that the rules allow only five minutes' hunting time. Any searching beyond that limit warrants an additional two-stroke penalty. So he borrowed a wristwatch before beginning the search. Nothing would be left to chance.

Such incidents are typical of Player. No top-level golfer, with the notable exception of Jack Nicklaus, is more precise in considering all factors involved in a given shotmaking situation, even if it be a mere two-foot putt. Gary once expounded to this writer on reasons for looking closely at the actual hole before putting. These included:

Checking the depth of soil above the cup itself (if the cup is set upright so the flagstick doesn't lean, more soil will appear above it on the high side).

Checking for unusual wearing of grass on one side of the cup (this will be the low side, he says, because more putts will have rolled into it than against the grass on the high side).

Checking for dead blades of grass on one side of the cup (a good indication that the grain runs cross-cup in that direction because the cutting of the hole necessarily severed the root system of those particular blades).

Only an inquiring mind like Player's, fuelled by the desire to gain an edge no matter how slight, would conceive of, absorb and apply such detail. He was not out of character, therefore, when early in his career he filmed and studied movies of players like Snead, Hogan and Cotton. It is not out of character today that he will give at least outward attention to almost any improvement suggestion, whether it comes from a reliable instructor or merely a friendly type in the gallery who happened to have 'noticed something when you were hitting those practice balls'.

Physical fitness. Player realized as a youth that to become the world's greatest golfer he'd need to get everything he could out of his small body and ever since has been conditioning himself accordingly, running miles daily to build his legs and his endurance, pushing himself up with his fingertips – seventy to eighty times a day – to strengthen his hands, arms and back (later he would minimize upper-body exercises for fear of losing suppleness).

After finishing sixth in the 1960 Masters, he reflected on a comment made by Peter Thomson. The Australian had said that he did not think he (Thomson) could ever win at Augusta because he wasn't long enough to reach the par-five holes in two shots. Player decided he faced the same problem, consulted a body builder on ways to add strength, added half an inch to the length of his clubs and otherwise changed his swing to generate the necessary extra yardage. The next year he reached all four par-fives in two and won the tournament.

During the 1960s this writer helped Player with two instructional books. Invariably the taping sessions were held in his motel room starting about 6 am, partly because often he was still functioning on South African time, partly because the rest of his day and evening were generally filled with golf and business functions. At various times during these meetings I was encouraged by Gary to:

Eat lots of fruit (there was always plenty in his room).
Eat my bacon burned (to avoid digestive problems).
Avoid showering with soap (bad for the body's natural oils).
Take wheatgerm pills ('Great for your love life').
Stand on my head (to improve mental alertness through better circulation).
Skip (to add distance through faster footwork).

While I chose not to follow most of these inspirational suggestions (though I did give the wheatgerm a good chance), I am convinced that such habits have contributed greatly to Player's success as a golfer, not only by directly improving him physically, but also by giving him the confidence and psychic well-being that goes with a clear mind and a strong body.

'I really enjoy exercise,' he once confided. 'Sometimes after a bad day on the course I come home tired and discouraged. But then I do my exercises before going to bed and I feel clean and strong again... (or) sometimes I'll deny myself something I really want, like ice cream. This does wonders for me both mentally and physically.'

Concentration. 'During every major championship I've won,' Player has said, 'I concentrated so hard that I played rounds without knowing my score. I've often been in a "don't know who I am" sort of daze – total relaxation with complete control.'

Just as Player keeps pushing his body into better service, so too he demands the utmost from his mind, almost to the point of self-hypnosis. He tells me of an incident just before the 1965 US Open at Bellerive Country Club near St Louis, Missouri. He was passing by a board on which the names of former Open winners were lettered in gold. The last entry on the list was '1964 – Ken Venturi'.

'I'd been past that board before,' Player said, 'but this time I looked up at it and I saw – I mean I really saw – my own name under Venturi's. There it was in gold lettering just like his: "1965 – Gary Player".'

A few days later Player's name was, in fact, lettered in gold on that board.

Another form of mental gymnastics that Player performs is convincing himself that the golf course where he happens to be competing is an outstanding example of architecture and conditioning. At times this appears to be the height of self-deception, but it is merely his way of establishing friendly working conditions for himself. It helps him avoid the trap of self-pity, the attitude of 'Who could possibly play good golf on this cow pasture?' that further escalates so many tournament golfers' scores when the going gets tough. It is also an attitude that endears him to tournament sponsors and ensures a friendly gallery from among the club's membership.

Competitiveness. This is a factor of success in golf that is difficult, if not impossible, to learn. It involves attitudes and behaviour patterns that were well established in the individual long before he ever swung a club, and it seems to reach an especially high level in players of small physical stature – Player, Sarazen, Hogan, to name just three.

Some years ago this writer asked a fellow competitor what, in his opinion, was the number one reason for Gary's success. His simple answer is still clear: 'Gary is a great success', he said, 'because he likes to beat people.'

Player is, indeed, one of the most competitive individuals ever to play the game. He has, for instance, added tens of thousands of dollars to his prize winnings over the years simply by never letting down when having a poor tournament or a bad round. He tries his utmost on every shot, whether he be contending for first prize or fiftieth position.

Though it will never come to pass, the only true way to determine who is indeed the 'world's greatest golfer' would be to stage a gigantic tournament in which all leading contenders would play each other, head to head, at least a dozen times in all the various golfing areas of the world. The winner – the man who finished ahead by the most holes – would necessarily have: (1) a well-rounded game that would stand up under all types of course and weather conditions; (2) an intensely competitive spirit; and (3) the physical and mental stamina to sustain numbers 1 and 2. In this writer's opinion, the winner of such a contest would be Gary Player.

Masters of Golf, Stanley Paul, 1976

Player v. *Lema*

Gary Player

As we walked from the green to the seventh tee (in the 1965 World Match-play), a most extraordinary thing happened to me. It was as though I was in the midst of a revelation, some spiritual experience which had a physical effect on me. This is almost impossible to explain, but I suddenly felt drenched in adrenalin. My mind became perfectly clear, my memory was sharp and precise. I became totally aware of my physical strength and the one thing I wanted to do was to get to that tee and play golf like I had never played before, like no man had ever played before. I felt tremendously charged up and yet absolutely calm and self-possessed at the very same time. It was a very strange experience.

We halved the next three holes, and at the ninth I had to hole a hard fifteen-foot putt to make the half. So it was five down, nine to play, instead of three down as I had hoped for, and to any rational person it was all over. My father told me afterwards that when he heard the radio news at that point, the twenty-seventh hole, he thought well, that's over. At the very same moment, as I walked to the tenth tee, I thought of him, and wondered if he would be getting the news. And I thought of my country, South Africa, maligned, misunderstood, pilloried by people who can tell us how to order our affairs from a range of 6,000 miles without ever coming down to South Africa and seeing for themselves, and trying to understand. I thought of my friends, the people who have helped me along the way, and all this added to my incentive to win this thing and put a fantastic achievement in the record books. Everything seemed to be tying up, in my mind, with the fact that I simply *was* going to win.

On the short tenth, Tony missed the green again and this time didn't make three. Four down. At the eleventh, where I had come unstuck in the morning, I poured the drive right down the middle, pitched it up to above five feet, and holed the putt for a birdie. Three down. The twelfth we halved. Three down. Six to play. Better. On thirteen, again I was down the middle with a stinging drive. Tony snap-hooked into the bushes, knocked it out about forty yards down the fairway, and I had to play next. This is one of the hardest challenges in match play, when your opponent has made a mess of things, to get down to it and have the guts or character or nerve or will-power or whatever you like to call it, to play the shot, to get down to it and take the advantage that has been offered to you by getting down and playing a perfect, or at least a telling shot. So often when you think you have the thing in your hands, you in turn make a mess of it and hand the advantage right back to him. It's like needing a four on the last hole to win a tournament. That's what makes match-play match-play. It happens all the time. This time I hit a ripe shot with the 5-iron, finishing some ten feet from the hole. Lema pitched it on, but at the front of the green and a good twenty-five feet away. And by crikey, he holed it. A real lifesaver. That is exactly what Tony Lema was thinking. After we had hit our tee-shots, and after I had hit my second, he was convinced he had lost another hole. Now in goes a beautiful putt, and he thinks he is off the hook again. My putt is going to break a foot to the right. After his saviour putt, I have to hole mine, I just have to hole it, there is no other way. And I did. I aimed a foot to the left, and it swung in smack in the middle of the hole. Just when Tony's spirits have risen a little, I have crushed him down again. Two down, five to play. Better and better.

Now Tony Lema is very worried. He's long since stopped talking, and now he is thinking all kinds of things. He is thinking, probably for the very first time, that it is possible for him to lose the match. And at the same time he is working very hard on resisting that very thought. He thinks he might lose and he refuses to think he might lose, at one and the same time. His thinking is confused. He's trying to make himself think positively, but in the depths of his mind there is a little negative pulling at the positive. On the other hand, I am now thinking very clearly, very positively at this stage, over the next two holes. I have only one thing, positive, working for me. All I have to do and think about is go, go, go. Keep on going. You have him. You have him worried and muddled and confused, and you have five holes in which to nail him. These next two holes, fourteen and thirteen, we halved. Two down, three to play. Now the gallery is swarming round us, as we go to the sixteenth tee, a tight drive and pitch hole at which I have used a 3-wood because of the precision needed from the tee. The sixteenth at Wentworth is definitely not a driver hole. Lema had played a 3-wood in the morning round, and in that practice round. It was my honour and I thought – all this flashed through my mind very quickly – 'take a driver and really bash it right down the middle and that will really shake him'. Then I've got him, really got him. So I step up on the tee and take out the driver with a flourish and belt it like a bullet right down the middle of the fairway, right into position A. Now comes Lema. He's thinking and wondering what to do, the 3-wood or the driver? Even if he didn't think that way, this is how I think he is thinking, if you follow, and this is how my own confidence is being solidly stiffened. And if he does elect for the 3-wood, no force on earth, after my big drive, will prevent him from hitting a fraction harder, to get close to me. Tony took his 3-wood, and snap-hooked it right in the trees. And he has to play another off the tee and eventually concedes the hole and I am one down, two to play. The crunch is nigh. The crowd is in near-hysteria.

The seventeenth hole at Wentworth is something of a hoodoo for me. That's not entirely true either – I don't believe in hoodoo holes – but I have never, let's say, played it particularly well. It is 555 yards, turning to the left, downhill, then uphill slightly, with a little dip in front of the green and a bank down from the right side of the green. In the landing area for the drives the fairway slopes from left to right and it is something of a monster hole, mainly because of that. I hit two very big shots, the second with a 4-wood, and came up about fifteen yards short of the green. With a 3-wood, Tony was some eighty, ninety yards short and he hit a gorgeous wedge shot, about twelve feet from the hole. How do you follow that? Well, my nerve was still good. I pitched my ball inside his, about eight feet from the hole, a good missable distance, but still inside his. Advantage still to Player.

Now I began to think that Tony Lema had to be so flustered that he would be doubting if he could hole his putt. But here again I was very lucky. Suddenly my mind filled with a tip my father-in-law, Jock Verwey, gave me when I was a very young boy starting professional golf in South Africa. He was a great match player – he won the South African Match Play Championship three times – despite the fact that he was a rather poor striker of the golf ball. He was probably the worst driver of a golf ball that I ever saw, he couldn't drive worth a toffee, but he was a great battler with the irons, and a tremendous chipper and putter and, above all, he was a great thinker about a match and had tremendous guts. He always said that in match play you should never anticipate mistakes from the other man, never rely on him missing a shot, missing a putt. You must always expect your man to make every putt, so that when you go up to putt, you are convinced in your mind that the other fellow will certainly hole his. Thus it flashed through my mind that Lema, no matter what strain he was under, would hole this one – and dammit, he did. But I still felt strong enough, confident enough, to go up and knock mine right in on top of him. Now if I had missed that putt, the match would have been over and I would have been out of the World Match Play Championship.

So we come to the thirty-sixth hole, I am one down, one to play. The entire drama of this long and momentous day seemed to have been packed into that putt on the seventeenth, the thirty-fifth hole. Now it was maintained and transferred to the eighteenth, the thirty-sixth. By this time I must have been absolutely exhilarated. Many people might have thought how terrible to be one down, with one to play. But after being six down the last time I played this hole, and seven down at the nineteenth, I just had to be feeling exalted.

We both hit probing drives down the centre of the fairway. Lema was away, and he hit rather a poor, low, hooked second, about fifty yards short of the green, with a bunker between his ball and the pin. I really launched myself into my second, with a 4-wood – the hole is 495 yards – and everyone screamed and yelled at what a great, great shot it was. Apparently, on television, it looked like the shot of a lifetime, but in fact it just proves that you never can tell in these matters. When I hit the ball, I thought it was an awful shot. I came off the ball a little bit, and it seemed to go through the top of the trees (trees from the right side on this last hole at Wentworth crowd right in on the line of the second shot) instead of just narrowly missing them, as I had planned. It looked to me to be slicing, but it went through the trees, pitched short of the green, took a break to the left, squeezed past the right-hand trap, and took the curve of the ground nicely down until it finished about ten feet from the hole. The result was magnificent. Of course, I was swinging a golf club, and not firing a rifle, but the ball had taken a line some eight feet to the right of the one I had hoped for. However, it had a perfect ending.

Tony Lema swung into his third shot – and was a little unfortunate. He hit a good-looking low pitch at the green, over the bunker, but it bit into the front of the green and stopped. Now if you look at that green at Wentworth closely, you will see that the front of the green is invariably a little more damp than the rest of it. This was certainly something I had noticed in practice, and Tony may have missed. If he had played a high pitch right at the hole, or pitched it short of the green and made it run, he might have been more successful. He didn't hole the putt. I used my 2 for it carefully, and we were all square. Unbelievable. We went into extra holes.

The thirty-seventh hole. Two normal drives, my ball finding a slightly cut lie on the right side of the fairway. Tony low-hooked his second again, into a deep bunker at the left front of the green. I knocked mine on the front of the green. Tony exploded out, way past the pin. He failed, only just, with the putt. I had two to win one of the most astonishing golf matches ever played. I hit my first putt two feet past the hole – and made the return. I had won.

I shook hands with Lema, and then for the first time in that long, hard day, I felt shot through with nerves. I started to tremble like a leaf in a storm.

Grand Slam Golf, Cassell, 1966

Moe Norman

Born 1930, Kitchener, Canada.

Amongst the ranks of the mighty there should be space for a man who marched to a different tune.

Moe Norman has few major successes to his name. He won the Canadian Amateur twice in the 1950s and the Canadian PGA in 1966 and 1974. The rest is silence. Our next author tells why.

A walk in the park

Peter Dobereiner

The crowd behind the eighteenth green cheered as the leader's approach shot smacked into the turf. The ball took two hops and then reversed under the effect of backspin, finishing three feet from the flag. The leader, now with three strokes for victory, walked briskly on to the green and deliberately clipped the ball into a bunker with his putter.

He splashed the ball back on to the green and, with his usual perfunctory glance along the line, stroked it into the hole.

Can you name the golfer? Well, a bit more of the story. With radio reporters vamping madly and promising to have the winner at the microphone any minute now and, with distraught tournament officials unable to delay the presentation ceremony any longer, the hero of the hour was hiding in a toilet until the hullabaloo died down and he could slip away quietly into the night in his battered old Cadillac.

You may never have heard of him, but mention that incident, or a hundred more like it, to any of the great players in North America and identification will be instantaneous.

'It could only be Moe Norman.' They speak his name with awe, and affection, and amused exasperation, and sometimes with a hint of envy, for Norman is blessed with a talent for striking a golf ball which is as legendary as his eccentricity.

Ever since I first began to hear weird and wonderful tales of Norman

I have been trying to track him down, but he is a will-o'-the-wisp character. Where do you start looking for man who habitually sleeps in his car, who keeps on the move and is so suspicious of strangers that he refuses to entrust his money to a bank?

Moe drifted into golf the way most boys of his generation did, by hanging around a golf club and earning pocket-money as a caddie. The club in question was in Kitchener, Ontario, and Moe was coached by the pro, Lloyd Tucker, who was responsible for bringing on quite a few fine Canadian players.

The one element which Tucker did not drill into Norman was a classical style. All his life Norman has stood to the ball stiff-legged, knees braced back, with a pronounced stoop from the waist and with his hands as far from his body as he could get them with fully stretched arms.

His impact on Canadian amateur golf was sensational. He would not have a caddie, remarking 'bag's not heavy, bag's not heavy,' much to the tight-lipped disapproval of establishment figures in the Royal Canadian Golf Association. He won everything, Canadian Amateur Championships and provincial championships seemingly as he pleased.

The town of Kitchener turned out in force to hail the local hero at a Moe Norman night, with the full ceremonial of civic speeches, presentation and fanfares. Needless to say Norman did not turn up.

In match-play events he often conceded ten-foot putts – 'that's good, that's good' – and then won the hole by rolling home his fifteen-footers, a devastating psychological gambit which finally left opponents unable to hole the vital two-footer and which stood him in good stead in his coming career among the rich pigeons.

Lesser amateur tournaments put up the usual prizes such as TV sets, furniture and other household appliances. Norman won four rocking-chair first prizes in successive years. He began to get cute and it was at this time that he learned how to produce the exact score he needed, a facility later to win him many bets as a gypsy pro touring the resort courses down South. He would ask around if anyone wanted to buy a radio for instance, and then, having made the deal and set the price, he would contrive to finish in the place which carried the radio as the prize.

Officialdom frowned on such covert professionalism, drawing from Norman the classic response: 'What do you do with twenty-seven toasters?'

However, Norman was persuaded to do the decent thing and turn pro. He made the Canadian PGA Championship virtually a Moe Norman benefit but in other professional events he sometimes seemed completely uninterested.

'Don't know if I want to win. Just a walk in the park, just a walk in the park.'

Eventually Norman was persuaded much against his inclination to venture into the big pond of the American tour. He was so overawed at first that his main interest was in diffidently asking the star players for their autographs. His friend Bert Turcotte was exasperated: 'Moe, what the hell are you doing? You're out here to whip these guys' asses.' 'Me?' said Norman in astonishment at the idea. 'Oh no. I'm not supposed to beat them.'

Norman is a Coca-Cola addict and at the Los Angeles Open he walked on to the first tee carrying a bottle, which he placed on the turf. Then, to the delight of the gallery, he put his ball on the top of the bottle and drove off. On another occasion he balanced his ball on a pyramid tee marker and drove off from that. Sometimes, to relieve the tedium of practice rounds, he would throw down a ball and leap into the shot while the ball was still rolling, cracking it 250 yards down the middle.

At Augusta, Norman made history as the only player ever to walk out of the Masters. He had caused something of a stir behind the scenes by sacking the caddie allotted to him before the poor man had even picked up the bag and then, when a breeze blew up for the third round with Norman in fifth position, he said: 'Too windy for golf. Back to Canada, back to Canada,' and disappeared.

Norman and the big time were clearly incompatible and mutually happy to end the association. For one thing it was not too good for the image of professional golf to have a player striking side bets with the gallery, such as whether he could keep a ball bouncing on his club face as he walked along the fairway (his record was 193 bounces) or whether he could get down from a bunker in two strokes with one hand.

For me, Norman's greatest claim to fame lay in one of his favourite sidelines. I have told this story before and repeat it without shame. When the opportunity arose, or could be contrived, he would strike a wager that he could break the course record, without ever having seen the course. He has collected on seventeen such bets to date and on this particular occasion was playing with the local pro. He came to the last needing a four to win his wager and asked the other pro what kind of hole it was. 'Drive and 9-iron,' he was told. Norman took out his 9-

iron and hit the ball off the tee, following it with a full driver shot off the fairway to the flat for a birdie three.

If you are ever in Ontario (in summer) or Florida when the snow makes golf impossible in Canada and a scruffy, portly man in his early fifties asks if you would like a game of golf with a little bit of interest on the side, settle for a wager you can well afford to lose and jump at the opportunity. You might just be in for a golf lesson from one of the game's consummate masters.

The Observer, 8 March 1981

Tony Jacklin

Born 7 July 1944, Scunthorpe, England.

In June 1970 Jacklin won the US Open and so became the first British player since Harry Vardon to hold both British and US titles simultaneously and the first British player to win the US Open since Ted Ray fifty years before. It could be argued that here was the best player in the world.

Thereafter decline. He finished well up in the Open for a few more years and had one or two wins annually in tournaments, fading to only a couple of victories after 1974.

What went wrong? Theories have been many and curious and have alleged lack of attendance on the practice tee or the dangers of 'too much too soon', and all have observed that the man's putting leaves a great deal to be desired.

My thought is that he was never quite as good as the press and the British public wanted him to be, he was always a player of good and bad streaks and the latter became more and more frequent while the former petered out altogether. Yet we do not count an athlete a failure because he won only one Olympic title or a tennis player only one Wimbledon. It is perhaps kinder and more true to see Jacklin as a man who won two Opens, and the list of those who have achieved that is very short indeed.

Splendour in a cow pasture – the 1970 US Open

Michael Hobbs

The players were not happy with the Hazeltine National course at Chaska, Minnesota. That fact was the key to the winning and the losing of the 1970 US Open. For a start Hazeltine, at 7,151 yards, was the second longest course ever used in this championship and as an inland course that had had plenty of rain – some three inches – it was playing its full length. Normally most professionals look on a par five as a clear birdie chance, requiring at most two woods to the green. But at Hazeltine those par fives were out of reach. This alone made a par round of 72 far more difficult to achieve.

Then there was another problem the players were not used to. The landscape at Hazeltine was undulating and targets were often not visible from the tee and sometimes not for the second shot either. In all, there were eleven holes at which the green was invisible from the tee, and the use of elevated greens by architect Robert Trent Jones meant that the flag was partially hidden at ten holes for the second or third shot. This posed an additional problem in that the greens themselves were particularly large, on occasion forty yards in length, so that it was not possible for a player to have a precise feel of the pin position as he went into his shot.

Nicklaus summed up opinion when he said that the course was as difficult as any used for an Open. Dave Hill, one of the most successful competitors on the US tour that year, went a little farther. He said, 'All it needs is eighty acres of corn and some cows,' and further defined it as a 'pasture with flags'. The locals were proud of the cattle and wheat plains of their native state but did not relish this description of their course. They mooed at Hill as he made his way along the fairways during the championship. Hill himself was fined $150 for his remarks, which he found a fair charge for the pleasure of voicing his feelings.

But many of the entry were even less happy than Hill after the first round was completed on 18 June 1970. Anyone with a round as good as a seventy-five was content, able to feel that he had mastered the blustering thirty to forty mph north-westerly wind. But few did as well as this. Only eighty-one of the 150 qualifiers were under 80. The 'big three', Palmer, Player and Nicklaus, took 79, 80 and 81 shots respectively. Even Trevino, with the reputation of being the best wind player in the world, could manage no better than 77.

For most players throughout the world, golf is a game played in a shirt and perhaps a light pullover if there is a slight nip in the air. It is a game played in the humidity of Singapore, the dry heat of South Africa and indeed every variation of warm climate you care to think of, but if there is a winter season it is usual for courses to close down during it. A Swiss course may be open for a few months of the year only and there is a lengthy closed season for much of the US – a reason for the US Tour 'following the sun'. Only in Britain do a high proportion of golfers feel that golf is a game for wind, rain, frost, hail and snow – if it is not too deep, you can paint a few balls orange and carry on!

In these circumstances, it was not surprising that the holder of the British Open, Tony Jacklin, was the one player to beat par, which he did by one shot. He started 3, 5, 5, 2, 3, 3, three under par, and had one other birdie during the first nine holes. (The first threeball were fourteen over par on the first four holes!) In the second half he had only one more birdie but throughout kept at bay all but one of the double bogeys that were plaguing so many of the field. Jacklin is a good front runner and not afraid of winning. His temperamental fault rather is to become disinterested if he feels he has lost the chance of winning, when perseverance can often mean that opportunities to capitalize on the falterings of others will present themselves.

Despite his two-stroke lead on Julius Boros and four shots on the nearest other competitor, Jacklin was still nobody's favourite for the championship. Although he had won a tournament in the US and was British Open Champion, first-round leaders seldom win and the weather was now relatively calm. Even those who had started with 80s by no means felt out of contention, because of the freak weather of the previous day. They would throw everything to chance to make up lost ground. Such a player as Nicklaus is often at his psychological best when freed of an inborn conservatism, an unwillingness to take risks, a tendency to aim for the centre of the green rather than at a flag menaced by bunker and water hazard. Surely the sixty-fives and sixty-sixes would now become fairly commonplace, despite the length of the course.

At the end of the day Jacklin was the halfway leader. Only Dave Hill, with 69, had made up ground on him, and then by only one stroke. None of the high scorers of the first round had forced himself up the field. Hazeltine National, and the testing course architecture of R. T. Jones, was winning the battle, for apart from its length there were other menacing features of the course. It is heavily bunkered – more than one hundred in all – and very many of them are out of sight as the player makes his shot. Most of the par fours and fives are dog-legs, demanding a drive both long and accurate if the player is to have a clear shot to the green for his second. And as Nicklaus put it, there were no 'position Bs' at Hazeltine. An off-line iron or wood from the tee usually meant a shot dropped – unless the player could make up for his error with a chip-and-putt finish. Most of the players disliked the greens and few were getting down in a single putt from more than four or five feet. The putting surfaces were dense and wet, and the ball had to be rapped firmly and confidently over them, but many had lost confidence on that first day – strong winds can be said to affect putting more adversely than they do the longer shots. Nevertheless, Jacklin was averaging only twenty-eight putts per round at that point.

During the third round he maintained his momentum. His putting was slightly less effective but his swing was now perfectly poised and rhythmic and he was perhaps playing in that kind of trance experienced by those at a peak of form. If he made an error, he made up for it with a precise floating wedge to the green, a good chip or a fine putt. He was not, as I have said, afraid of leading, and when in trouble, like Palmer, would be driven by temperament to a bold, sometimes rash or desperate, counter blow. One moment of crisis came on the 344-yard seventeenth when his 2-iron from the tee finished behind trees. He considered merely playing out toward the green, for the trees were really too near and too high for him to get both the height to clear them and the length to reach the green. He selected an 8-iron as likely to give him enough height and lashed into the shot. Up and over it went and on and on for 160 yards before settling about twenty-five feet from the hole. Without further alarms he finished the round and signed for a 70. Hill had fallen a shot farther behind, firmly in second place but still four shots behind Jacklin. The remainder were seven (Brewer), eight, nine, eleven and worse behind. Gay Brewer had drawn to within two strokes of the leader halfway through the round but his challenge had faded over the second nine holes.

Many tournament players see the third round as being particularly crucial; it is then that a leader must consolidate a good opening. If he does so, it is up to the others to take risks in the final round while he can play the 'safe' shots – play short of a water hazard or line of bunkers, aim for the middle of the green, putt to be sure of getting down in two rather than go boldly at a downhill putt.

Jacklin could not yet disregard Dave Hill, but the course would probably protect him against the 63s and 64s that any other challenger would still need if Jacklin should stumble to over par for his final round. The trouncing of the field that Jacklin had in his grasp was only once threatened. He was one under par for the first six but dropped shots at both of the next two holes. Thoughts of Palmer losing no less than seven strokes to Billy Casper in the 1966 Open always recur in the minds of championship leaders at times like this. At the ninth he was in the rough from the tee but managed to get his 4-iron on to the green about ten yards from the hole. Now to get safely down in two. But his putt was too bold, at least five or six feet too strong, although dead straight. It hit the back of the hole, jumped up in the air and disappeared from sight.

The rest was a triumphal progress. Jacklin stood on the eighteenth tee with a six-shot lead. He drove safely down the fairway, put a 4-iron on to the green and holed a long putt.

This is how they finished:

281 Tony Jacklin (71, 70, 70, 70)
288 Dave Hill (75, 69, 71, 73)
289 Bob Charles (76, 71, 75, 67)
289 Bob Lunn (77, 72, 70, 70)
291 Ken Still (78, 71, 71, 71)
292 Miller Barber (75, 75, 72, 70)

Jacklin had broken no records in winning this championship but he had joined a number of select companies. The only foreigners to win the US Open are Harry Vardon (1900), Ted Ray (1920) and Gary Player (1965). Jacklin's winning margin of seven shots was not the highest on record – Jim Barnes finished nine shots ahead forty-nine years earlier – and others had led throughout, but not many – only Walter Hagen, Jim Barnes and Ben Hogan. Bobby Jones (twice), Gene Sarazen, Ben Hogan and Jack Nicklaus have also held both the British and the US Open Championships at the same time (although only Jones, Sarazen and Hogan have won both in the same year).

All of Jacklin's rounds except the first had been a 70. It is interesting that but four players recorded a single round better than this. There were three 69s and a 67 from Bob Charles, who came home strongly with the best round of the tournament. It was, of course, the consistency of his scoring that brought Jacklin home; all his rounds were below par – an achievement he shares with Lee Trevino in the US Open records.

Jacklin returned to England a national hero to defend his British Open title three weeks later. He might have succeeded. On the first round he went out in twenty-nine and was maintaining a momentum towards something between a 62 and a 64 when the weather broke. When he completed the round the next morning the mood was gone.

For Tony Jacklin at Hazeltine in 1970 the future seemed to hold a secure place with the 'big three'. His performance there was one of the supreme achievements in golf history, but since then he has barely held his position as the best British golfer – not enough really in a country that does not often have more than one golfer of the highest world class, and Jacklin today has slipped below this level. If he has the appetite, there is still time.

The Great Opens, David & Charles, 1976

Catherine Lacoste

Born 27 June 1945, Paris, France.

The daughter of tennis champion René Lacoste and Thion de la Chaume, a golf national champion, Catherine Lacoste's genes were hardly unfavourable, and it seems now inevitable that she became a champion. Yet in the odd way that fame sometimes quickly fades she is now relatively little remembered, only a decade after she was the best woman golfer of her time.

On marrying she retired with a formidable record built up in very few years. Between 1966 and 1970 she won the French Closed championship twice, the French Open thrice, the British Open once, the US Amateur once and the US Professional Open once. In the latter she remains the only amateur to have won, one of only two overseas winners and, aged twenty-two in 1967, the youngest.

Catherine Lacoste – championne du monde
Peter Ryde

Golf demands humility of its followers. Some of us never cease to pay our tribute. Others may seem to escape; the game leads them up to exaggerated pinnacles of fame and wealth; it may – it almost certainly does – grant them moments of infinite pleasure and satisfaction; but before the end, by some means or another, even the mightiest are humbled by it.

The full drama of these occasions is only felt when the champion is at the height of his powers, and the débâcle is in full view of the public. Not every famous calamity may satisfy those conditions, but there is one champion for whom the moment of tragedy was all too completely staged. In the autumn of 1969 Catherine Lacoste let it be known that she was retiring from international competition. It was not to be a clean break. She was to marry a Spaniard, but since she would be living in that country she could hardly turn her back on the women's world team championship which was to be held there the following autumn. But her decision to pull out kept nearer to the truth than most announcements of that nature. It looked, then, as though she might escape unscathed, as though she might be the one champion whom the game would allow to remain unhumbled. Her successes had been so numerous in her five-year career that she had hardly had time to throw a championship or quit on a tournament. Her whole story was one of dazzling success, proudly borne.

She had, of course, known defeat, as any great golfer must. Quickly, as she rose to supremacy, she had first to establish herself against three of the finest golfers in Europe at that time. The Vicomtesse de Saint-Sauveur was coming to the end of a long and distinguished career; Brigitte Varangot and Claudine Cros were approaching the summit of theirs. All of them were French, and taking the long view her rivalry with them was the making of her as a champion; without such a tough initiation into the competitive world she might never have prevailed in America.

Although she had at the age of nineteen contributed most to the victory of France in the first world team championship, she needed time to prove her superiority. It was not until two years later, in 1966, that she won the championship of France for the first time, overcoming an inhibition about beating Brigitte Varangot that was threatening to turn into a mental block. The following year she suffered what I have always supposed to be her most vexing defeat. At Harlech she led the qualifiers for the second year running in the British championship, only to find herself beaten in the first round by Martine Cochet, a compatriot who had scraped into the championship sixteen strokes behind Catherine over the two qualifying rounds.

Vexing, yes, but that defeat hardly entered into the realm of grand drama. In the ultimate test of strokeplay Miss Lacoste had already made her mark; the hazards of matchplay were another matter and had always frustrated the best. Bobby Jones, we hasten to point out, had won two British and three American Opens before he succeeded in winning the British Amateur. Moreover her main triumphs lay ahead; against the background of that historic Welsh city, she was not yet ready to play the leading part of tragedian.

From her childhood she had been cast in a heroic role, having champion's blood in her veins from both sides of the family. The ability to win does not of course depend necessarily on inherited talent in that particular field. Sheer adversity may force the genius out of a performer, and sometimes the parents of a champion may excel in another field. But with a father who had been singles champion at Forest Hills, and with a mother who, as Mademoiselle Thion de la Chaume, won a British championship in Catherine's favourite sport, it was not long before Catherine felt at home in the competitive atmosphere which some excellent performers never get used to at all. Her father, René Lacoste, confined himself to shrewd observations about her technique. A great theorist of this and other games, he perhaps had the good sense to realize that his daughter needed, not instruction, for she was too good a natural ball player for that, but an outside eye that could supply what most players need, a diagnosis when things go wrong. Many a good golfer who can detect faults in others and correct them, can remain curiously blind to the fault that has crept into his own game.

Catherine's string of successes has its roots in the children's tournaments her mother used to organize during the summer holidays at their home course of Chantaco, down the road from St Jean de Luz. Madame Lacoste did her best to see to it that her daughter did not collar the first prize all the time, but it was hard work. They had given birth to a winner. She was young, she was powerful, she was scornful of opposition to the point of giving offence. Add to this some blunt remarks, remarkable more for their honesty than for their tact, and it is hardly surprising that, over and above her maddening habit of winning, she roused occasional animosity. She once admitted to being perhaps 'un peu cabochard'. We must make what we can of that, but 'caboche' is a hob-nail, and riding-roughshod over people's feelings might not be wide of the mark.

But how exciting a trait that was when translated into action on the course! She came to the first world team championship for women at the age of nineteen, junior champion of France and that was about all. The team event, the only one of its kind in which a player represents his country in strokeplay, is the most exciting of all. Yet Catherine played the last decisive round as though it were the height of enjoyment to her. We said that it was the innocence of youth, but even in full maturity she never lost that quality. Patty Berg, the famous American professional, was quick to observe it. She wrote: 'She enjoys playing golf and anyone can see that sport is far from being the most important thing in her life. . .' This completely amateur approach helps to explain her victory later in the US Open where so much was at stake for the others, and it also helps to explain her ability to play her best when it mattered most. 'I need a high stake to bring out the best scores in me,' she once said. Such a remark may sound like tempting providence, but almost until the end of her career she made it look as though it were the right way to treat providence, and as though an assurance so complete had enabled her to earn exemption from the golden rule of humiliation.

In 1967 came the first thunderbolt, completely unexpected and almost unwitnessed and unreported from this side of the Atlantic. I was in Portugal watching the European women's team championship in which Catherine, to the irritation of her colleagues, declined to take part. They were standing in a huddle in the hotel lobby, and when I said in reply to their question that I had not heard the news, they told me that I must first be seated or the shock would be too great. Catherine had won the United States women's Open championship. The surprise has worn off for all of us by now because we are familiar with the brilliance of her game. We accept that she can hit the ball harder and straighter than any other living woman, that she has more confidence in playing the 1-iron than do most men. We know, or thought we knew until that last act in Madrid, that she will always knock the putts that matter in.

What lingers in my mind of that victory is the courage she showed in going over there and maintaining her game to the end. I sometimes pass the time thinking of the great occasions I have missed and would like again to have the chance of seeing. Catherine's triumph at the Cascades club in Virginia is high on the list. She herself is not easily drawn on the subject but a French journalist, Renaud de Laborderie, in *Les Reines du Sport*, has reconstructed the ordeal with sensitivity. For days at the motel and at the course Catherine was completely alone. The championship journal, the press, the players ignored her existence. The only exceptions were two young girls seated at the next table to her. They got talking as Catherine sat munching her lonely cornflakes, and they persuaded their parents to stay on until their new friend had won. Her 70 the second round hoisted her five strokes clear of the field and established her on the road to victory. It was one of the great rounds of her life, comparable to the fabulous 66 which she had scored at Prince's the year before in winning the Astor Trophy. Before the final round on a day of clouds and humidity she went to Mass, praying no more fervently than usual, for golf is not essential to life. It was this air of detachment that carried her through the final round, that enabled her to keep hold of a slipping lead, to drive across trees at the seventeenth, hole a three-yard putt, and make sure of the title.

Her victory was as complete as was to be that of the next foreigner to win an American championship, Tony Jacklin. She was the first foreigner to win the US women's championship, the first amateur to do so and the youngest player. It was the championship she most wanted to win, *ça va de soi*. But it was not the one she found hardest to win; that was the American Amateur; nor was it the one that gave her the greatest pleasure in winning; that was the British Amateur. She had to wait three more years for these two and one depended on the other. The British had been the stumbling block in her career, for here her predominance in strokeplay could not assert itself. But in 1970 she went early to the green shores of Northern Ireland to prepare for the championship that still eluded her. Already that year she had won the French championship and also, for what it was worth, the Spanish by 10 and 9. She allowed her mother to accompany her; in America she had wanted to make her own way to fame, apart from her parents. Now she wanted her mother with her, because it was down the coast from Royal Portrush at Royal County Down that she had won the same championship forty-two years before. Only Ann Irvin looked capable of stopping Catherine that week on a giant course worthy of a true champion. Ann was three up on her after seven holes, and luck went against her when Catherine's approach to the ninth was deflected by a spectator's handbag from the rough to the edge of the green. But luck comes to all, and it is the ability to take advantage of it that marks the champion. Catherine holed that putt and banged her tee shot to the next hole ten feet from the pin.

Coming back to London in the plane afterwards she was uncertain what to do next. She was contemplating marriage, but reluctance to return to America, where, to put it mildly, her triumph had been received with mixed feelings by players and press, was losing ground to the vision of her completing the grand slam of winning the American Amateur. This time she would land in that country not an unknown at the start of a great adventure, as had been the case in 1967, but as someone who was expected to win and whom every American would take delight in beating. 'When you are a champion, if you win *c'est normal*; once you lose everybody says you are over the hill.' Moreover, the championship was being held at Texas at the hottest time of the year. From the relaxed country-house atmosphere of the Côte Basque she would have to go forth into the furnace, summoning up for a final effort her great competitive spirit. In a temperature of more than one hundred degrees in which the iron clubs under the sun became too hot to handle, she clung like a leach to par. As had happened in the British she found herself three down in the final; as in the British she extricated herself, this time against Anne Welts, a golfer in the highest class, but one whom she had beaten when their Curtis Cup team visited Paris, and one who was beginning to show signs of having been so long at the top.

The grand slam was complete; that year she had won the French, British and American in succession. She was now ready to withdraw from top competition, with the finest record of all time and also the proudest. But by one of those quirks of fate the world women's team championship was the following year to be held in Madrid, the city where she was going to live and on the course of which she had recently become a member. Complete as her achievement was this was one last international championship on which she could not turn her back. In the six years of its history her individual record of tied first, third, and first was second to none; and of all the leading countries France alone had kept her team intact from the start.

She might joke that, being now married to someone who was half-Spanish, half-Chilean, she had a choice of three countries to represent; and it was certain that since the championship would take place a few weeks after her marriage she would not be in full competitive trim. Still, no matter; half a Lacoste was better than no champion. Slowly and inexorably the situation built up. In that type of championship, where the best two rounds out of three count for four days, the climax sometimes passes unseen out on the course, and the result becomes a matter of statistics. In this case there was never any doubt where the climax lay, and the insignificant crowd that found its way out from Madrid, reinforced by members of other teams who had finished, watched the long drawn-out agony of those last nine holes. Catherine Lacoste blew up. She would not, I feel sure, with her own tremendously high standards, want to hide behind words. There were all kinds of extenuating circumstances and she finished with a plucky par at the seventy-second hole which even in ordinary circumstances is not an easy four, but she blew it. I am concerned only to make the point that at the eleventh hour the champion who looked to have got away without being humbled by the game she loved, was made to pay the tribute demanded of all other great players.

We can gloss over the details. The three strokes' lead Catherine held with nine to play vanished and the United States retained the title of world champions by one stroke out of 598. By ordinary standards the French girl did not collapse, but she would not forgive herself the shortness of the putt she missed on the eleventh green or for having been short with her pitches at two relatively easy holes. Her opponent, Martha Wilkinson, was a lovely swinger of the club – one of those juvenile sun-tanned products of the American conveyor belt, who had done nothing but play golf since January and who had played in 72-hole tournaments week after week through the summer. She did not have, as her opponent, packing cases full of unopened wedding presents in a still unfurnished home, and when she does I have no doubt she will not be playing for the United States. Sometimes as a spectator it is possible almost to hate the game one loves when one sees the full burden of a team event proving too heavy for one person. There had been an example of that the day when Catherine first burst upon the world and won the team championship for France six years previously. Then Barbara MacIntyre's failure to retain America's lead sent a chill through the hearts of the spectators. Today the boot was on the other foot as Catherine, waiting for Martha to take two putts and get her four, sat on the bank, at the back of the green, her head in her arms.

When the pain has worn off, comes the realization that this is part of the greatness of the game; one comes to admire its cold impartiality. Catherine, whatever that day may have cost her feelings, is not diminished by it as a golfer. She remains nonetheless the greatest woman champion of our times; and it would be surprising if the experience had not left her a more complete person.

The Golfers' Bedside Book, Donald Steel (ed.), Batsford, 1971

Johnny Miller

Born 29 April 1947, San Francisco, California, USA.

At the end of the 1981 season Miller stood twelfth on the US money-winners' list. He had completed a comeback from the worst slump experienced by a supreme golfer. At the nadir he had sunk to 111th amongst money-winners in 1978.

From his victory in the 1973 US Open, climaxed by a sequence of superb iron shots that gave him a 63, to his victory in the 1976 British Open, Miller was unchallenged as a tournament winner on the US circuit.

His peak period was from the beginning of the 1974 season until a month or two into 1975. In 1974 he won the first three tournaments and, including them, went on to play twenty-three consecutive rounds under par. In all that season he won eight and began the following year by taking the first two once more.

Apart from Byron Nelson's achievements at the end of World War II and Horton Smith's fifty years ago, no golfer has so dominated the US circuit, and during that year Miller probably found golf an easier game than anyone else has done before or since.

Miller's year of the American eagle
Peter Dobereiner

The bare bones of the story of the 105th Open Championship was that Johnny Miller, the twenty-nine-year-old American who has won more than $1 million in his golfing career, added another £7,500 to his tally by equalling the course record of 66, six under par, to win by six strokes. It sounds easy and in the end it was, but for nine holes the most cherished prize in the golf world was there to be taken by any one of half a dozen players with the skill and nerve to thread his way round Birkdale's treacherous narrow and fiery fairways.

For most of the day the main contenders were Miller and Severiano

Left It's not possible but it's a fact: this finish is the result of exceptional swing velocity. Severiano Ballesteros was attempting to drive a par 4 en route to his 1979 Open win. *Below* The most prolific winner on the US women's circuit, Nancy Lopez-Melton, at impact.

Above left The simple balanced method of Peter Thomson helped him to five Open Championship victories. *Above right* Tom Weiskopf has won a major championship just once – the Troon Open of 1973 – but the power and elegance of his swing ensure that his name will last.
Below left Trevino splashes from sand: the simplest shot in golf.
Below right Greg Norman, a player on the edge of greatness.

Ballesteros, the nineteen-year-old Spanish prodigy who led this illustri-
ous field of international superstars by two strokes at the start of the
day.

The key to the day's play proved to be the sixth hole. It is a par four
of 468 yards, dog-legged to the right and with a cross-bunker set in the
elbow. Ideally, the tee markers are adjusted to present the player with
the dilemma of whether to lay up short of that bunker, followed by a
long and blind second shot to the green set in a fold of the sand dunes
and guarded on the right by a clump of ferociously thick bushes, or
whether to go for broke with the driver and try to carry the bunker,
leaving a relatively straightforward second shot.

For this last round the markers had been set too far back to give the
players any valid option; they had to play short and that caused all
sorts of problems. Of the leading twelve players, all but three (one of
whom was Miller) dropped at least one stroke to par here. Christy
O'Connor, Jnr, lost three shots; Jack Nicklaus lost two shots and a ball;
Ballesteros lost two.

That was the point where Miller went into the lead for the first
time, but he was far from home and dry. Ballesteros came back with
a renewed challenge, but the eleventh hole settled the issue. Here,
Ballesteros ripped off one of his uninhibited drives, leaning back and
giving it everything with the careless abandon of youth. The ball
found a patch of willow scrub, which is a unique feature of the
course.

The youngster smashed at the ball as hard as he could and failed to
move it out of his own shadow. Two more shots to the green and three
putts gave him a seven and left Miller five strokes ahead. That is
exactly the situation which Miller thrives on. He had been trying to
put Ballesteros under pressure and now, as he said, 'I wanted to give
him some of the stuff I know I am capable of.' That stuff followed in
the form of a birdie at the twelfth, and a chip in for an eagle at the
thirteenth, and Miller knew for sure that he had his second major
championship.

One of Miller's main strengths as a competitor is his uncompromising
attitude once he gets on top. No matter how large a lead he may
amass, he remains hungry for more. It never occurs to him to ease off
and play safe, which is the Nicklaus way in such situations. Miller's
policy is to take no prisoners. His one idea is to go farther and farther
ahead, to crush his rivals and humiliate them and rub their noses in
the superiority of his golf. This is when he plays his best, and he pro-

ceeded to do just that with immaculate birdies at the seventeenth and eighteenth.

In fact, for a player of his class in this killer mood, these two holes are fairly simple birdie chances downwind. By now he was playing easily and fluently, with his willowy six-foot-two-inch frame bending into every shot with the fullest swing in golf.

Inevitably, memories were revived of 1973 when he came from behind with that historic 63 to win the United States Open. This was not quite the same style, since a burnt-up Birkdale is a different proposition to a waterlogged Oakmont, but the growing impetus of his round and his unchallenged domination of the championship over the closing holes were similar and typically Miller.

By the roll of a putt, Miller missed the added flourish of a course record. An hour earlier Mark James, the former British Walker Cup player, in his first full professional season, had also scored a 66 to lift him well up the field.

Reviewing the round, Miller said that he had formed the opinion that Ballesteros was a bit too aggressive for his own good. Miller, who had been playing conservatively in the first three rounds, had to revise his policy in the fourth after the first hole, where Ballesteros was in all manner of trouble, in willow scrub left of his drive and in rough right after his recovery. However, the Spaniard pitched to thirty feet and holed the putt for his par.

Miller had played the hole exactly according to the book, which is quite a trick on this narrow S-bend of a fairway winding 450 yards between the dunes. His drive split the fairway and his approach just ran through the back owing to a sudden switch in the wind. He chipped up and two-putted. 'I was afraid that this would give him confidence, which was exactly what I did not want. Now I decided to throw my iron shots right in there.'

Even so, Miller tempered his tactics with caution. He used his 1-iron off eleven tees, and this was one of the factors which brought him that rare par on the dreaded sixth. Then when he had seen off Ballesteros, and had appraised the leader board, with neither Nicklaus nor Ray Floyd making enough of a charge to worry about, he reverted to his driver and let rip for the dénouement. 'I was just going to enjoy it from there on in.'

All week Miller had been confident that he would play well. He arrived at Birkdale last Monday, which was cutting it a bit fine for thorough preparation and adjustment to the time change, but that did not bother him. 'Sometimes I just feel bubbling with enthusiasm and strength. I just felt like I was ready to go.'

In the past Miller has been scornful of the special status of the major championships. His ambition, he has declared, is to win tournaments: any tournaments and as many as possible. In his moment of triumph he softened his views somewhat. 'I am not going to revolve my whole schedule round the four major championships, but if I do not do anything else this year I feel I will have achieved plenty in 1976.'

The Observer, 11 July 1976

Decline and fall
John Ballantine

Nothing in golf, not even Tony Jacklin's inexplicable loss of form, equals Johnny Miller's fall from grace. The handsome, fair-haired Mormon from San Francisco was playing a different brand of golf from anyone else, even Jack Nicklaus, for three golden years – from 1973, when he won the US Open title at Oakmont with a record last round of 63, to July 1976, when he beat Nicklaus and Sevvy Ballesteros into joint second place at the British Open at Birkdale. In this season's first event at Tucson, by contrast, he scored two final rounds of 70 and he finished last but one of seventy-five qualifiers.

Golf can be the cruellest task-master in sport. The game's foreshore is littered with wrecks that captains like Tony Jacklin, Bruce Crampton and Arnold Palmer once sailed proudly. But the hulk that is Miller's game is the most horrific because, of all golfers, he alone looked to have mastered the game and so be ready to score regularly in the low 60s.

'A lot of things contributed,' he said the other day in Tucson. 'I had some swing problems. I don't know if it was because I gained weight, or just worked myself into a slump.

'I was aiming too far to the right, with the ball too far forward and my hands behind it. I was taking the club back slightly inside and too far. I was hitting with a mad rush – no lateral movement, breaking down after impact. I was finishing flat and without balance. Nothing major,' he added sardonically, 'just a bunch of little things.'

On a foggy evening in San Francisco six months ago, Miller realized how far he had gone back. 'I was watching old movies of myself as a kid of fifteen and sixteen. They'd been kept in a cupboard by my father, who was really my only coach. Pictures of myself swinging then, and in the 1966 US Open at the Olympic Club, showed I used to have a real good compact swing. I hadn't seen the movies for eleven years, and now I've started working on my present swing with those in mind.'

Perhaps, having made so much money, and having so many business interests, he had lost his desire, I suggested. 'I've always been easy-going, casual,' Miller admitted. 'That's my approach to life. I don't look at '77 and have a scar on my heart. But my swing should last for ever, like Julius Boros's.'

'And when I played well,' he reminisced, 'I knew that even my worst shots weren't going to be all that bad. So I could aim at the centre of the fairway and know that I wasn't going to get into trouble. Now that's confidence,' Miller said, sighing wistfully.

If he doesn't find form again, Miller hinted that he might go into teaching. 'I think I have a talent for it, and I enjoy sorting people out and starting juniors off on the right track. Golf is basically a matter of sound fundamentals. I want a sound set-up at the address, and then relaxation. If I was to teach my oldest boy, I'd want him to have a fluid swing like Sam Snead's or Jerry Pate's.'

What about the rest of us hackers? I asked him. Miller gave some advice that could have cost £5,000 (his reported clinic fee) if given professionally. 'Only one out of a thousand club players grips the club lightly enough,' he said. 'You've got to turn yourself into a material as soft as putty, and then just sort of slop the clubhead through. You'll hit much farther and with less effort.'

'I know,' Miller concluded, 'that when I play my best, I can play as well, if not better than anyone out here.' But isn't that just the problem that the rest of us face?

The Sunday Times, 15 January 1978

Tom Watson

Born 4 September 1949, Kansas City, Missouri, USA.

Many superb players have lacked the will, ambition and narrow vision to be dominant amongst their contemporaries. Not so Tom Watson. At the age of thirty, though he has won a formidable number of tournaments, his appetite seems undiminished whereas others after comparable success have tended to concentrate more on the major titles. Of the latter, Tom has won five: the 1977 and 1981 US Masters and the Open three times between 1975 and 1980.

In all tournaments his record is more formidable still. On the US circuit he has been leading money winner for the years 1977 to 1980, passing $300,000 in each of the first two years, rising to $462,000 in 1979 and $530,000 in 1980. He finished ahead of the second man by $181,000 in 1979 and by $145,000 in 1980. Enough perhaps of money, but it is now widely used as a measure, at least of consistency. A better gauge perhaps is that he has, no surprise, for the years 1977-9 also won the Vardon trophy, which is awarded to the man with the lowest stroke average per round – and that is an award that Jack Nicklaus has omitted to win throughout his career.

Head-to-head
Dudley Doust

Tom Watson fought back from an early three-stroke deficit yesterday to overtake Jack Nicklaus, his playing partner and fellow American, with an astonishing finishing rush to capture the Open Golf Championship in baking sunshine at Turnberry. Watson scored a 65 for a four-round total of 268, to his fellow American's 66 and 269. The total also smashed the existing record of 276, held jointly by Arnold Palmer and Tom Weiskopf.

Watson showed signs of nerves when, on the first tee, he brushed aside the traditional photograph with his playing partner. These nerves seemed to continue when, on the first and fourth greens, he missed shortish birdie putts. Nicklaus, meanwhile, was playing like a dream and, going down the fifth fairway, enjoyed a three-stroke lead amid a tumultuous crowd which the Royal and Ancient Golf Club failed to control.

Watson fought back. He birdied three of the next four holes to draw level. Nicklaus nudged ahead at the turn and appeared set for another Open victory after Watson missed the green on the short fifteenth.

Then the tide turned. The young US Masters champion holed gloriously from off the green there and for the first time all day moved ahead on the long seventeenth. Here he reached the green in two massive blows, while Nicklaus, playing off an awkward uphill fairway lie, pushed his iron shot twenty yards to the right of the green.

He chipped four feet past the cup and after his opponent was safely set for his birdie, the Golden Bear sent his ticklish putt racing past the cup. It was all over, or so we thought, for both players ended the epic battle by scoring birdie threes on the formidable home hole.

Inescapably, the pairing of Nicklaus and Watson yesterday was seen as a match between the king and the pretender, a young man who at twenty-seven already has two major championships and this year is heading for the greatest money-winning season of all time. Almost as inescapably, the players themselves, who after all went into the day three strokes clear of Crenshaw and six of a trio of players including Tommy Horton, saw it in the same light. Nicklaus, with his flair for the deadpan psychological riposte, chose both to accept it and shrug it off.

'I've faced the same challenge for fifteen years,' he said after he and Watson had scored 65s playing together in the third round. 'And I enjoyed them. Palmer, Player, Trevino, Miller...' Nicklaus let his sentence tail off as though there would be other challengers and each would be summarily put down. 'It's fun,' he added.

Watson is no mug either when it comes to the confidence game. He followed Nicklaus into the press tent to talk about his 65 and straight away pointed out that it was a better 65. His was more solid, and later he inferred that Nicklaus might have been a little lucky to get away with a half-dozen drives pulled off line into the brown, threadbare rough.

'That's what I was saying the other day; British seaside golf is a test of the man, whereas in America golf is a test of the skill alone. On our courses where bounces are mostly true, you are directly rewarded for a good shot.' Watson had passed that test, survived Nicklaus's scrambling and come out of the third round a stronger man for it.

Watson has been fiercely competitive since his private day-school days in Kansas City. 'I hate to lose in anything, even at checkers [draughts], or chess or snooker,' he said. 'I hate to ease up in any game. Easing up breeds quitting.'

It became increasingly obvious through the week that young Watson was gifted with more than this blunt, animal aggression. He has one of the keenest, most absorbent minds in the game, and whatever the outcome of the championship, he was planning to use every scrap of experience to improve himself as a golfer. This was only his third Open; he won his first, at Carnoustie, in 1975, and playing on British seaside courses was an experience not to be wasted.

'The key to British links golf is the word "frustration",' said Watson; 'you can hit the perfect shot and, all of a sudden, it will bounce straight right or, for no apparent reason, jump beyond the hole. It is frustrating. Even a lucky break can add to the frustration. But that's good. It's a test of your concentration and your guts.' He grinned. 'Having said that, if I played over here four straight weeks I'd be a raving lunatic.'

Final Scores
268 T. Watson (US) 68, 70, 65, 65
269 J. Nicklaus (US) 68, 70, 65, 66
279 H. M. Green (US) 72, 66, 74, 67
280 L. Trevino (US) 68, 70, 72, 70
281 G. Burns (US) 70, 70, 72, 69
     B. Crenshaw (US) 71, 69, 66, 75
282 A. Palmer (US) 73, 73, 67, 69

The Sunday Times, 10 July 1977

Perceptions of St Andrews
Dudley Doust

Tom Watson, who this week defends his Open championship, arrived at St Andrews last Thursday morning, and straightaway went to the balcony of his hotel room and gazed for about ten minutes over the famous links. It was his first view of Mecca, and he was struck by the staggering size of its greens. The hallowed ground, moreover, looked very, very flat as it stretched far out toward the Eden River. 'My first impression of St Andrews was one of strange ambiguousness,' Watson later said slowly. 'I didn't like it nor, for that matter, did I hate it. I still don't know enough about it.'

Watson was not going to lure himself into some pitfall of pre-judgement. First impressions, while memorable, are often misleading, and perhaps no course in the world suffers as much from premature abuse as does the Old Course at St Andrews. In 1946 Sam Snead remarked that the sacred place 'looked like an old abandoned golf course', and he added, back home they wouldn't plant cow beet on such land. Snead stayed only long enough to win the championship that year and never went back. In 1921, when he first played the Old Course, Bobby Jones felt a 'puzzled dislike' for the seemingly anonymous wasteland, with its low, treeless tumble of dunes and sudden bunkers. Jones's conversion was complete by 1930, the year of his Grand Slam, which included his Amateur triumph at St Andrews.

'I had taken great pains to learn the location of all the little pot bunkers,' Jones wrote in *Golf is my Game*, 'and felt that I had a complete familiarity with all the devious little slopes and swales which could deflect well-intentioned shots in such exasperating ways.'

The locations of St Andrews' numerous bunkers, some one hundred and ten of them, are enough to befuddle the first visitor, and in their subsequent practice round neither Watson nor his caddie, Alfie Fyles, bothered to note these hazards on their score cards. Nor, for that matter, did Fyles follow the St Andrews form by precisely charting the driving line for each tee. 'Off the fourteenth tee, sight on the church spire to the right of town,' the great local caddie, Tip Anderson, once said, coaching Tony Lema to the 1964 championship.

Watson was more interested in the surprisingly steep slopes that introduce many of the greens. 'This was something I couldn't see from the hotel balcony,' he said later, 'but they will be crucial to my game. Downwind, I'm going to have to run-in my shots while, into the wind, I'll probably float them into the greens. I've still got to work out exactly where to land the ball.'

Old hands at St Andrews, aware of the capricious winds that spring up to rake the old links, shudder at the thought of pacing out yardages in the style of this generation. After all, what may be a 5-iron on one day will, almost inevitably, be a 3-wood or a 7-iron the following day. Still, seeking some absolutes in such an alien land, Watson and Fyles marched out and marked down the distances from tee to burn to bunker to green.

The flags hung limp, and there was no shifting of the whin bushes, which keenly disappointed Watson. 'Without the wind,' he said, 'St Andrews is even shorter than I expected.' The defending champion was especially anxious to play the seventeenth hole, the famous Road Hole, with the wind blowing left to right off St Andrews Bay. 'From the hotel balcony, I could see it was really a great hole,' he said. 'The shot in the narrow green, with the road beyond and the wind at your back, is going to be one of the key shots of the championship.'

Jet-lagged and untested by winds, Watson was not satisfied after his first day at St Andrews. 'I'm puzzled,' he said before dinner. 'I've never been so puzzled after a first practice round in my life.' He dined, contemplatively, with his wife Linda, and turned in at midnight with the novel, *Trinity*. The air was mostly still, too, on Friday, and after a second practice round the Watsons flew off to Switzerland for a pro-am event, planning to return to St Andrews tomorrow.

Puzzled, perhaps, but Watson already is far ahead of his usual Open preparations. (The first round is on Wednesday.) 'This is the first time Tom's come over this early,' said Fyles, who caddied in Watson's victories at Carnoustie in 1975 and Turnberry in 1977. 'You know, we never had a practice round at Carnoustie at all, and we only played Turnberry a couple of times before the championship.' Fyles laughed as he said: 'Tom usually leaves the preparation to me.'

The Sunday Times, July 1978

The golfer who can do the impossible
Peter Dobereiner

Tom Watson is the world's leading golfer. He is also the world's leading golf perfectionist. In order to get some inkling of what that means it is necessary to understand a little of what is required to drive a golf ball down a fairway. Having raised his club, the golfer must complete the following precise sequence:

For the first 17/100 second in the downward movement he must apply a pull on the club which increases smoothly from two to six pounds; in the next 15/100 second that pull must increase explosively to seventy pounds and then drop to zero in the last 4/100 second before impact. This surge of energy, amounting to 1.45 horse power, accelerates the

7½ oz clubhead through centrifugal force from zero to 166 feet per second. The clubhead, which now 'weighs' 110 pounds in pull directly down the shaft, strikes the ball with an impact of 1½ tons.

The force of impact compresses the ball on the club face, distorting it to about two-thirds of its normal diameter of 1.68 inches. Contact is maintained for 4/10,000 second over travel of .67 inch, with the ball skidding up the clubface one millimetre, and then taking up a reverse rotation as the compressed elasticity is released and the ball is despatched at 225 feet per second. Under those forces, average for a good professional, the ball travels about 280 yards.

Of course, it may not go in a straight line. The criteria for a straight shot are that the clubhead must meet the ball along the target line (a two-degree error will send it into the rough); the centre of mass of the clubhead must meet the target axis of the ball within a tolerance of ⅜ inch or the force will be dissipated; the face of the club must be square to the target line (a three-degree error will impart enough sidespin to slice or hook the ball into the rough); and the angle of attack of clubface to ball must be within these same exacting limits.

Several scientists who have set out to analyse the game of golf have concluded in all seriousness that it is impossible for a human being to combine such degrees of power, timing and accuracy within these precise margins.

Watson has devoted much of his life to the proposition that it is not only possible to achieve these criteria every time he swings a club but these tolerances can be refined even further. He has an obsession to conquer the game.

All professional golfers want to improve, it goes without saying, in order to further their ambitions. In most cases that means to acquire as much money as possible. In rarer cases the motivation is to accumulate major titles and establish themselves as giants in the annals of golf. Jack Nicklaus is the supreme example of a golfer who is spurred to secure unassailable credentials as the greatest golfer who ever lived.

Watson is chasing self-satisfaction. His aim is domination of that 1.62 oz white sphere to the point where he can manoeuvre it at will, high or low, flighting to the left or right, with such perfect precision that it will land within feet of his chosen target some 200-odd yards distant and still retain control of the ball's bounce and roll after it has pitched into the turf.

His quest is hopeless, of course. There are too many variables beyond the player's control to achieve theoretical perfection. A golfer can judge the effect on a shot of wind strength and direction but once the ball is in the air it is at the mercy of capricious gusts. It is impossible to judge precisely what the compression of grass between clubface and ball will do to alter the distance and trajectory of a shot. Golf balls themselves vary one from another, in symmetry and surface imperfections.

The texture of the landing area is another imponderable, since it may be soft or hard and the golfer unable to tell which. Humidity and barometric pressure affect the behaviour of the ball, as do changing biological balances within the golfer from shot to shot. The best the golfer can do is to make an intelligent guess about these variables and then make a perfect contact.

Ben Hogan, the ultimate perfectionist as a striker before Watson came along, devoted his life to refining his technique. By common consent he got closer than anyone to mechanical precision and at the peak of his powers Hogan reckoned that he hit no more than two shots exactly the way he wanted in any round of golf.

These two men, who grappled with the intricacies of golf technique for its own sake rather than as a means to an end, could hardly be more different. Hogan was the son of a blacksmith whose ill health and inability to find work in the Depression drove him to take his life at the age of thirty-seven, when Hogan was nine. It took Hogan eighteen years to fight (sometimes literally) his way to security in golf, through the ranks of the caddies and years of desperate privation as tournament gypsy.

Watson came from middle-class, middle America and had all the advantages of a middle-class education – private schooling and Stanford University, where he graduated in psychology and played golf. He was a typical heir to the American dream, and everyone, himself included, assumed that he would go into the family chemical business, settle down to marriage with his childhood sweetheart in a desirable suburb of Kansas, and start the whole cycle over again with a brood of heirs to that American dream. Watson's nearest and dearest were less than ecstatic when, late in his college career, he decided to make golf his profession.

Perhaps vocation is a better word because Watson had no yearning for fame (he is still uncomfortable in his role of celebrity and hates being lionized) and no lust for money. He thus joined the most ruthless free-for-all in world sport with neither of the motivating forces normally considered to be essential for survival.

Watson survived because he had his personal challenge with the golf swing to spur him through endless hours on the practice ground. His obsession is a priceless asset because it allows him to play golf for its own sake, without the destructive pressures which afflict the hungry and the ambitious. He just about covered his expenses in his first year, did rather better than that the second season, but he still had not won a tournament when he played himself into a potentially winning position in the US Open championship at Winged Foot in 1974.

It is almost axiomatic in golf that nobody succeeds at the first attempt. Everything has to be learned from painful experience, and that includes the technique of winning, which requires balance between aggression and caution, control of nerves and judgement under exceptional emotional pressures, and marshalling of rebellious physical and mental resources. Watson, a stranger to this turmoil, scored a last round 79 and was instantly labelled a 'choker'. The cruel tag stuck as Watson fell out of contention again in the US Open the following year and in several regular tournaments.

By this time he was winning tournaments, but when he was pipped at the post it was assumed that he had simply blown it again or lost his bottle. The best golfers do not play themselves into a winning position every week, by any means. On those occasions when a golfer is in contention after three rounds, he is doing exceptionally well if he wins one tournament in three. Watson was achieving that level of success by the time he played the 1977 Masters, that great golfing classic at Augusta, Georgia. Toward the end of the last round there were only two players in it: Watson and Jack Nicklaus. Watson won by a stroke and finally shrugged off that choker label.

British golf fans could not understand how the calumny had ever started. In the 1975 Open championship at Carnoustie, Watson showed no frailties in winning a tense play-off against Jack Newton, nor in his Ryder Cup matches two years later. And again in 1977, during a historic week at Turnberry, Watson proved himself to be a man with nerves of tungsten. He and Nicklaus were paired together for the last two rounds. Nicklaus, the most formidable golfer the world has known, kept seizing an advantage of one, two or even three strokes. Every time Nicklaus went ahead Watson clawed his way back on to level terms. On the seventy-first hole Nicklaus faltered and the fresh-faced kid from Kansas had his freckled nose in front. By a titanic effort of will Nicklaus salvaged a birdie from the wreckage of a poor drive at the last hole. Watson topped it with an impeccably played birdie of his own.

That week Watson had a glimpse of his goal of golfing mastery. He has expressed his ambition like this: 'I am waiting for the day when everything falls into place, everything makes sense, when every swing is with confidence and every shot is exactly what I want.

'I know it can be done. I've been close enough to smell it a couple of times, but I'd like to touch it, to feel it. I know it's been touched. Hogan touched it. Byron Nelson touched it. I want to touch it. Then I think I would be satisfied. Then, I think, I could walk away from the game.'

Watson certainly smelled it on the last hole at Turnberry and the records show that he is getting closer. He has been the number one golfer in America (which means the world, in effect) for the past three years.

Watson is subject to the normal fluctuations of form, which appear rather more pronounced in his case because of his Charge of the Light Brigade approach to golf.

Most professionals can fiddle their way round in respectable figures when they lose their edge. The only way Watson knows to play the game is to go for the flag, a philosophy shared by the prodigious Spaniard Severiano Ballesteros. Golf courses are arranged so that such shots, unless executed perfectly, are punished most severely. When Watson is off his stick his scores zoom up to the 78–79 levels, but when he is sniffing close on the scent of that elusive quarry his golf is sublime. It happens about six times a year.

Will he ever fully achieve his ambition and hit every shot exactly the way he wants? The quest seems hopeless. Hogan did not come close to it. For one summer Byron Nelson approached nearer to it than anyone and the strain broke him; after winning eighteen tournaments in that one year he was physically sick and his nerve could not take any more. Watson might well surpass them both, possibly to the point of hitting one perfect shot in five. If he could achieve such a level of performance he would indeed be the greatest golfer of them all. But the world would not recognise him as such, because golfers are judged by their accumulation of victories and, at thirty, he does not have enough time left to crack the records. It is just as well that self-satisfaction will be reward enough for him. I hope he gets close enough to his impossible dream to enjoy his private triumph, for in his searchings along the way he has given enormous satisfaction to millions.

The Observer, July 1980

Nancy Lopez-Melton

Born 6 January 1957, Roswell, New Mexico, USA.

Of her first fifty tournaments Nancy Lopez-Melton won seventeen and at that point already ranked eleventh in the list of all-time money winners. She won the most US LPGA tournaments in both 1978 and 1979 and in the latter year set a stroke average record at 71.2 per round. Having at that time won $400,000, one of her main aims was to be the first woman to reach $1 million in tournament winnings.

This emphasis on money would be denied by most modern golfers, who place the emphasis on major championships as the ultimate measure of a man; but for women only the US Open carries major prestige – the British Open once did for women but only for amateurs, and the top Americans do not compete.

Super Mex
Dudley Doust

When Nancy Lopez holed her last putt on the final green at Hershey, Pennsylvania, last Sunday, the gallery exploded into cheers, and a woman spectator, wriggling free, sprinted across the green to accept the ball and a wan smile from Miss Lopez. It was all over. She had lost at last. Nancy Lopez, who had won five successive tournaments in America, finished way down the field in the Lady Keystone Open.

The world's golfing eyes had been fixed for weeks on the sturdy, dark-eyed young Mexican-American, and not surprisingly dozens of news and television men swarmed around when she failed. Was she disappointed not to have stretched her winning streak to six? Lopez sighed and grinned, revealing those wonderful white teeth. 'No,' she said, 'it only shows that I'm human and, God, that's all I want to be.'

Human she is, and this already has made her the most popular woman golfer since Babe Didrikson Zaharias after the Second World War. Lively, warm and generous, she is beloved by her fans and her foes. 'Nancy has everything,' says rival Jane Blalock, who doesn't lightly dispense praise. 'She is attractive, but not a sex symbol. She has talent, but isn't cocky. She has class. I just can't find it in me to be jealous.'

There is reason enough for jealousy. Over the last several weeks, since Lopez began her record run at the Baltimore Classic, she slowly, inexorably had begun to look invincible. She had won her five tournaments in just about every possible way: from five strokes back, from four in front, battling neck-and-neck to the wire and, again, after a sudden-death play-off. 'If that girl realizes how good she is,' says Lee Trevino, a fellow Mexican-American, 'they may never beat her again.'

At twenty-one Nancy already is being prematurely placed in such all-time company as Zaharias, Mickey Wright and perhaps even Britain's Joyce Wethered. It's cruel, but certainly no player, man or woman, has dominated a season so completely since Byron Nelson won eleven tournaments on the trot in 1945. Lopez's record this year is astonishing. In fifteen tournaments she has won seven times, finished in the top ten four more times, returned a stroke average of better than 72 a round and officially won $131,128. No player, of either sex, has won so much money so quickly in a Rookie year, and Nancy has three more tournaments before her year ends at the end of this month.

We have seen Lopez twice in Britain. In 1976 she won a singles and a foursome, not spectacularly, in the Curtis Cup matches at Lytham, and last summer, freshly turned professional, she was runner-up to Judy Rankin in the Colgate European Open at Sunningdale. She now looks a different player. Seeing her last weekend, one was struck first by her figure; gone is the baby fat. Since January she has trimmed from eleven stone six pounds to ten stone on a diet of fish, chicken and vegetables. As a result, she attacks the ball with a much fuller swing.

Above all, Lopez still has that 'touch' which is rare among women. Carol Mann, one of the nicest and most perceptive of women players, recently explained this elusive gift. 'The strongest part of Nancy's game is that she plays by feel. All her senses come into play. That's when golf is an art. She has a sense of self, and that's all you need, really.'

Nancy is totally composed, too, and generous of her time to a fault. At Hershey, for instance, she made four changes of clothing before teeing up for the second round, thus accommodating a *Sports Illustrated* cover photographer, and national television, who wanted her on the course in bright red slacks. Tired, dogged by a headache, she played poorly that day, showing a curious lapse in her sense of distance. Her caddie had an excuse. 'The flagsticks are two feet shorter than normal on this course,' he said, 'and that ruined her judgement of distance.'

Lopez made no excuses. The scribbles on her scorecard told the story: a rare star, signifying a birdie, and several picket fences drawn round a bad score. Nancy makes no apologies, either, for her swing which is anything but classical: arms out-stretched, hands too high in the takeaway, a little loop at the top. 'As long as your swing works, use it,' Trevino once told her. 'When it stops working, change.'

That piece of advice was offered when Lopez was twelve years old, when she burst on the world as a child prodigy by winning the New Mexico Women's Amateur Championship. She soon won two US girls' titles and, at eighteen, came second in the American Women's Open. Sensational as she was, chubby little Nancy never was warmly accepted in the exclusive clubs of her home town of Roswell, New Mexico. The bitterness lingers.

'Because I was a Mexican, there were a lot of Anglos in Roswell who weren't ready to accept the kind of golf I was playing,' she recently told *Time* magazine. 'Now a lot of them like to say they are my friends. But I don't feel I owe them my friendship because they didn't give me theirs when I was young. My parents gave me all the chances I ever needed.'

Nancy Marie Lopez was born on 6 January 1957, the daughter of Domingo, an autobody mechanic, and Marina Lopez. For their daughter they made enormous sacrifices. He put aside $100 a month for her golfing expenses, her mother excused her from the washing-up ('Our Nancy's hands were made for golf'), and when his daughter turned professional last summer after completing her second year at Tulsa University, Domingo sought and was granted a $50,000 bank loan to underwrite her fledgling years.

Nancy never needed it. As a pro, she went winging away, finishing second in her first three tournaments. Then tragedy struck. Her mother died unexpectedly at fifty-four from complications following an appendectomy. Nancy dropped out of the tour for a month, shattered. 'I'm lonely sometimes,' she says, 'a deep, hard lonely. The other day I looked into the crowd and saw a woman who looked just like my mother – same arms, same mouth. It hit me.'

There is, of course, another kind of lonely, one that chiefly arises within the clamour of crowds. Nancy Lopez recognizes it. 'I'm now going to dye my hair blond,' she said last Sunday, 'and then I'm going to get lost.' The next day, however, she was unlost, giving interviews, posing and preparing for the tournament that started yesterday in Indianapolis.

The Sunday Times, 2 July 1978

Severiano Ballesteros

Born 9 April 1957, Spain.

For twenty years Nicklaus has drawn the golf galleries as, successively, the most powerful and then the best golfer in the world. For much of this time Palmer was his competitor who, even when his great days were long past, was still followed by 'Arnie's Army'. There is not yet a 'Sevvy's Army', but he is regarded by all as golf's best hope of reviving the falling TV ratings. Watson is seen as Nicklaus's successor but he does not arouse awe, affection or compassion.

I recall Ballesteros playing in a British tournament about three years ago. He came to a hole some 400 yards long and refused to drive because players were still putting on the green. The stewards intimated that he should get on with it, that the green had never been driven. Ballesteros had his way; it was downwind and he knew that if he hit one flush he might reach. Indeed it is this élan in his hitting that has made him such a crowd pleaser, though more impressive still is his ability to get the ball close to the flag from all manner of unlikely places. And then to hole the putt.

His career so far has been fit for a *Boy's Own* story. Quite a few relative unknowns have led the US and British Opens after one round, have been content with their glorious moment and been heard of no more. Ballesteros was totally unknown when he led the 1976 Open by two strokes going into the final round, and then faded away, yet finished eagle, birdie to tie with Nicklaus for second place. He then proceeded to plunder the 1977 tournament season. When the 1979 Open began, Ballesteros was given no chance. All the pundits declared that at Royal Lytham you just had to keep the ball on the fairway. Ballesteros's driving was too erratic. Ballesteros proved them right – at least in part. Few were the fairways he hit and few the holes he failed to par. And then it was all climaxed by a drive into a car-parking area and another par.

In due course there followed Augusta, Georgia and the Masters, and Ballesteros with a dominant lead with just a few holes to go. Suddenly there came a five at a par three and then a half-hit iron shot into a stream. The temperature rose but the Spaniard, just past his twenty-third birthday, rallied and the green jacket was his.

That was two major championships under his belt and the golf world agog to see how he would fare in the US Open a couple of months later. Ballesteros got the next element in his life-script exactly right – disqualified amidst a buzz of comment that the Americans hated a foreigner winning in their own country and had stabbed the lad in the back with a technicality. (They had not. The USGA has a strict rule that if you start early or are not on the tee at your starting time, disqualification is automatic.)

What then does the future hold for Ballesteros? His talents could give him successes to equal Nicklaus's but I doubt that he has the solidity either of physique or of golf game to do so. If I'm wrong, he will be as good for golf as Vardon, Hagen, Jones and Palmer were in their day.

On to the world stage

Anon., *The Observer*

Until yesterday he had played as if leading a cavalry charge, flourishing his driver like a sabre, hacking with inspired aggression out of all the trouble his boldness brought him, daring the finest golfers in the world to match his pace. Then quite abruptly in the final round of the Open championship, young Severiano Ballesteros was no longer a leader but a quarry, panting and scrambling ahead of his betters, all but unnerved by the gathering heat of the pursuit.

The pain of his ordeal was viciously compounded by being paired with Johnny Miller, who turned that last round into a regal procession toward his first British Open title. As Ballesteros struggled, looking at last like a nineteen-year-old stumbling dishevelled from a dream of glory, Miller attacked Birkdale and the hopes of his rivals as uncompromisingly as a flamethrower. The cost of the Spaniard's six at the sixth hole and seven at the eleventh was multiplied by Miller's own birdies and most spectacularly by his eagle three at the thirteenth. All the time there was an almost palpable pressure bearing down on Ballesteros from the presence of a great player stimulated by the knowledge that this was his day.

It could so easily have become one of those small tragedies of sport, a trauma so profound that the victim would have been left scarred for life. Instead Ballesteros forced the wheel round full circle. First he compensated defiantly for that disaster at the eleventh by extorting birdies from the thirteenth and fourteenth and then, responding to Miller's sincere urgings, he recaptured his earlier exuberance and stormed the last two holes with an irresistible bravado that would have done credit to Audie Murphy on a good day.

The seventeenth fell to an eagle three, the eighteenth to a birdie four and, although Miller's brilliant shot-making had long since taken him far out of reach, Ballesteros had the immeasurable thrill of finishing in joint second place with Nicklaus. If he could not be the youngest champion since Young Tom Morris won at Prestwick in 1868, this was a wonderful next best. He had lived a lifetime in a handful of days, and made himself a genuine hero at the end of it all.

Some had argued that Ballesteros might go all the way because his youth and his background automatically prevented him from carrying the burden of strain borne by the other contenders in the field. He is part of the new tradition of peasant golfers from Spain (his father is a farm labourer near the course at Pedrena, where Severiano learnt the game while caddying to his brother Manuel, who is the Spanish Close champion) and, despite his obvious intelligence, his attitudes to money are still largely innocent. 'He cannot comprehend the enormity of a £1,000 deal with a golf clubs firm,' says his American manager, Ed Barner.

Such insulation against the consequences of winning must indeed have helped the prodigy to walk calmly toward the fire at lunch-time, but once out on the course Miller had his own way of making Ballesteros aware of the kind of contest he was engaged in.

Miller had been immensely complimentary after the third round, but showing through the seams of his praise had been a clear belief that this apprentice could be brought to heel before Saturday was over. 'I am going to catch him,' said Miller. 'He's a threat and I have respect for his game. He's got a lot of courage, maybe sometimes too much. He's not afraid to go out there and fire. He takes a good cut at it.' Then came the telling reference to the Spaniard's 'phenomenal' scrambling out of difficulties while Miller, with no greater waywardness, was being severely punished.

What the American seemed to be saying was that the final round would be another story, that the course could be expected to take some revenge on the young man who had treated it with so little reverence – and that he, Johnny Miller, would be around to take a personal vengeance.

It did not take us long to see that the action yesterday was to follow Miller's script. As early as the sixth Ballesteros must have known that the championship would not be his. What he had there was a moment of realization, not of resignation, but it was unmistakable and irrevocable nevertheless. That was where Miller went into the lead for the first time, and once in that position his domination of the Open grew rapidly beyond challenge.

At the following hole, the short seventh, he took a flawless, easy swing, and sent the ball to the heart of the green. Ballesteros smiled almost shyly at him, then biting his bottom lip in his habitual expression of concentration, fought his way to a matching three. His tenacity was maintained, but there can be little doubt that he knew as we did that second place was the best he could hope for from then on.

Such a finish could hardly be considered less than magnificent for a golfer at his stage of development, and the way he battled for it will remain, almost as much as the glittering achievements of Miller's climactic round, one of the lasting pleasures of this championship. His closing rally of eagle three and birdie four represented a triumph of skill and nerve to stand alongside any finish the Open has offered in more than a hundred years.

The crowd around the eighteenth green welcomed him into legend with a vast, warm-throated roar. In that moment he looked almost diffident again, a dark, extraordinarily handsome boy from the fields of Northern Spain, at the centre of a classically British scene that will never fade from his mind or from ours.

It is difficult to say how far he can go in the game from here. 'There can be a lot in golf for this boy,' Miller said last night. 'Apart from his power, he's got the pitching and putting to be a really good one. He's already a really good one. But I mean we could be hearing plenty from him right at the top level. If he had played more cautiously out there, maybe more like I did, taking irons off some tees, he might really have won. Yet, though it's easy for me to say so as the champion, I really believe it was a good thing for Sevvy that he lost.

'In 1971 I nearly took the Masters, but the best thing that could have happened for me then did happen. I came second. I was good enough to win the Masters then, but I wasn't ready to back it up. Sevvy will have many doors opened to him by coming second here. If he had won there would have been so much pressure on him he might have been swamped. This result is a plus for him, not a minus. He's got a great career ahead. He's got the golf to be a star and he's a terrific-looking fella, too, which does no harm.'

It is his approach to golf rather than his appearance that appeals to men. In action he strikes toward each shot with an impatient vigour, and when he strikes the ball it is with every ounce of power he can summon. His drives are uninhibited slashes and, though his basic swing has quality, that aggression often carries him off line. At Birkdale on Friday and yesterday he was constantly having to rescue his ball from mounds of willow scrub and hollows of rough.

Until yesterday he coped with those problems superbly, finding sufficient physical strength and technical resourcefulness to complement his bottomless morale. Even yesterday the morale withstood the barrage of his own mistakes and Miller's relentless excellence.

All the hours he gave to practice a few years back repaid him fully. 'Ten, twelve hours a day, this was normal,' he says. 'From ten years' old I am caddying for my brother Manolo, Saturdays and Sundays. When I am thirteen I shoot 65 when I win the caddie's championship of our region by sixteen shots.' He won the first of his two Spanish under-25 championships when just turned seventeen over his home course of Pedrena, the Bilbao Open, the Catalonian Open and the Tenerife Open, which do not attract touring pros. But he is already a seasoned competitor outside his own country. He failed in his first attempt to qualify for the American circuit, but he will surely be seen there to some effect soon enough.

The Observer, 11 July 1976

A prodigy continuing
Peter Dobereiner

In just two weeks, on 9 April, Severiano Ballesteros will celebrate his twenty-first birthday. He will spend the day playing the last round of the Masters at Augusta, Georgia, where it is the custom for the starter to introduce each player to the gallery with a review of his notable achievements during the past twelve months.

It will take a deep breath to complete the inventory: 'Swiss Open champion, French Open champion, Japanese Open champion,

Kenyan Open champion, winner of the British Uniroyal tournament, winner of the German Braun tournament, winner of the Japanese Phoenix tournament, winner of the New Zealand Otago Classic and, in partnership with Antonio Garrido, winner for the second year in succession of the World Cup.'

In the history of golf only three players, Byron Nelson, Ben Hogan and Sam Snead, can boast as many major victories in a year, and for a golfer to achieve such a record playing all over the world is quite unprecedented. It is no coincidence that all four of them came into golf through the hard apprenticeship of the caddies' pen.

If by some unlikely chance I found myself given the responsibility for distributing economic aid on behalf of the United Nations I would not waste my time looking at statistics for gross national products or per capita annual income. I would travel to the applicant country, go straight to the nearest golf course and count the number of urchins fighting for the privilege of carrying my bag. Ten of the little beggars? Right, then that will be ten billion dollars for the local exchequer. Spain and Portugal are the only European countries which would get a ha'penny out of me these days.

Five years ago, had I gone to Santander golf club in northern Spain, Severiano Ballesteros might have claimed my bag. He was a strapping lad and strong enough to subdue any rivals but he was not exactly a fanatic about humping twenty pounds of scrap iron over five miles of rough country.

It was not poverty which took him to the golf club so much as the lure of the game itself. His elder brother Manuel, a moderately successful tournament player, had given him an old 7-iron and taught him how to use it. Severiano earned his pocket money by chipping and pitching against the other boys as they waited for clients. Hour after hour, day after day, he played for five-peseta bets, pitching off concrete paths, or out of rough, cutting the ball up high or pushing it low into the target. In the evenings, in defiance of the club rule, he would sneak out to a quiet corner of the course and play a few holes.

When he won the annual caddies' tournament he was given special dispensation to play the course in the evenings, and a member became his patron. Within three years he was disputing the world's premier championship with Johnny Miller, thrilling the golf world with the power and foolhardy boldness of his play and devastating the teenage female population with his hundred-kilowatt smile. Perhaps it is just as well that he did not win that Birkdale Open, for too much success too soon might have destroyed him. As it is, his confidence sometimes borders on arrogance.

Experience was the deciding factor at Birkdale. Miller played a canny last round, knowing when to play safe and when to apply the pressure. Ballesteros played full throttle all the way, as he always does.

Today things are rather different. Miller's swing, the product of the country club teaching tee, is slightly out of tune and he is struggling. Ballesteros has never had a long game to compare with the accuracy of Miller's but he does have that precious legacy from his caddie days, the ability to get the ball close to the hole from the unlikeliest places.

Luckily for us Ballesteros is not going to take the logical step of transferring himself to the American circuit, at least not just yet. He is a Spaniard before he is a golfer and does not relish the idea of spending most of his time in a country where he does not speak the language and separated from his friends and family. Besides, he resents the requirement to go to school and demonstrate his ability to play golf before being permitted to compete on the US circuit. It is easy to sympathize with this view since there is hardly a player of note in America who has not finished behind him.

Possibly he could win more money in America, but that is a slightly academic point for a youngster whose income over the past twelve months was equivalent to a first dividend on the pools in a good week. He prefers to try and repeat his triumphant routine of 1977, playing in Britain and Europe with occasional forays farther afield.

It is scarcely conceivable that he could have quite such a good year again, although his last-round 66 on a course as tough as Muthaiga to win the Kenyan Open was a recent reminder of the dangers of setting a limit to his talents and to his will. He believes he can win every tournament he plays and that absurd notion is just what makes a champion.

His exploits last year made a profound impression on some of his fellow professionals. Tony Jacklin, for instance, watched Ballesteros's progress and it persuaded him to return to Britain and Europe for this season. Bob Charles also did some mental calculations and decided that golf on this side of the Atlantic offered a more attractive proposition than the grind of the US circuit. Graham Marsh is wavering. He was once the number one world traveller, racking up a fortune without playing in America, and I would not be surprised to see him back. Dale Hayes could be another prodigal son.

Some twenty years ago Arnold Palmer took American golf by storm and in the process he led the professional game into a new era of affluence and popularity. Severiano Ballesteros is no evangelist for British and European golf. He is motivated by self-interest as much as everyone else in the game, and more than most. But he has many of the qualities of the young Palmer, and pro golf could well be drawn along in his slipstream.

At the very least, he has made people stop and question the assumption that the grass is greener on the other side of the fence. That is a start. I would just love to see him with ten tournaments this year, including that one on his twenty-first birthday.

The Observer, March 1978

PART II
MISCELLANY

All collections of writing tend to centre on one or two particular themes. To finish, here is a selection with just one thing in common: good writing.

Vacancy

Sir Walter Simpson

Excessive golfing dwarfs the intellect. Nor is this to be wondered at when we consider that the more fatuously vacant the mind is, the better for play. It has been observed that absolute idiots play the steadiest. An uphill game does not make them press, nor victory within their grasp render them careless. Alas! we cannot all be idiots. Next to the idiotic, the dull unimaginative mind is the best for golf. In a professional competition I would prefer to back the sallow, dull-eyed fellow with a 'quid' in his cheek, rather than any more eager-looking champion. The poetic temperament is the worst for golf. It dreams of brilliant drives, iron shots laid dead, and long putts holed, whilst in real golf success waits for him who takes care of the foozles and leaves the fine shots to take care of themselves...

When a putter is waiting his turn to hole-out a putt of one or two feet in length, on which the match hangs at the last hole, it is of vital importance that he think of nothing. At this supreme moment he ought studiously to fill his mind with vacancy. He must not even allow himself the consolations of religion. He must not prepare himself to accept the gloomy face of his partner and the derisive delight of his adversaries with Christian resignation should he miss. He must not think that it is a putt he would not dream of missing at the beginning of the match, or, worse still, that he missed one like it in the middle. He ought to wait calm and stupid till it is his turn to play and putt as I have told him how – neither with undue haste nor with exaggerated care. When the ball is down, and the putter handed to the caddy, it is not well to say, 'I couldn't have missed it.' Silence is best. The pallid cheek and trembling lip belie such braggadocio.

The Art of Golf, David Douglas, 1887

Golfers are more prone to curse their clubs and balls than praise them. These authors argue that a different attitude can pay better dividends.

Love the ball

Lawrence Morehouse and Leonard Gross

Your attitude towards the ball affects the flight of the ball when you hit it with an implement. If you're batting and you think of the ball as an antagonistic object coming your way to make a fool of you, your tendency will be to conquer it by hitting it as hard as you can. With that attitude, you're more apt to miss the ball; you have no control over where it's going, and even if you hit it hard it's not a gratifying, harmonious experience. The ball is your partner, not your enemy. It wants to succeed as much as you do. It wants to fly as far and as straight as it was designed to.

You and the ball are one in the system of golf. It's an extension of you, just as the club is an extension of your arm. Help it take a long ride. Help it set down gently. Help it find the hole. Feel the hole welcoming the ball.

The next time you're on a driving range, experiment with the different reaction you get with 'unfriendly' and 'friendly' balls. Dump a bucket of balls into two piles, one 'friendly' and the other 'unfriendly'. Pick up an 'unfriendly' ball, put it on a tee, tell it you hate it and you're going to murder it. Then proceed to kill it. Now take a ball from the 'friendly' pile, and address the ball as though you're going to give it a lovely ride. It's your messenger in effect. It's working for you, and you're working for it. Pick a reasonable target and send it off. After you've hit a dozen 'unfriendlies', and another dozen 'friendlies', notice what's happening. Hitting the unfriendlies you're most likely clutching the club too hard and trying to push your muscles at the ball, in spite of the fact that muscles can only pull. Your swing is anxious, because you want to get the ball before the ball gets you. Your muscle action with the friendlies, by contrast, is graceful and rhythmic. Your timing is good. You're letting the forces summate naturally and harmoniously, so that the clubhead gradually develops the maximum acceleration, the shaft bends as it gives in to the pressure of the ball, the ball compresses, recoils and flies out to your mutual target.

Maximum Performance, Granada, 1978

The main reason for American dominance in both amateur and professional golf is undoubtedly that a very great number of people play the game and all derive from an intensely competitive society. But the courses that people grow up on have something to do with it too. As a left-hander I believe I know the answer to the question: why are there so few good left-handers when the brood produces its fair share of outstanding tennis players, boxers, cricketers, while left-sided footballers are much in demand? It's the courses.

All are designed from the perspective of a right-hander with the result that as we left-handers stand on the tee at a par three, we seem required to yank the ball around our bodies to project it there, while on other holes the fairway similarly requires us to try to hook the ball round or else line up at an angle.

This author discusses a feature of American courses he believes contributes to US dominance.

Water

Peter Dobereiner

Water is the golfer's enemy in the matter of hazards, much more so in America than elsewhere. American golf architects use water for tactical and aesthetic purposes to great effect. The flattest and most unpromising site is transformed by digging lakes and using the spoil to contour the land and build tees and greens. The courses which result certainly introduce an element which is lacking in many older British clubs.

There is a finality about having your ball splash into a lake which can never be duplicated by the roughest rough or the densest woods. The sight of water is enough to make the golfer grip his club a little more tightly, to swing a little quicker and a little harder. And if the architect has done his work with due cunning these unconscious reactions will be enough to dispatch the ball into the drink.

In some cases – and Pebble Beach with its run of holes along the rocky ocean shore, and most especially the dreaded eighteenth is a notable example – the anticipation of water to come can throw a golfer's swing out of kilter. If a golfer is brought up on courses where card-wrecking water hazards exert their unique threats on seven or eight holes, a fair average for modern American layouts, then he

179

must learn to control his nerves and his swing if he is to survive.

I believe that this constant exposure to water is a contributing factor, a minor tributary if you will, to what I accept as the fact of American superiority as competitors. I do not believe that the general run of American professionals are superior strikers to their British and Continental counterparts. Indeed, I tend toward the view that there are more indifferent strikers in American pro golf than there are in Europe. Where the Americans score is in their almost fanatical commitment to the game.

It is rare to see a disinterested shot played during an American tournament. The man in sixtieth place is busting his guts to finish fifty-ninth, whereas in Britain and Europe it is patently obvious that half the field is interested only in finishing the round and getting the hell out of here.

Of course there are exceptions. We have young players who are just as dedicated, just as keen to practise and improve, but they are in the minority. So in the continuing debate on what is wrong with British and European golf I would like to suggest that in addition to better courses, better practice facilities, better competition, we might consider taking a little more water with our golf.

There are few courses in my experience which would not be improved by the addition of a few water hazards. Maybe it is not possible to reproduce the high-voltage shock of standing on the sixteenth tee at Cypress Point facing a 220-yard carry across the foaming Pacific, but it is surprising what a tingle can be produced by a modest pond in the right place. Water is the stuff to turn boys into men.

The Observer, 22 January 1978

Company golf outings, appearance money, hotel expenses, retainers, advertising sponsorship, the name on a golf club – all are part of the commercialism that has increased apace since Mark McCormack grasped that Arnold Palmer was a name which could be marketed in all manner of ways as he became *the* leading American sportsman in about 1960.

The name of a superstar on your golf club adds a percentage to its price and seldom does the star have anything to do with the birth of the project, other than supply a specimen of his signature. It came to me as a surprise that one of them, David Graham, does actually do the job himself and a name duly appears on the back of the blade – Jack Nicklaus!

Of course, we do not, most of us, believe that X or Y actually designed our implements but the knowledge that X or Y really does play with them is strangely comforting – we do know that they can be used effectively.

For the superstar comes the problem that he is often contracted to use the clubs of different manufacturers as he jets his way around the world, in part the topic of the piece that follows.

Tony Jacklin's new companion
John Ballantine

When Tony Jacklin reappears on the British golfing scene in his first home tournament in May, which will be either the Martini at Epsom or the Colgate PGA Championship at Royal Birkdale, he will be accompanied by a strange-looking figure. The stranger is not a thing of flesh and blood, however, but an advertising symbol as blatant as the stick figure with a halo that the detective novelist Leslie Charteris used to push the sales of 'The Saint'.

Jacklin's 'companion' is the trademark of an American manufacturer in Arizona whose clubs Jacklin now uses in place of the British 'sticks' with which he won the British and US Open titles in that marvellous and memorable calendar year of July 1969 to June 1970.

The story of Jacklin's defection from Dunlop to Ping, or from pounds to dollars in the last year, personifies the key clue in the mystery of the great little Englishman's unparalleled decline and fall in the Royal and Ancient game. It is a story of bitterness and triumph, of optimism and accusations of lack of loyalty, of commercial jealousy and prag- matism; in short, a summing-up perhaps of the attributes of the game itself.

From the time that he started on the tournament trail in 1964, Jacklin used Dunlop clubs. In 1967 he achieved fame as the smiling black-haired twenty-two-year-old who won the Dunlop Masters at Royal St George's with a hole in one on television. In 1968 he became a national hero as the first Briton to win a modern US tournament, at Jacksonville in Florida. He followed this up by winning the Open at Royal Lytham St Anne's, his 160-yard walk down the centre of the last fairway, after he had hit the green with what was obviously the winning stroke, being as triumphal a procession as that of any Caesar in Rome after a victorious winner.

His admirers watched their TV screens with choking pride in the next June as 'Jacko' won the US Open at Hazeltine, Minnesota, by a stunning seven shots. Who can forget that arrogant James Cagney look when he canned the thirty-five footer on the last green? Our overwhelming feeling was: Here's a chap who can beat the Yanks on their own midden.

Jacklin became not only painfully famous but painfully rich; fitting out his big houses, Hollywood-style, with wall-to-wall carpeting and power-driven shower baths, first at Elsham, near Scunthorpe, Lincolnshire, then at his stately hilltop home at Winchcombe in the Cotswolds. He reduced the hillside behind the house to build an indoor swimming pool, built himself a personal driving range, and yet was so *nouveau riche* that he didn't really know exactly what he owned. I recall his asking one of his retainers what a line of sheds on his property was for. 'Eee, Master Tony, they're for the machinery and the garden tools.'

The organisation set up by Mark McCormack, a lawyer from Cleveland, Ohio, to help sporting prodigies like Arnold Palmer, Rod Laver and Jacklin to cash in on success and public acclaim, brought in staggering sums from endorsements, advertising, writings and guarantees. I asked Jacklin once whether it was worth paying the substantial percentage. 'It's a matter of getting a percentage of millions or of thousands,' he said frankly.

Throughout all that, Jacklin, although far busier, remained a likeable, wisecracking, entertaining, faithful friend. About his move to tax exile in Jersey in 1972 his argument that 'I've only got ten or twelve more years at the top, and don't want them to take eighty-five per cent' was irrefutable. But his game suddenly went sour, and from then until now, that has been a source of constant discussion and disappointment, especially to the golfing press, who suddenly saw their golfing golden goose turned to straw.

Jacklin left the US tour, then returned; did appallingly badly one year, even in the Masters; persuaded willing critics that he'd got his game back, and then as abruptly and frustratingly lost it. Alibis, alibis.

Last winter he began experimenting with the American clubs. After some misgivings he grew genuinely to like them, and a bonus scheme for performances was an added incentive. He was under contract to Dunlop for a far higher annual increment than is paid to almost any professional in America, to use the British clubs everywhere but in America. It was rumoured that Jacklin had wanted Dunlop to extend his contract worldwide, but that this was rejected. Even so, his defection induced alarm and despondency; one British executive criticized me for mentioning it in print. Expediency and patriotism, he implied, came before news.

Another problem was that golf clubs, unlike tennis rackets, must be changed carefully. Brian Barnes, for instance, tried the same American clubs here last winter, but refused to practise with them, arguing with strange logic: 'I don't want to get too used to them because it would be more difficult to revert to my Slazengers back in England.'

Using the American clubs, Jacklin nearly won the Bing Crosby event at Pebble Beach, California, last January, and his caddie, Scotty Gilmour, told me, admittedly with the caddie's eternal optimism: 'He's never hit the ball better.' So were the clubs the keys to new success? Alas, Jacklin did little else all year.

A row blew up when he returned home. At the Benson and Hedges Festival in York, he was criticized for carrying his US clubs in a Dunlop bag. Did he want to show some loyalty, however misguided, toward the British company, or had they asked him to do so? It is anybody's guess. The next time he appeared on TV in a British tournament, he had his new clubs in an American bag. Dunlop could have sued him for breach of contract, but the publicity would have hurt. It was all settled reasonably and amicably behind the scenes.

Last month, Jacklin got back to very nearly his best form, again in the Crosby, where he finished joint eighth and won a total of £4,200. In the first round in San Diego last week, however, he scored a disastrous 77, dropping five strokes in two holes. 'He went mad, hooking a 6-iron down a bank, and then hitting out of bounds over a cliff,' groaned Gilmour. A second round 73 could not save him.

Jacklin and Dunlop appear to have reached a diplomatic agreement for the coming British and European season that the player's name should not appear on the American bag. This gentleman's agreement, if true, could boomerang on Dunlop, for Jacklin's massive white bag will bear a symbolic figure as distinctive and increasingly well known as Donald Duck.

The Sunday Times, 12 February 1978

The all-round sportsman and the 'ordinary' golfer have occupied little space in this book, although there are some events on the golf calendar when an amateur player can arouse more interest than the pros – if he's celebrated far and wide as comedian, singer, politician, actor...

Once there, our ordinary golfers will hope for words of comfort and advice from their companions. Alas, as Norman Mair and the late Patrick Campbell explain, it is not always so.

Of games and golf
Norman Mair

The tall and friendly stranger fell into step with me among the gallery following in the wake of Bernard Gallacher during the 1967 Youths' championship at Copt Heath. 'How is that electric blanket of yours doing then?'

The Murrayfield blanket is, of course, one of the wonders of the sporting world; and, though none too pleased at thus having my attention diverted from the business in hand, I nodded enthusiastically: 'It really is marvellous – it means we can get cracking no matter what the weather and it is so much less bother than all that business with straw and braziers...'

He looked at me, as I thought, very oddly. And did not reply. At lunch my wife – we had been married some six months – pointed him out to me as having been a guest at our wedding. I did not have to ask what he and his wife had given us by way of a present.

Such an occasional crossing of the wires is, I suppose, an inevitable hazard of being interested in, and associated with, more than one sport. Yet, for myself, I think a love of other games, if anything, sharpens a man's appreciation of golf. For instance, you recognize more readily that there is more than one form of courage.

I remember in my student days playing cricket for Edinburgh University against Durham University, who had a fast bowler – then almost wholly unknown – by name of Frank Tyson. My fellow opening bat survived perilously, for an over or two, this totally unexpected and hair-raising experience, then was comprehensively castled, the air alive with spinning stumps and flying bails. Whereupon he turned and ran like the wind all the way back to the pavilion.

'What's the hurry?' his colleagues asked, as he clattered up the pavilion steps.

'I was afraid,' he explained, peering fearfully back over his shoulder, 'I might be given not out!'

Save that the cry of Fore! may not always come in time and that there are golfers whose rapturous practice-swing is always liable to catch the unsuspecting the mother and father of an upper-cut, golfers are not obviously exposed to physical danger.

Bob Charles is indisputably a devil of a chap to tackle in his own New Zealand, as the like of Arnold Palmer and Tony Jacklin have found to their cost. But it is still not quite the same as arriving to play rugby against the All Blacks.

'Is it true,' the New Zealand press reputedly inquired of Bryan Thomas, the alleged hard man of Welsh rugby, 'that you have come to New Zealand to sort out Colin Meads?'

'Not me!' exclaimed Thomas. 'I want to die in Wales...'

Yet, in a different way, as much or more is required in the way of guts to hole the kind of agonizing short putts that Brian Huggett sank on the seventeenth and eighteenth greens in his match against Billy Casper on the last day of the 1969 Ryder Cup at Birkdale – believing as he did, alas erroneously, that he was putting for an overall and overdue British victory.

There is a close analogy between kicking goals in rugby and holing putts in golf. And when, like the writer, you have missed a penalty goal from almost straight in front to lose a comparatively important representative match, you are that much less likely to write, of a three-footer in the realm of golf, that the player in question 'had only...'

Jack Nicklaus – who, at Wentworth in the autumn of 1970, greatly surprised me by observing that even if it hadn't been golf, he would still probably have turned professional at some other sport – was a promising place-kicker in American football in his youth. However, when I think of Nicklaus in terms of courage, it is of the Old Course and the Road Hole in his Open Championship play-off with Doug Sanders.

Earlier in the round, that masterly American golf writer, Herb Warren Wind, and I had agreed that the winning of the Open that day could presage for Nicklaus – who had not won a major title since the 1967 American Open – a kind of second coming.

Four strokes ahead with five holes to play, Nicklaus was now only a shot in front. And Sanders' cunning 5-iron had escaped by a whisker the veritable whirlpool of green and sand that is the Road Bunker to finish some eighteen feet past the flag. As Nicklaus settled to his approach, the world shrank to a man, a green and his ball. In my ear, Herb Warren Wind prophesied softly: 'Jack's career has reached a turning point, a crisis. . .'

Nicklaus' answer was a 7-iron, sumptuously struck, inside Sanders. A stroke which, whenever I play the Road Hole, seems still to linger in the air.

Jack Nicklaus himself tends to make light of that unflinching riposte. 'My lead was slipping, but I was still playing well. And so long as I was still confident, it was not that difficult a shot.'

He did something similar later in the season in that unforgettable final of the Piccadilly World Match-Play Championship at Wentworth. Having played the first twenty-seven holes in 98 strokes – 33, 33, 32 – he was twelve under par and five up on Lee Trevino. Nevertheless, by the thirty-third there was only one hole in it and Trevino, having greened a glorious 3-iron, was home in two. Nicklaus – just when almost any other golfer would have been about to crack wide open, his lead evaporating, his opponent rampant – replied with as lovely a 4-iron as a man may hit. And, for good measure, holed the putt for an eagle.

It is, for all the milling crowds of great championships, a lonely courage that golf demands. Though he carried a nation on his shoulders, was ever a mortal more alone than Tony Jacklin as, with a two-stroke lead over Bob Charles, he shaped to the drive from the seventy-second tee of the 1969 Open, the terrain before him pitted with lost hopes yet framed in the swelling optimism of a vast multitude?

Golfers of fibre come in so many different temperaments from the highly combustible Tommy Bolt – whose clubs, so swears Paul Hahn, have got in more flying time than the average Pan-Am pilot – to so engagingly resilient a character as Fred Daly, who has the Irishman's traditional ability to improvise whether it be on the links or in repartee.

Some time ago, a brother member of the Fourth Estate happened to come across Fred Daly in a golf outing. Afterwards, in the bar, Daly amiably questioned my friend: 'With a grip like that, I don't imagine you're normally very straight?'

'As a matter of fact, in my own golfing circle, I am rated remarkably straight. . .'

'With a grip like that,' pursued Daly, 'I don't suppose you hit it very far?'

'Actually, my chums reckon me surprisingly long...'

'I suppose,' said Daly blandly, 'you play an awful lot of golf?'

'In point of fact,' came the reply, not without a certain smug satisfaction, 'I hardly play at all...'

'Well,' exclaimed Fred triumphantly, 'the more you play, the worse you'll b—— well get!'

It is often said, with much justification, that professional golfers are the new élite of the sporting firmament. Nonetheless, if the odd one does succumb to delusions of grandeur, many remain refreshingly down to earth.

None more so than Eric Brown, for all his deserved Ryder Cup fame and other exploits. Recently a chap I know chanced upon Eric Brown shortly after the Ryder Cup captain and his family had moved from Bearsden in Glasgow through to Edinburgh.

'This,' indicated Eric, with a jerk of his thumb, 'is my new house. Do you like it?'

The other was visibly impressed. 'It looks terrific – and you know, Eric, this is a very select district.'

'We will,' promised Eric cheerfully, 'damn soon change that!'

A great competitor in his heyday when in the mood – for all that he is so highly strung – Eric Brown has always been quick to anger. And seldom minded who knew it. But he has always had, too, the ability to laugh at himself.

Once when he was a professional in the south, a retired Colonel stumped into his shop and deliberated between the tray of tees priced at a penny each and those at a halfpenny. In the fullness of time, he selected one solitary halfpenny tee.

Eric Brown was genuinely outraged. 'No Scot,' he told that military gentleman indignantly, 'would have had the brass effrontery to do that. No sir! – no matter how long he had to scrub round on his knees to find one!'

One of the best of all rugby stories is that of the French referee whose control of a match involving a British team was sadly handicapped by the language barrier. Finally, after several warnings given with the aid of much Gallic gesticulation, he sent the worst offender off.

'Get stuffed!' advised the said transgressor warmly.

'Zee apologee,' insisted the referee firmly, 'eez too late...'

Yet, though the game is spreading, rugby has not yet developed globally to anything like the same extent as golf, to whom almost no frontier is closed. Consequently, for one who spends his winters reporting rugby, one of the great pleasures of the world of golf is the positively cosmopolitan conglomeration of a major championship.

The much-loved Roberto de Vincenzo's rendering of the tongue that Shakespeare spake is essentially his own; but I have known him, more improbably for a South American, even have problems in making himself understood in Spain – most memorably when, in the 1965 World Cup in Madrid, he hooked out of bounds and an over-zealous official refused to let him back on the course without a ticket.

With the coming of the holiday package deal, you don't have to be either fabulously rich or a world-class golfer 'to follow the sun'. It is not so easy for those – for example, that wonderfully accomplished shot maker, Neil Coles – who have a rooted aversion to flying; but then they can always emulate the famous boxer – the entertaining Terry Downes, if memory serves me aright – who always preferred to go by sea on the very logical grounds that 'while I can swim a bit, I can't fly at all'.

Golf spans the generations, from the astonishing octogenarian Mrs Charlotte Beddows, who was still reporting for regular lessons when well past her eightieth birthday, from Gordon Durward, 1970s Club Professional of the Year, down to that fetching little sprite, the seven-year-old Bridget Gleeson, who has already been round her native Killarney off the LGU tees in a gross one hundred and whose passion for the game is such that in 1969 she contrived 362 days golf out of a possible 365.

Not many games so readily as golf bridge the generation gap – though it is part of Scottish legend how Harry Haddock, the Clyde left back, when congratulating Stanley Matthews at the end of an international in which the ageing maestro had given him the run-around, made the immortal sally: 'Why don't you pick on someone your own age?'

Cricketers also, admittedly, have been known to enjoy careers of remarkable longevity – Jack Hobbs making, after all, a hundred centuries after his fortieth birthday. But reminders of the fleeting years are apt to come earlier and rather more humiliatingly than in golf – though victims of the twitch might disagree.

For my own part, I recollect with painful clarity the afternoon that finally persuaded me that the time was nigh when, as a participant, I should be well advised to devote my summers exclusively to golf. Thrice a ball from a bowler, whose victims over the years had included batsmen of world renown, was cut narrowly past me in the gully.

'Would you,' asked our wicket-keeper captain of the perspiring bowler, 'like gully squarer?'

'Not squarer,' retorted the bowler bitterly, 'but younger!'

Mark you, cricket and golf have more than a little in common – sharing, to cite but one obvious example, a degree of euphemism worthy almost of angling. The sort of careful phraseology epitomized by Sir J. M. Barrie's classic observation: 'In the first innings, I made nought not out, in the second I was not so successful.'

The only other sex that as yet we have play golf. And the image of the golfers of the distaff side as grunting creatures, hirsute and only with the greatest of reluctance not on all fours, is certainly no longer valid, if it ever was.

Most of them, too, take commendable trouble with their golfing attire even if the widespread introduction of slacks and Bermuda shorts cannot be a uniformly good thing, since that is, so to speak, a sphere in which, undeniably, some have larger handicaps than others.

Again, they can be alarmingly temperamental. Indeed, my wife still tells of the occasion she was playing in an open stroke-play competition and holing putt after putt – to the growing disgust of the girl with whom she was paired, whose token congratulations had long since died in her throat.

At last there came a time when the girl could stand the sight no longer: 'Hole just one more putt,' she hissed through clenched teeth, 'and I'll slap your face.'

The awe inspired by officialdom in women's golf does not always derive from exceptional administrative ability, far less golfing prowess. Not so long ago a couple of our more gifted young fillies were playing with an embattled matriarch of markedly inferior skill.

To their mingled horror, amazement and glee, she succeeded in depositing her drive smartly between her legs into the tangled rough adjoining the tee. Mercifully, she had not the foggiest notion where the ball had gone; and, frightened to tell her, the girls solemnly joined in the search a flattering 150 yards from the tee.

Not only does golf belong to both sexes and all generations but its exponents come in all shapes and sizes. From Frank Sinatra – to whom, in the singer's younger and skinnier days, Bob Hope wished to attach a red flag preparatory to putting him on duty in the hole – to those like the writer whose best irons are all too patently the knife and fork.

The curse of modern golf, it is often averred, is slow play; but, if it is getting worse, it is no new malaise. For was not the incomparable Bernard Darwin moved to observe tartly that 'golf is not a funeral, though both can be very sad affairs'. Of course, golfing galleries, even when irritated beyond belief by golfers whose activities on the green would be hard pressed to keep pace with coastal erosion, would seldom, if ever, dream of giving vent to their feelings, as did a gentleman one afternoon at Edgbaston when a cricketing companion of mine had taken root at the wicket.

'Whatever else you die of,' opined the aforesaid frustrated spectator in a voice of thunder, 'it won't be from a stroke!'

To practise a team game one so often needs either others or plenty of imagination. One afternoon, nearly a decade ago, I chanced, in the height of summer, to stroll across a famous rugby ground whose boundary wall fronts an asylum.

Although it was June, the First XV scrum-half was there, stripped to the waist and armed with a cluster of elderly rugby balls he periodically dipped in a bucket of water, before bouncing each ball against the wall and whipping it away to an imaginary stand-off.

Over the wall peered, with frank amazement, a long line of the inmates – obviously wondering just what on earth they had done to be put away. But no one looks askance at a golfer practising – not even, nowadays, in Britain.

It is sometimes said that only when he stands at the altar on his wedding day does a man experience quite the same sensation of impending doom as he feels each week on the first tee of a Sunday morning. In truth, others are much less interested in our golf than we incline to think they are.

Not that the matches fore and aft do not sometimes add to the store of memory. In fact, only recently, I happened across my own account of the day, immediately following the 1968 Curtis Cup at Royal County Down, that four itinerant golf writers sampled that majestic links. Among them myself.

We had come to the short seventh, measuring somewhere around 130 yards. One of our number, burly and bespectacled, hit what he modestly deemed a perfect shot, which that mischievous green shrugged off with a light laugh.

'There is,' he cried, wrathfully, 'no way to stay on that green!'

We left the tee arguing the pros and cons of links golf in general and the merits of that short seventh in particular.

The small gaggle of women playing immediately behind us included that marvellously repetitive technician, Mrs Jessie Valentine, six times Scottish champion, thrice British. Off the eighth tee, I let fly. 'By Jove,' yelped the bespectacled one, 'a hole-in-one.'

I must say I was surprised, for the eighth stretches some 425 yards and, despite a wider arc and a resolve to get a little more right hand into the shot, it seemed unlikely that I should have suddenly uncovered an additional 200 or so yards. Nonetheless, while it lasted, it was a pleasing thought, not sullied by the faintest knowledge of where the devil my ball had gone.

Wheeling round, I was, though too late to see the tee shot from the ladies behind cavorting merrily into the hole at the short seventh, in plenty of time to join in the spontaneous applause. 'That,' we pointed out to our disgruntled companion, 'is one very good way of staying on the seventh green!'

He, though, was now smiling happily. 'That is the first time I have seen a hole-in-one actually going into the hole. I did not,' he added, making his point neatly, 'see my own.'

The Golfers' Bedside Book, Donald Steel (ed.), Batsford, 1971

Pro-Ams
Patrick Campbell

Sooner or later, as the player advances along the narrow fairways leading to Scratchdom, he will probably find himself assisting professional golfers to win serious money in pro-amateur tournaments, the most socially glittering of which is the Bowmaker Tournament at Sunningdale.

Here, the professional plays thirty-six holes medal, so that he puts in three scores – one off his own bat, one his best ball with Amateur A, and one his best ball with Amateur B.

It often takes Amateurs A and B several hours of patient listening and questioning to understand the system, but an example usually makes all clear.

If the pro takes five at the first, which he usually does, and Amateurs

A and B take four and six respectively, the three cards will read:

Pro: 5
Pro plus A: 4
Pro plus B: 5

From this it will be seen that while the amateur can improve the pro's score, he cannot make it any worse, a comfort to the amateur when quick hooking breaks out, if not to the pro.

Last year at Sunningdale, on his own card, the pro stood to win £350, and with one of the amateurs £250, so that the pro has a sympathetic interest in his partner's progress. One year, playing with Ugo Grappasoni, from the Villa d'Este, I discovered how sympathetic this interest could be.

We played the first nine holes in complete silence owing, as I thought, to Ugo's failure to come to grips with the English language. I wanted to speak to him, as I wasn't playing very well. When I got one off the tee that finished on the fairway I put the next one into the woods. When I got one off the tee that finished in the woods I picked it up.

Ugo watched these enervating activities with a cold black eye that put me in mind of vendettas and the Mafia's revenge.

Held up briefly on the ninth, I decided to take a chance on speech. I asked him if, perhaps, I was doing something fractionally wrong. The right hand creeping a shade too far underneath? A minute fault in the stance – the ball, perhaps, half an inch too far back?

Ugo made his first and last observation of the day. 'Isa ponch, ponch,' he said. 'Isa noh swing. Isa whole t'ing isa noh good.'

That's the kind of discovery the budding Scratchman is liable to make when he moves up into the big time. Isa whole t'ing isa noh good. And the professionals do not hesitate to tell him so, with £250 slipping out of their hands into the bushes.

I played a year later with Leopoldo Ruiz, the Thin Crust of Bread from the Argentine.

In the first round Leopoldo, taking a 2-iron off the tee and hitting all of them 270 yards, notched a spirited 65, unassisted in any way whatever by myself.

In the second round, however, he got a bad kick with his pitch to the seventh and found an unplayable lie in a small bush at the back of the green. He prowled round it for some time with cries of, 'Carramba!' and 'Mamma mia!', had a hack at it, knocked it into the deep bunker on the left and finished with a seven. Things began to go wrong from then on until, after failing to get anything like a three at the short fifteenth, Leopoldo abandoned hope. He turned to me with charming Latin-American courtesy. 'Now,' he growled, 'I play no blahdy good, same like you.'

How to Become a Scratch Golfer, Blond, 1963

Wild slice or hook, the thinned shot that disfigures a ball and flying clods of earth are the province of the high handicapper, but worse than all these is the shank or socket.

It usually appears from nowhere at the worst of times: a fine drive has been struck and all that is left is a short pitch to the green. Out comes the wedge or 9-iron, a deft practice swing and away your ball shoots at right angles. Golfers of all standards have experienced the ire and chagrin that ensue.

An Attack of Socketing
Bernard Darwin

People who talk too much about their ailments are justly deemed to be bores. Yet there are one or two complaints the mention of which will, as a rule, produce a general and spirited conversation. If, for instance, one had anything the matter with one's knee or back and says so in company, one is at once overwhelmed by advice as diverse as it is sympathetic, since every one of the auditors knows the one man in the world who can cure knees and backs as if by magic. Similarly in the case of golfing ailments almost every golfer has at some time or another had an attack of the fearful disease called 'socketing', and will take his part in the talk if the latest victim starts the subject. Some, indeed, refrain not so much because they think the topic tiresome as because they think it too dreadful. Having been stricken and cured, they wish to forget all about the attack lest the mere thought of it should bring a recurrence. Such people had better skip the rest of this article, because I propose to describe a short, or at least I hope short, and severe attack of socketing which lately befell a golfer whose game I know better than I do anyone else's in the world.

This golfer, who has played the game now for a depressingly long time, has never been seriously troubled by socketing. He once had a mild visitation, in consequence of which he bought a crook-necked mashie and mashie-niblick supposed to make impossible the hitting of a non-existent socket. He grew so fond of them that he has played with them ever since – that is, for twelve or thirteen years – and, in cases of extreme mental anguish, has even gone so far as to putt with the mashie. Just once, for the space of a shot or two, he discovered that it was possible to socket with the socketless club, but he had been practically immune from the disease. Suddenly, like a thunderbolt out of a blue sky, it descended on him.

I believe that pride nearly always comes before a fall in such cases, and my golfer was playing, or thought he was playing, rather well with that crook-necked mashie. He was hitting the ball with plenty of 'nip' and confidence: he was in a complacent state of mind and inclined to take liberties. One day he went out into the field next door to his house to play a few shots for air and exercise. He had on a good many clothes, and his braces felt rather tight, but what did that matter? He knew he could hit the ball, and for a few minutes he did hit it so accurately that he was lost in admiration of the perfect grouping of the bails in the smallest possible space at just the point he was aiming at. Then without the least warning a ball sped skimming the grass in the direction of cover-point. He laughed – a little uneasily and artificially – and addressed himself to another ball. That one went nearer the point than cover-point, and of the next dozen balls nine or ten did exactly the same thing.

Anybody who has ever suffered will know what were his sensations. He felt as if Heaven's worst curse had suddenly fallen on him and he had gone mad. In other respects he appeared to himself to be normal; the scenery had not changed; the field and the dripping trees and the depressed cows in one corner looked just as they had ten minutes before. The thing in his hand was almost certainly a mashie (warranted not to socket); the thing on the grass was a ball which he was addressing in what he believed to be his usual way; he was looking at it very hard and swinging very slow; and yet – there went another one, farther to the right than ever. The hour of lunch was approaching. When he went in to eat it, his family would probably discover that he was raving mad and would send for the doctor; he would be removed to an asylum. Meanwhile (O heavens! look at that one!) he must and would hit one ball not on the socket before the gong summoned him to his doom. In the nick of time a notion came into his disordered brain, and one, two, three balls were hit straight; his deportment at lunch was not detected as being insane; perhaps he was not mad, after all.

He rushed out again afterwards, having first taken off some of those superfluous garments, and, except for one horror, there were no more socketings; but he played each shot with a most elaborate carefulness, even as a drunken man speaks when he is uncertain of his powers of articulation. Whether he is really cured it is too early to say, and in any case it is doubtful whether he will ever be the same man again. The shock of that sudden visitation is not easily forgotten, and the undeniably humorous circumstances of his socketing with a socketless club will not mend matters. I am apprehensive about the poor fellow's future.

It is conceivable that others who have suffered may ask how the attack was cured. Well, I am not quite sure. Socketing comes and goes, and I have always observed that golfing doctors are chary of prescribing for it. 'A medical winner,' remarked Sir Walter Simpson, 'unable to hit with any part except the socket of his iron is no uncommon phenomenon.' But he laid down no precise treatment. As far as I could discover in my poor friend's case, both his previous complacency and his superfluous clothing had something to do with it. Both because he was self-satisfied and because he had too many clothes on for proper swinging, he tried to hit the ball with too much wrist and too little of anything else. Also, I fancied that his right elbow was not clinging to his side as it ought, but flying out from the body on the way down. At any rate, it was by trying to be very stiff and to keep that elbow under control that he checked the pestilence; but, for all I know, both the cause of the attack and the manner of its arrest were really quite other than those I have described.

I recollect that a good while ago this poor man won a certain tournament. In one of the rounds the enemy had come to such sad grief at the last hole that my friend could not fail to win if he kept topping the ball down the middle of the course. He remarked to an onlooker: 'Thank Heaven, I've got a mashie without a socket,' and by trundling the ball in inglorious safety with this weapon he duly won. If he had known then what he has learned now I doubt whether he would ever have reached the green at all. Meanwhile, I do hope that, by describing his torments in such detail, I shall not have put socketing into somebody else's head, especially into the head of somebody who has socketless clubs. That would, I admit, be an impish, not to say a malignant thing to do.

Country Life, 12 January 1935

Tales of the caddie are legion. The one that ends George Plimpton's piece is my personal favourite.

The role of the caddie
George Plimpton

The main attribute of the caddie, almost all professionals seemed to agree, is to reinforce their pro's decisions, or even to dispute them, and make the golfer think hard before making his shot. Naturally, some golfers feel a caddie's importance is overrated.

Claude Harmon was scornful of a caddie's advice. He said his instruction to them was always very simple. Clean the clubs and the balls and show up on time and be in the right place and always be quiet. 'My idea of a caddie is the one I won the Masters with. Never said one word. Hell, he won two other Masters that I know of – with Ben Hogan and Jackie Burke – and I think he won a fourth one. We compared notes and only Burke could remember him saying anything. That was on the seventy-second hole, the last of the tournament, and Burke, who was looking over his putt, heard this calm voice just behind him say: "Cruise it right in there, Mister Burke. Cruise it in." And he did, too.'

Harmon said he never could recall asking a caddie's advice. He said: 'How can a boy know what you spend your life learning? Take a ball's lie. Just how the ball's sitting on the ground, whether it's hunkered down or sittin' up can mean a fifty-yard difference in a shot's length using the same club. How's the caddie going to know? Is he good enough to make the right allowances for the weather – that a ball isn't going to go so far in the cold...that it's going to die up there – he's going to know *that*? And how's he going to know about adrenalin – that great power you get under pressure, that strength, y'know, that allows one-hundred-pound women to lift Cadillacs off children? That's why you get such great pitching performances in the World Series from those speed pitchers – guys like Gibson of the Cards. Why he throws the ball faster than he ever *knew* he could. In golf the same thing...you come down those last fairways in contention and you find yourself hitting the ball thirty yards more than you know how. Well, how's a caddie going to judge *your* adrenalin quota? Think of Trevino in the '68 Open. He comes down the stretch just about ready to take the whole thing and he asks his caddie to club him and the guy suggests a 5-iron. Trevino's all hopped up, crazy strong, and he knows it so he grabs himself an 8-iron and hits the flag with it. Well, imagine where a 5-iron would have taken him. Right out of the whole caboodle, that's where.'

I asked: 'Are there golfers who don't have the courage of their convictions? Who really rely on caddies excessively?'

'Well, Sam Snead's too dependent on his caddie, and he's gullible – which is a combination that can add up to a couple of mental errors a round. I can remember once at Oakmont on a round we come up to the eighteenth hole and we both hit the middle of the green with 6-irons. Well, the next day we come to the same hole and Sam asks his caddie, "Boy, what do you think here?" He hasn't got his mind on it, I guess. His caddie clubs him with a 5-iron and Sam flies the shot over the green. He stares after it, and then he says, "Hell, boy, that ain't no 5-iron shot!" Well, hell, it's Sam should have known about that shot, not the caddie. It's typical of him, though, I always reckon I can have a good time with Sam on match play. I work up a little conversation with my caddie, just pretending to be all-fired confused about a shot, and I take out the 3-iron, and then the 2, and then finally I choke up and hit an easy two that just clears the river and coasts up the green. The fact is, the shot's a natural 4-iron. Well, Sam steps up and he says, "Boy, what do you think?" and his caddie, who's been keeping his ears open, knows that I used the 2-iron, so he says, "It's a good two, Mister Snead." So Sam laces out a 2-iron and it clears the river, and green, and maybe some trees beyond. And Sam, he stares after it, and he says, "Hell, boy, that ain't no two-iron shot." Well, the fact is, you got to learn to depend on yourself. Hagen had the great system for penalizing opponents who eavesdropped on him. He had a jacked-up set of irons – the four-iron was marked five, and so forth, and you could get into big trouble relying on him.'

Gay Brewer, the 1967 Masters champion, also felt a caddie's value was overrated. It was fine to have his reassurance on club selection, but a professional would be foolish to rely on anything but judgement based on knowledge of his own game. Brewer had a different caddie every week on the tour, never really trying to keep one on a regular basis, and indeed he had won tournaments with boys who had never been on that particular course before. He took the Masters in 1967 but he couldn't remember the name of the caddie with whom he won.

'But I'll tell you when the caddie is important,' he told me. 'In England. The caddie seems more devoted there, and God knows he has to be. The weather is such a factor – weird stuff – that the courses can change overnight. You'll have a hole which one day requires a drive and an easy wedge, and the next day it takes a drive and a 3-wood to reach the green. So yardage doesn't mean a thing – I mean, unless the conditions are absolutely perfect and static, which in that country is rare, hell, *unknown*. So you rely more on your caddie. They not only know the course but also how your ball is going to act in the air currents above, and how it's going to bounce and move on the turf. I think I was clubbed on nearly every hole in the tournament I played there. Those caddies are incredible.'

Certainly the English caddies were self-assured. Bobby Cruickshank told me that on his first practice round at Muirfield in 1929 he had a seventy-five-year-old caddie, Willie Black. Cruickshank hit a good drive on the first hole. 'Willie,' he said, 'give me the 2-iron.' 'Look here, sir,' Willie said, 'I'll give you the club, you play the bloody shot.' I've always liked the story about the caddie at St Andrews who interrupted his 'boss' (which was the current term) at the top of his backswing, and shouted, 'Stop! We've changed our mind. We'll play the shot with an iron!' Frank Stranahan had a terrible problem with such caddies in one of the British Amateur championships at Muirfield. He fired a number of them, mostly because pride on both sides got the best of the situation. The caddies were furious and sulking because their advice was ignored, and Stranahan was upset and oversensitive because he could not, under the circumstances, keep his mind on his golf game. The climactic moment in their strained relationship came on a hole with the green hidden behind a high ridge. Stranahan sent his caddie up on the ridge to point out the direction of the green, indeed to place himself so that a shot soared over his head would be on the correct line. The caddie went up there with the golf bag, moving around on the ridge, sighting between Stranahan and the green, his head turning back and forth, and finally he waved Stranahan on. Stranahan hit directly over the caddie and then toiled up the hill to discover that the caddie had lined him up with a thick patch of bracken, waist-high, where it would be a miracle if he found the ball, much less knocked it out; the caddie looked at him and very carefully, like a dog laying down a bone, he dropped Stranahan's golf bag at his feet and set out for the golf house, saying over his shoulder, 'Now, sir, if you think you know so much about it, let's see you get yourself out of there.'

The Bogey Man, Deutsch, 1969

Caddies on manoeuvres
Peter Dobereiner

A reader in Holland writes to tell me of a young man from a good caddie family who wants to make a career in golf and asks if there is anywhere he can go to learn the business and acquire good golfing manners.

For a youngster just out of school there could hardly be a better apprenticeship for life than to spend a year or so as a touring caddie, and in the years to come, if golf develops the way it should and must, there will be even more scope for travelling the world, earning a living at a healthy outdoor occupation and acquiring a cosmopolitan breadth of mind.

If a teenager has ambitions to become a player, and has an aptitude for the game, I would think that a spell of caddying on the major professional circuits would be a better preparation than a year of amateur golf.

There is a new breed of caddie on the circuit these days. The good ones are highly professional, well behaved and make a genuine contribution to the play of their employers. In recent years I have known a newly qualified doctor, a lawyer and two other university graduates, both business executives, on the tour for a season of caddying before settling down to their humdrum professions.

However, there remains among the ranks of the caddies another element, the type of man Horace Hutchinson knew when he wrote in *The Badminton Book of Golf* that a caddie should never receive a tip greater than sixpence, for he would assuredly dissipate it in drink.

Such raffish social misfits still survive in golf despite attempts to form an association of tour caddies, with a code of practice, and licences granted by the European Tournament Players' Division of the PGA, and a disciplinary committee to weed out the bad hats. It will come to that sometime, no doubt, but for the moment the caddies remain a mixed lot, and about the only thing they have in common is resourcefulness.

No training establishment could begin to teach the kind of survival techniques which caddies have to employ from time to time. The recent German Open provided a case in point. This immediately followed the Irish Open and one of the caddies had providently saved £100 to get him from Dublin to Berlin. However, he improvidently lost it all playing dice on the boat trip across the Irish Sea, thereby putting him at risk of missing two weeks' work in Germany and Switzerland.

They are a clannish and cunning lot, these caddies, and his friends decided to smuggle him through East Germany and into Berlin by train. And that is exactly what they did, concealing him under a pile of suitcases on the luggage rack.

Six armed East German police and immigration officials came into the compartment to check passports and issue visas, and that crisis, although causing palpitations among the other caddies, was safely negotiated. A woman passenger who entered the compartment almost fainted when the luggage began to heave.

When the Vopos had moved on to the far end of the train one of the caddies took the stowaway's passport to them and said he had been ill in the toilet and could he please have a visa stamp. That worked. He reached Berlin home and free.

At the end of the German Open there was another problem, involving a different caddie from the same group. They had enjoyed a good week, sleeping in the locker room and therefore having the means for a larger quota than usual of foaming German beer.

Their luck stayed with them, for the mobile office belonging to the company which organizes continental events was going to move on to Switzerland and they could all hitch a ride in it. But this caddie had meanwhile lost his passport. How many people have been shot trying to get from East Germany to the West without the necessary papers? Nothing daunted by such questions, eleven caddies piled into the camion, with ten passports and a French driver who spoke not a word of any other language, most pertinently not English, nor German nor the curious patois by which caddies communicate among themselves.

They had zipped themselves into the golf-bag covers off their employers' bags, as makeshift sleeping bags, and were lying on the floor of the camion like so many chrysalides when they reached Checkpoint Bravo. When the guards entered the camion the caddies emerged in the manner of caterpillars and engaged in a routine which was part barn dance and part pass-the-parcel. That worked as well. Eleven caddies were passed through the checkpoint, having convinced the East Germans that they were only ten. The camion started down the autobahn towards Bavaria, along that narrow strip of neutrality from which travellers are warned not to deviate under pain of severe penalty.

Unbelievably, for it is quite difficult to confuse the autobahn with the side-turns, as I knew because I was driving the same route, the

French driver managed to get off the autobahn and was happily driving through East Germany towards Poland when the caddies realized that they had gone astray.

With extreme difficulty they managed to persuade the driver that he had taken the wrong bleedin' frog and toad. There was nothing for it but to ask help from the polizei.

Fortunately, the police found the episode amusing and kindly escorted them back to the motorway, where the camion driver, with the panache which distinguishes Parisian taxi drivers, swung the vehicle onto the carriageway leading back to Berlin. Well, it was very dark by now.

More highly flavoured dialogue ensued and the driver was eventually persuaded of his mistake, an error which he rectified by the slightly unconventional expedient of making a U-turn across the central reservation. As luck would have it there was a police patrol car lurking nearby and that cost the party a stiff fine on the spot, without the option.

The real danger came when they reached the border, a bleak collection of customs sheds and barriers in the middle of nowhere with the border itself stretching away on both sides, a swathe of mined and fenced nothing, lavishly illuminated and cut through the forest like an obscene scar.

Once more the caddies went through their impromptu vaudeville act and once more the guards were completely foxed. The party drove into freedom. First chance they got they unzipped their golf-bag covers, crawled out and stopped to celebrate the Great Escape in the time-honoured manner of caddies everywhere. It took them the best part of a day and a night to make the rest of the journey through the Alps to Switzerland, but the show went on. The roustabouts of the golf circus had made it.

If there is an educational institution with a curriculum covering this kind of specialized training, and which is willing to accept a young Dutch boy as a pupil, I will be happy to pass on the details. Indeed, if anyone has any constructive suggestions of any sort to help him I will pass them on as well.

The Observer, 1980

The last three pieces discuss the essence of the game.

The all-demanding endeavour

Peter Thomson and Desmond Zwar

Three times a year I say goodbye and my small son weeps and says he doesn't want to go to school. He doesn't know why and it tears my heart so that I wonder why I am doing it to him, and whether it is worth the anguish.

Golfing is an all-demanding endeavour that has no beginning and no end. It can devour a man with its insatiable appetite, or slowly torture and destroy him as surely as a disease. And there is no cure. Some say a man must have a goal and it must be the highest or it is not a goal at all. Others have another God that beckons them farther and farther from home. Golf is different things to different people, and if you don't watch out it becomes all things before you know it. It is a good servant but a bad master.

The professional's life is an odd mixture of maestro and virtuoso. Not so long ago he was a teacher and club-maker, a servant of the game. Now it is possible to be an actor, an entertainer, an entrepreneur and a manufacturer all at once. And if you're lucky, very, very lucky, you can turn your back on it early enough to enjoy living a life like normal citizens and live to a ripe old age watching your children grow.

First you have to forget it's a game. If you play at it they'll murder you and the critics will call you all manner of names except champion. It's an age when society measures achievements by noughts and the size of your house. It's money you're after, not pleasure. You've got to work at it. Strain and strive as much as your senses will allow you, and never will you be able to rest until the day you turn away and leave it to the unlucky ones.

But you'll learn things on the way. You'll learn about life and human frailty, and wickedness and cunning and craft and all the other short cuts social man has contrived. If you're lucky you'll learn about honour and trust and other high levels of behaviour. Most of all you'll learn about yourself.

At the end you may have something to show for it, something to pass on, something to share. And if you succeed, you will have, above and beyond all that, a warm and healthy respect for life and love for your family.

A golfer has to travel. You have to go where the tournaments are. They won't come to you. As far as is possible they have been arranged in a convenient sequence, so that one can buy a ticket at a reasonable cost and fill the months playing one event after another. This is the making of many of us. No amount of practising at home can substitute for active tournament play.

Making a success at golf is not composed of perfecting by repetitive practice, but of understanding how to compete. The former assists the latter but it doesn't assure it. Amongst us there are practising addicts. With one or two exceptions these people are chasing something different in life. Target practice doesn't make you a good guerrilla.

Competing and winning has to be your make-up before you start. You don't learn it. You just bring it out. The few exceptions, of course, possess what I am writing about. The practising developed their confidence. The combination succeeded.

Succeeding, it goes without saying, is more important to some people than others. Competition with other people for certain goals may even be a little show of insecurity, like young monkeys scrambling for peanuts. For some it is a desperate effort to win recognition from the rest of the tribe, or to gain power and status. With golf, since there are huge prizes at stake, it can be a chase after financial wealth. Nobody would say in this day and age there is anything wrong with this. Everyone amongst us, whatever activity he engages in, must be chained to the same wheel.

A young man starts out in golf with no accurate picture of what it involves, except that he knows by observation and newspaper reading that somewhere at the end of the rainbow is a pot of gold. He adopts an idol who is wealthy by now, beyond his wildest dreams. If he emulates him he thinks he might end up with the same opulence.

So he sets about copying him in practice, trying to swing like him, adopting the same rhythm, wearing the same clothes and shoes. If he makes progress he is full of praise for the great man and attributes every advancement to him. He may even draw close to him.

If he does, familiarity will more than likely destroy his image of his benefactor. He will realize his god is merely human with human failings that might even be repulsive.

At that stage he takes off on his own, flushed with a strong ego that tells him he is as good or better than his rivals. Success is likely to come fast and free at that point. Events fall into his lap. He becomes a new 'find'. His scrapbook fills up. He is wooed by manufacturers, magazines and hangers-on. Now he may be sponsored, ending his financial problems. No longer will he have to worry about money. It will always be available if he runs short. He may even be able to afford a manager.

If he doesn't quite make it, however, if his ego gets a rude deflation at the hands of an experienced veteran, he is in for a bad time. *Nobody* woos him. Manufacturers feed him with the barest minimum of balls and equipment, magazines never mention him and no one hangs around.

Loneliness is his worst enemy. It saps his confidence and drains his spirit. His life becomes an aimless wandering in search of a purpose only he can remember. He becomes resentful and morose and his road to the top now takes detours in the opposite direction.

The successful ones can become almost unbearable, shouting advice, philosophizing and generally building up an unpopular image. It would be inconceivable that all the spoiling, writing up, following, hysterical adulation should not have some effect on the strongest make-up. It is understandable if a young man leaves the ground and starts floating around in the clouds. The hangers-on will do their best to keep him up there, keep his image polished, hoping some of the reflection will hit them. It would all be revolting except that once in a while you see a young man who goes through it all and comes out unscathed. If you enter into big races you have big hurdles to jump. Some get over the first lap then crash the second time round. It takes a big man to finish.

Boredom is another enemy. It takes about four hours to play a round of golf and maybe one hour to be shod, practised and ready to tee off. That leaves another nineteen hours to be filled. Assuming one sleeps for nine hours (my own figure) there are ten vacant important hours to fill every day. It is enough for some to spend two hours or more of this time on the practice tee training the muscles to respond to trigger mechanisms. Very satisfying, I'm sure, to those that find it fills their needs but boring beyond words for others. It is dangerous to read too much. It might tire the eyes. One mustn't do anything too athletic, at least before tee-off time. Better by far to save every ounce for the real thing. So what is there to do?

The ones who solve this problem best are the most consistent winners. Boredom is the curse of intelligent man. It destroys interest, incentive, concentration and eventually application. It wrecks a golfer.

There is a strong temptation to waste time; fill it with trivia, comic company or just plain twiddling thumbs. Even this eventually becomes mentally unbearable. Drink, make fun, play cards, matches, dice, anything, to pass the awful waiting time. Count your money, dream of riches, think up schemes to get more, plan your pleasure, indulge until it too becomes a colossal bore.

Go to church, pray, read the Bible, talk about it, preach until someone tells you to keep your problems to yourself. Try everything in turn. *The truth* is it can't be done for long, for months on end. It palls. The mind collapses under the weight.

It must surely dawn on even the dumbest in time that golf playing, demanding as it is, is not the whole of life or even an adequate substitute for some creative satisfying occupation. Those who try to make it so end up disappointed if not a little disillusioned. For the professional player, all that counts in the end is what he has to show for his time spent, in the way of security, money in the bank. Played year in and year out it is not a game but a profession, a life-supporting craft with the richest spoils going to the craftiest.

This Wonderful World of Golf, Pelham, 1969

The ugly game
George Plimpton

As I sat there, listening, perhaps taking a drink too many to dispel my gloom of the afternoon, the golfers seemed to take on heroic, if slightly tragic, proportions. Thompson was right only in a sense: golf had its compensations, perhaps, such as the easy evenings of hitting golf balls into a practice field. But the exercise of the game itself in top competition was an ugly combination of tension and frustration, broken only occasionally by a pleasant surprise, but more often by disaster. The game required a certain cold toughness of mind, and absorption of will. Perhaps it was only all right when you were done with it and could sit around and reminisce, with the music in the background, like the military people at the post dance after a hard day in the field.

There was not an athlete I had talked to from other sports – the roughest of them: football, hockey, basketball – who did not hold the professional golfer in complete awe, with thanksgiving that golf was not *their* profession. The idea of standing over a putt with thousands of dollars in the balance was enough to make them flap their fingers as if singed. They would have none of it. Golf was the only major sport in which the tension remained throughout – where each shot was far enough apart in time for doubt to seep in and undermine one's confidence, so that there was no way of establishing an equanimity of mood. Other sports were not similar; the tension would mount, but as soon as the first whistle blew, or the contact began, that was the end of it. It was the familiar business of jumping into cold water – it was all right once you got in.

The Bogey Man, Deutsch, 1969

Golf blight
Michael Parkinson

The scientists and the doom-watchers have got it wrong. The greatest problem facing the world today is not overpopulation, or nuclear proliferation or pollution, it is golf blight. This disease, which has reached epidemic proportions over the past decade, means that our natural habitat is rapidly becoming turned into one huge golf course.

One could, if one so desired, play golf from coast to coast across the United States. A man getting off a train in Newcastle could tear up the return ticket and golf all the way home to Torquay.

Recent research shows that in Britain an increasing number of people play golf more times each week than they have sex – and, in the main, get more enjoyment out of a hole in one. Moreover, it is calculated that more man-hours are lost through executives practising their golf swings in office hours than accrue during an outbreak of typhoid.

But, most significantly, there are now more golf clubs in the world than Gideon bibles, more golf balls than missionaries and, if every golfer in the world, male and female, were laid end to end, I for one would leave them there.

I am president of the Anti-Golf Society, a position I have held for many years in the face of stiff opposition from friend and foe alike and in spite of the aforementioned spread of golf blight.

My Society would not ban golf, it would simply provide rehabilitation centres where people could be taught that there are more important handicaps than golfing ones, that practising swings in public places is anti-social and that the reason why golfers' wives soon lose their girlish enthusiasm for love and marriage is that they know better than most exactly what a golf bag is.

Unlike other human beings golfers do not live at home, they live at the golf club. They are happier in these establishments because they guarantee their peace of mind by barring outsiders and only giving shelter to people of similar pigmentation of skin, background and religious and political views.

Thus there are clubs exclusively for Jews, and clubs where a Jew could only gain admittance if he arrived on the doorstep with Moshe Dayan at his side supported by a regiment of Israeli paratroopers.

This unhealthy state of affairs can only damage the move toward better international understanding and will undoubtedly lead to dire consequences. Indeed, it is my belief that the Third World War will start at a golf club – probably the deliciously titled Honourable Company of Edinburgh Golfers – when Sammy Davis Jnr arrives at Muirfield unannounced and uninvited with Arthur Scargill as his partner.

It is difficult to find any justification whatsoever for golf. The people who play it might disagree with the criticism that it is simply an elaborate device for ruining a good walk. But they would be hard pressed to convince me of its claims as a sport, particularly one to be watched.

One of life's great mysteries is just what do golfers think they are playing at, but even more mysterious is what those spectators who traipse around golf courses are looking for? They, at least, can claim the exercise as an excuse, but what about those noddies who sit at the eighteenth hole all day long? All they see – and I know because I observed them on television – is an alleged athlete fretting over sinking a two-foot putt.

There is more excitement and spectacle in a competition to decide the world's largest parsnip.

It is during events like those of last week that some of us despair for the future of the human race. The golfers are taking over, vast regiments of people whose only justification can be that they provide employment for people who make sad and gaudy trousers.

At such times I feel isolated but not alone. There are a few of us left to fight the rearguard action. Not all of us have been brain-washed.

Watching the Open on television – actually I was fretfully waiting for them to go back to a real game, cricket – my wife came into the room as some golfer was practising his swing. 'He missed the ball,' she exclaimed. I felt a new, stirring love for her. She looked more closely at the box. 'Also he's lost a glove,' she said. At that precise moment I knew I had married the right person.

If there is hope it is in my wife's unsullied innocence plus the expert backing of people like the environmental correspondent of *The Observer*, who recently suggested that in the national interest, all golf courses should be ploughed up and made into allotments.

There can be no arguing with this outstanding piece of common sense. Vegetables are more important than golfers and, aesthetically speaking, I'd rather watch a cabbage grow than a man worrying his guts over a two-foot putt.

The Sunday Times, 13 July 1975

Index